D0854003

Doing More
with Less

Jacob B. Ukeles

DOING MORE WITH LESS

Turning Public Management Around

amacom

A Division of
American Management Associations

To "M" and the other
midnight diners, with thanks
for your love and encouragement

Library of Congress Cataloging in Publication Data

Ukeles, Jacob B.
  Doing more with less.

  Includes index.
  1. Public administration.   2. Organizational effectiveness.
I. Title.
JF1411.U37   350.007'5   81-69352
ISBN 0-8144-5741-X   AACR2

© 1982 AMACOM
A division of American Management Associations, New York.
All rights reserved. Printed in the United States of America.

This publication may not be reproduced, stored in a retrieval system, or transmitted
in whole or in part, in any form or by any means, electronic, mechanical, photocopy-
ing, recording, or otherwise, without the prior written permission of AMACOM, 135
West 50th Street, New York, N.Y. 10020.

First Printing

Preface

This is a book about how government can do more with less—how through more effective public management, better services can be delivered at lower cost, and revenue can be increased without increasing taxes. Public management can become more effective when it adapts many of the concepts and methods used by large private companies. Sensitive adaptation is crucial, because of the political environment of decision making in the public sector.

The emphasis is on state and local government, the largest segment of public activity, and particularly on the problems and opportunities of management improvement in the larger central cities of the Midwest and the Northeast. This work draws heavily on more than fifteen years of experience with state and local governance. The specific approach of the book—the emphasis on private management tools in the public management arena—is based on two assignments which brought me in contact with some of the best managers in the private sector attempting to help their counterparts in the public sector. As executive director of the Mayor's Management Advisory Board in New York City at the beginning of the fiscal crisis and later as study director for the Citizens' Committee for Effective Government, Inc. in Hartford, Connecticut, I had an unparalleled opportunity to observe what works and what doesn't work in this transfer process.

This book is directed to anyone who is involved or would like to get involved in the effort to help make our government work better. First and foremost, it is intended to be a source of useful ideas and perspectives for public servants on the firing line: elected officials and professional managers in state and local government. You are largely unsung warriors, struggling to meet the competing demands of complex constituencies, usually under the most difficult circumstances. Much of what is written here you know already. Some of it will make you angry; all of it is meant to stimulate broader understanding and better capacity to respond.

The second group that might find this book helpful are those tax-payers who are baffled at the apparent inefficiency of public services but are too sophisticated to be satisfied with name-calling or theories of conspiracy or idiocy. Hopefully, this book can help make you more informed citizens with a better understanding of what citizens can legitimately expect government to be able to accomplish for them.

The third audience for this book is a student audience, those courageous enough, idealistic enough, and perhaps foolish enough to want to join the public service at a time when the public service is under broad attack. Students in public administration or public management, policy analysis, public and urban affairs, city planning, or public law should find this practical exposition a useful supplement to the more basic works of theory that are required reading. Though based on practical experience, it is more than a collection of war stories.

A word or two about what this book is and is not. Governments in the United States face two challenges that are often confused. There is pressure to do less: this is a political policy mandate, reflecting in part the belief of the Reagan administration that the 1980 national election was a signal from the body politic for a smaller civilian government. "Cutback management" is an attempt to respond to this mandate. This book is not about cutback management.

There is a second mandate: to do the best possible job with the available resources, whether resources are being cut back or increasing. Improving public management should be an imperative for liberals and conservatives alike. This book *is* about "turnaround management." Much as a corporation or government that is headed for, or already in, fiscal trouble can be turned around by an effective management strategy, so too can public management in the United States be turned around.

While the examples are drawn from local and state government, the management principles espoused appear to be relevant to federal civilian programs and the nonprofit world of university, hospital, and social welfare agency. Managers in this sector, too, are under increasing pressure to do more with less; in this world, too, measurement is difficult and the decision-making process complex. There are even those who believe that there are some lessons here for private industry. With the increasing concern about the inability of American industry to compete with Japanese and other foreign counterparts, the focus here on the interaction between management processes and concepts on one hand and political decision making on the other may in fact be helpful to those who worry about American productivity in the private sector.

Many of the examples in this book are drawn from New York City. Considering the dim reputation of New York City's management, perhaps this should be explained. A great deal has now been written about how New York City got into financial trouble, but relatively little has been written about how New York City got out of trouble. I was a participant in the successful rescue of this deeply troubled municipal government. The story of how New York avoided fiscal collapse has many strands. It is a story of close cooperation between traditional adversaries: management and labor; public and private leadership; federal, state, and local officials. It is a story of political courage and a citizenry that bore sacrifice, of a community pulling together. It is also a story of a surprisingly strong local economy shored up by international investment in a cosmopolitan city. But it is also the story of one of the most ambitious efforts at management improvement in the history of urban governance. It is this last strand—the N.Y.C. management improvement story—that is used here as illustrative material. In long-range financial planning, in financial accounting and control, and in management by objectives, New York City did break some new ground. As a former participant I am both well informed and not objective. Readers will have to draw their own conclusions about the way that subjectivity and information balance out.

Two apologies are in order: First, in stressing the relevance of lessons from the private sector, it is conceivable that I understate the contribution made to thinking and practices within public management by those who have devoted their careers and lives to its improvement. In particular, the International City Managers Association and managers in such places as Phoenix and Kansas City have made an outstanding contribution and have arrived at many of the same conclusions through their work that I have through mine.

Second, at times readers may feel that they have stumbled on a tract exhorting the sinner to abandon evil ways and to seek the true righteous path. I started out as a skeptic on the general question of whether state and local government management could be improved and, more specifically, on whether the private sector could be of any help in this area. Convinced now of the error of my former ways, I sometimes have the fanaticism of the convert. I hope that an occasional excess of zeal does not obscure the content of the ideas.

Many people have contributed to the strengths of this book, but the weaknesses are mine alone. In particular, I would like to thank Herbert Schoen, a friend and mentor, who read the manuscript with great care, and whose comments were invaluable. I would also like to thank Fred Lane, whose thoughtful reading of the full manuscript provided useful guidance in final revisions. Michael Brown also reviewed substantial portions of the draft, and his insights were of great assistance. Jim Capalino, Wheeler Smith, and Robert Schrank made very useful comments on individual chapters. My thanks also to Donald Kummerfeld, Lee Oberst, Richard Shinn, and John Zuccotti, who were effective leaders during the fiscal crisis in New York City. The members of the Citizens' Committee for Effective Government in Hartford and the Mayor's Management Advisory Board in New York City were important partners in the development of these ideas. And last but not least my appreciation to Jim Hayes, Anthony Pisano, Allan Ferrin, Ernest Miller, and John Budlong for their interest and involvement at various stages of the effort that led to this book's becoming a reality. Eileen Lyons, Judy Kalisch, and Susan McCue provided very helpful research assistance at various points along the way. Sonia Kamph and the staff of the AMA word processing center provided high-quality support through the various drafts of the manuscript; I thank them for the thoroughly professional way in which they worked.

Jacob B. Ukeles

Contents

1

Introduction

During the late 1970s a strong public groundswell for putting the lid on public spending emerged in the United States as an incredibly powerful political force. Early tremors of what became an earthquake appeared in the mounting refusal of communities across the nation to approve bond issues. The passage of Proposition 13 in California signaled an explosion of tax revolt sweeping the country from coast to coast, and including states and localities with budget surpluses such as California's as well as those areas where shrinking public resources are a way of life.

In every region and at every level of government, the people signaled dissatisfaction with the value of government services and spending. More than a conservative backlash, Proposition 13 was a "meat-ax" response of a frustrated electorate convinced of government's inefficiency and not quite knowing what to do about it. This view of the meaning of the tax revolt of the late 1970s is substantiated by a poll of 1,500 adults nationwide conducted by Lou Harris for ABC. This poll found that 85 percent of those polled interpret the vote for Proposition 13 as "a strong protest that people running government will have to respond by trimming a lot of waste from government spending."[1] It was front-page news in *The New York Times* (June 28, 1978) that "there is a growing perception of government waste." The New York Times–CBS News poll of 1,093 Americans of voting age outside California found that 78 percent of the respondents think government wastes a lot of the monies they pay in

[1] Louis Harris, "Tax Revolt Not a New Phenomenon," *The Harris Survey*, June 29, 1978, p. 1.

1

taxes. In comparison with earlier polls by the Institute for Social Research at the University of Michigan, this was an increase from 42 percent in 1958. In only 20 years, the percentage of Americans who believe there is extensive waste in government had almost doubled.

In short, Americans do not believe that their government—federal, state, or local—works very well. To put it bluntly, the average American thinks that public management is inefficient. One of the most interesting polls that supports this view was a survey of business executives in 44 cities around the United States.[2] They were asked, "How do you rate the quality of life in your home city?" They were asked to evaluate the school system, transportation, restaurants, night life—altogether, 14 factors that might affect their decisions to stay or to relocate. One of the areas that they were asked to rate was the municipal government. There were 3,000 answers, and in *no city* did the quality of the government compare favorably with the overall quality of the city as a place to live. Even for Indianapolis, where 69 percent of the poll respondents felt the municipal government was very good or excellent, 85 percent thought that overall as a place to live Indianapolis was very good or excellent. In other cities the gap between the quality of the government and the quality of the city overall was much greater. In Seattle, for example, 91 percent rated Seattle highly as a place to live. Only 43 percent rated the municipal government highly. In short, these business executives liked their city a lot more than they liked their government. In general, they didn't think that their municipal government does a particularly good job. Of course, there is wide variation. Some cities appear to be a lot better managed than others. For example, none of the poll respondents in New Orleans thought the municipal government very good or excellent, whereas in Houston 59 percent did think that the government was good or excellent.

While there are those who would speak of the myth of government mismanagement, it is wrong in a democracy to ignore the perceptions of the people. It is also not very practical. The reality of government's situation lends an urgency to the case for management improvement even beyond these popular perceptions. Particularly in the older cities of the Midwest and the Northeast, local and state governments are caught in a significant bind. Inflation and the legiti-

[2] *The AMBA Executive*, Vol. 6, No. 6 (1977), p. 2.

mate needs of the poor increase the cost of services. If a city cuts its costs by reducing the service level the downward spiral is reinforced—poorer services lead to a less attractive city, to fewer jobs, and fewer self-sufficient households. As a result of these combined trends, the services from each dollar of investment need to be maximized. In other words, cities and states must provide good service at reasonable cost. Even in states and localities in the West and South, where resources for government appear to be more plentiful, spending is similarly constrained politically by the tax revolt. In the 1960s, problems were dealt with by throwing money at them. No city or state can any longer plan on spending its way out of problems.

Better management is no longer just a polite catch phrase. Increasingly it is part of the real agenda of any elected official. The argument has been made that the difference between government and industry is that business is concerned with "economic" efficiency while government is concerned with "political" efficiency. If this argument were ever true, it is certainly true no longer. Government, too, must care about economic efficiency. The tax revolt means that economic efficiency *is* political efficiency. Good service at reasonable cost is now a political as well as an economic objective, and the time is ripe to act to improve the management of the public sector.

Why It's Hard to Improve Public Management

The average citizen—and the average private sector manager with no experience in government—probably believes that the problem of government is that "all politicians are crooks," and that "all civil servants are stupid petty bureaucrats who enjoy creating red tape and strangling the citizen." Some elected officials, early in their administrations, have made remarks about "obstructionist bureaucrats" and "incompetent civil servants," but this limited response by otherwise intelligent and sophisticated people tends to disappear over time, and the private sector manager tends to develop a healthy respect for those who survive and function at all in the public sector. In a perceptive article in *Fortune* magazine, Michael Blumenthal, at the time Secretary of the Treasury and formerly chief executive officer of Bendix Corporation, makes this point: "At the level GS-15 to 18, you have officials who are very dedicated, who work as hard as their counterparts in private industry, or harder. They work extremely hard for relatively low pay and produce extremely well . . . . There's nothing inherent in a bureaucrat that makes him less efficient. It's the way the system is structured. So I'm not indicting the people; I'm indicting the system. It's an important distinction."[3]

The same perception has emerged in countless conversations with managers who have moved between the public and private sectors. Invariably, the view is expressed that the people in government are as bright and as capable as their counterparts in industry. The big difference is "the system." Many a private sector manager has entered public service at the federal, state, and sometimes even local level convinced of a cheap, easy, and quick solution, and slightly contemptuous of those who have come before. Months later, frustrated and sometimes bitter, such managers emerge baffled by an inability to move the system.

The American governmental landscape is littered with the wreckage of efforts to make government more effective. Planning-programming-budgeting system (PPBS), productivity programs, and management by objectives (MBO), all had their day. The model cities program of the 1960s was viewed by many as an attempt to integrate and coordinate and thereby improve services in the nation's urban slums. The Department of Housing and Urban Development sponsored limited efforts to support management information systems and a variety of other efforts to improve local capacity. This total effort has left only a modest mark on urban and state management.

Following is a discussion of some of the specific characteristics of the political environment and the management system that has grown up in response to it that make it difficult to improve management.

Crisis Management and the Pressure to Respond

The dominant attribute of public management is that it is reactive or responsive. Top management in particular spends most of its time

---

[3] Michael Blumenthal, "Candid Reflections of a Businessman in Washington," *Fortune*, Jan. 29, 1979, pp. 40–42.

and energy reacting to specific pressures from individuals and groups, often expressed via the media. Whether it is a housing sit-in, a TV program critical of the welfare system, or a series of phone calls from outraged school parents, the public sector in a democratic society demands that public managers respond. Private managers who move into the highest levels of government often complain that between the demands of the media, crises generated by outside events and by other levels of government, and appearances before important groups, there is little time left to manage. Operating in a fishbowl of public scrutiny, the manager may find that public appearances and other symbolic actions become more important than real ones. Symbols are important in a political arena where executive managers must face and communicate with a broad range of people.

Responding to public pressure as a method of management means public management *is* crisis management, and since the pressures from the public are constantly shifting, the agenda of action is constantly changing. As top decision makers respond only to peaks of public pressure or crises, there is little continuity in policy or program.

The Instability of Executive Management

Instability in policy and program is forced by another aspect of the political process. Instead of executive management maturing and developing over a long period of time, the top of the organization can change every two to four years, a circumstance that brings about virtually no continuity in management. Each new administration brings with it new leadership, new policies, new symbols. As Kenneth Axelson, a distinguished private sector manager, pointed out after a highly successful stint in the public service, the instability at the top makes it difficult for the middle managers in government to plan either their own work or their own careers.[4] A premium is placed on caution because one never knows when the new administration will signal a change in direction. If a housing official has "gone out front" on a program direction involving new housing, a new administration committed to rehabilitating old housing is not likely to be very enthusiastic about that manager.

[4] *The New York Times,* Nov. 19, 1976.

In state governments, most counties, and most large cities, the chief executive in our system is elected. It is highly likely that that person and the people close to the top are professional politicians and amateur managers. Being elected to high office in America requires a great deal of skill and experience. There is no evidence, however, that the skills required to get elected bear any resemblance to the skills required to govern. And if they do, they are likely to relate to the political rather than the managerial end of the job. It's as if, every two or four years, the leadership of General Motors were handed over to a new group of people whose experience with Chevrolets is that they once rode in one. Even in the 2,000 cities and towns that have an appointed city manager as chief executive, the appointment is in the hands of an elected city council that can change leadership quite frequently.

Politics and Constituencies

In government, every manager is involved in "politics." Constituencies and pressure groups, each with its own objectives and priorities, dominate decision making. The extent to which these groups interact not only with the symbolic but also with the real is often not clearly understood. The parks constituency, organized perhaps as a parks council, has very strong views as to organization, priorities, and measures of performance. This group, if politically connected, can make or break a manager; and if powerful and intelligent in its media relations, it can destroy a manager in the press. The political (symbolic) imperatives and the management imperatives in government are often in conflict. Many examples of this conflict can be cited. Setting executive salaries, setting policies on the use of automobiles, and contracting out some public service delivery are classic areas where the political imperative is likely to conflict with the managerial imperative.

Even at lower levels of government, the political process is pervasive in its impact. Patronage is not dead even in civil service environments. The file clerk in the next office may be connected with a politically important district leader, a powerful union official, or a mayor-elect.

The Bureaucratic Process

While top management attempts to respond to crises and problems, lower-level managers operate their services and programs using as their basic criterion "the way it has always been done." The concern for the appearance and reality of protecting against abuse of power often ties the operating manager up in knots. Ironically, those whom the public sees as responsible for red tape are most often the victims of it. In looking at New York City's civil service system for the Management Advisory Board, we wrote, "The current pattern of regulations and procedures is like the map of a hundred-year war between those seeking to abuse the public interest and those seeking to protect it. Every step in the city's multi-step personnel process— be it hiring, firing, or assigning—probably evolved in response to a particular abuse at a particular point in time. Over a long period, these attempts to safeguard the system's integrity have added an inordinate amount of steps."[5]

The Road to Improved Public Management

Can cities and states be managed more effectively? And can better management yield better services, lower costs, and higher revenue without increasing taxes? This book is based on experience which indicates that the opportunities for improving public management and thereby public services are substantial. It is the thesis of this book that a very good way—not the only way—to improve public management is to identify characteristics of good management in the private sector that appear to yield good services at reasonable cost. Once identified, these attributes of good private management have to be recast, often substantially, to fit the special political decision-making environment of government.

There are many people who have examined public and private management and concluded that they have more differences than similarities. For example, private management is supported in its efforts to do better by a market system that rewards good products and services and penalizes poor ones. Rather than dwell on such

[5] *Personnel* (New York: Mayor's Management Advisory Board, 1977), p. 21.

obvious differences, it is more useful to ask how much can be learned from the best-managed companies that *is* relevant to government. The answer turns out to be, a great deal.

This approach—borrowing ideas and techniques from the private sector—does not imply that all business is well managed or all governments poorly managed. Or that good management inevitably leads to good results. Rather, the argument is that many companies have made a major effort to perfect principles and techniques, and in the current reawakening of interest in public management effectiveness, government should not reinvent the wheel. Obviously governments can learn from each other as well, and should. Entire movements, such as the city manager movement spearheaded by the International City Managers Association (ICMA), have been promoting more effective public management for decades.

What are the characteristics that seem to make the difference in the well-managed company, as identified in the literature and in practice? Four factors stand out: (1) a concern for performance, (2) individual managerial accountability, including a system of rewards and sanctions, (3) methods of planning and control, and (4) close attention to operational detail at the nuts and bolts level of how things work. Each of these factors can be brought into the world of government.

The Focus on Performance

The fundamental characteristic of good management in the private sector is so basic that it often escapes notice. The key concept is performance. The question "How well are we doing?" is the starting point. It leads naturally to a second question, "How can we do better?" Therein is the concept of performance improvement. By extension, a third question emerges: "How do we know how well we are doing?" And therein is the concept of performance measurement. Current and prospective stockholders, the first-line supervisor, and the chairman of the board all depend ultimately on the company's financial and operational track record. Performance is to the private sector what responsiveness has historically been to the public sector: the basic criterion of success. "Responsiveness" in the public sector is usually particular. A citizen feels that government is working if a complaint to a city councilman about a pothole results in having the pothole filled within a reasonable period of time. Performance in the private sector is usually general: a stockholder is concerned with the overall performance of the company, the bottom line.

Many have argued that performance in the public sector cannot be measured because there is no analog to a company's profit and loss (P&L) statement. These arguments represent too simplistic a view. First, government does have a bottom line: revenues and expenditures should be in balance. Thus, the measurement of expenditure performance against plans (budget) and the measure of revenue performance against plans are hardly insignificant tools in the public sector. Second, even in the private sector, the P&L statement is not sufficient to assess performance. Managers in the private sector are evaluated in terms of a whole series of indirect measures—for example, their compliance with affirmative action targets. Particularly in service industries, measurement of output is not simple. In regulated industries such as utilities, the relationships between service, the regulatory environment, and profitability make the measurement of performance very complex.

Performance does not depend on a simple measure or a single measure. It depends essentially on the philosophical commitment to ask the performance question persistently and often—namely, "How well are we doing?" If the question is framed in a serious way, answers or at least clues can be developed even in the absence of a simple bottom line. Typically, in government many measures are needed, each giving only a partial view of performance.

A shift in orientation from the traditional approach to performance in the public sector is central. This traditional approach was described by a head of a major city department: when asked, "How do you evaluate performance?" he gave two answers: "When the mayor stops me in the hall to ask how things are going, I answer terrific. I always answer terrific. When the 11 P.M. news shows two of my men goofing off and I get an angry phone call from the mayor, then the answer is awful."

The Concern for Accountability

A second characteristic of modern management is the accountability of the individual manager. In the well-managed company, managers are accountable for a specific budget and for achieving specified results. They are likely to have some control over the resources necessary to perform effectively, including some role in the hiring and firing of people under their direction. In addition, there are rewards for doing well and sanctions for doing poorly. Promotion, with the implication of more money, status, or power, is probably the most powerful motivating force in the corporate structure. There is pressure on the individual manager at all levels to produce.

The major criticism of the potential transfer of the accountability emphasis from the private sector is that government can't develop the kinds of incentives and disincentives that are used in industry. If managers are given more control over the resources affecting their ability to perform, if performance is evaluated in relation to a clear definition of what is expected, it is possible to find and administer rewards and sanctions. It is sometimes argued that civil service makes it impossible to use promotion as a reward. This perception underlines the urgency of civil service reform (see Chapter 2).

The Emphasis on Planning and Control

Modern management in the private sector, though not immune to crisis, is predominantly planned management. It is initiatory and forward-looking. It is built around the specification of objectives and execution of controls to achieve objectives.

The well-managed company emphasizes systematic planning and control in every aspect of its activities. In the last 20 years there has been a virtual revolution in planning and control in private sector management. Clearly, these two activities lie at the heart of management as defined many years ago. But it is only recently that pervasive (often computer-based) planning and control systems have played a role in real decision making.

Planning in the private sector starts with strategic questions—the reevaluation of functions and the setting of priorities. Of two companies manufacturing horseshoes in the early 1900s, the one that reevaluated its product line in the face of growing use of cars was clearly better managed than the one that concentrated only on improving its productivity per person-day. Of the three major companies manufacturing propellers in the prejet era, only one saw far enough ahead to diversify before the contraction of the propeller market.

Many of the critics of the transfer of private sector approaches into the public sector have claimed that the difference between planned management in the private sector and crisis management in the public sector is generic. They have argued quite appropriately that the development of explicit goals and objectives which are the key in most planning systems is practically impossible to do in government, because arguments about goals and objectives are the very substance and heart of the political process. Thus a mayor who needs to build a coalition among groups with widely varying images of appropriate public policy objectives in order to get elected is undoubtedly reluctant to be too precise about his own objectives while in office lest he alienate three-quarters of the electorate. It is true: most cities and states have never been able to develop working mechanisms to define overall objectives and to translate these objectives into service delivery choices and operations.

For some reason the difficulty of planning in the public sector has not been clearly understood. When the mayor of New York City announced the management-by-objectives program in January of 1976, a widely read newsletter in New York City carried the comment, "What's new about managing by objectives—organizations always manage by objectives." While the development of planned, forward-looking management is desperately needed, it represents a major departure from deeply rooted traditions and practices and is in fact a formidable undertaking.

It is useful, however, to distinguish between strategic planning on one hand and operational planning on the other. Even in the private sector long-range planning is difficult in the face of significant market and technical uncertainty. In government, the level of uncertainty—political, economic, and social—is so vast that long-range strategic planning is not a good place to start.

The most promising opportunity to borrow from the private sector in the planning area is at the operational level. Most companies have sophisticated and complete programs within each functional area from data processing to marketing, from production to vehicle maintenance. Operational plans exist to structure the evaluation of results against plans and to explain and correct variations from plans. Financial management and personnel management typically involve large and complex systems for ensuring that the money and people resources of a company are focused appropriately on the broad objectives.

Close Attention to Operations

A fourth, sometimes overlooked characteristic of good private sector management is close attention to nuts and bolts operations. The interest in operations typically occurs at a very high level in the organization. In the public sector, there is a tendency to think of operations as something to concern lower-level managers, while higher-level managers focus their attention on policy and program matters. Decisions as to how resources are allocated—who gets served and at what level of service—are more likely to be addressed by senior public managers than are the more mundane issues of scheduling and deployment, use of materials, and specific work methods. Yet it is precisely at the level of operations that the grand policy gets undone in government, with unhappy consequences of high cost and low quality for citizens. Where senior government officials do concentrate on operations, it turns out that there is substantial commonality between what seems to work in the private sector and what works in the public arena.

One major area of operations that is particularly troubling in government is the area of operations support: the least visible aspects of public services. The average manager in private industry takes it for granted that purchasing, data processing, space management, and equipment maintenance view their missions as helping the line manager. In the public sphere, these support services often strangle the line manager—not because of evil intent but because they are perceived as being put in place to protect the public interest from the mistakes or malfeasance of the line manager. The support functions, such as purchasing or legal services, are set up as a set of checks and balances to keep the manager in line rather than as aids and support. The operations support systems are among the most adaptable from industry, as long as the significant legal and philosophical constraints are understood.

These four factors—the development of a performance orientation, a stress on individual managerial accountability, wide use of planning and control systems, and close attention to nuts and bolts operations—form the strategy for improving public management that is the focus of this book. These broad themes are applied within each of the broad sectors of public management.

In Part I (Chapters 2, 3, and 4), the rapidly changing environment for public personnel management is explored. Part II (Chapters 5, 6, and 7) analyzes the new tools of public financial management. In Part III (Chapters 8, 9, and 10), the focus shifts from people and money to service delivery: how to improve the way services are delivered through better management of operations. Then Part IV (Chapters 11, 12, and 13) includes a new approach to the frustrating, difficult, but urgent need to introduce performance-oriented planning and control into government. Finally, Part V (Chapters 14 and 15) offers an implementation strategy which rests on building a constituency for better public management.

Part I

Managing with People

Public employment has been one of the fastest growing sectors of the nation's employment picture. By 1978 almost as many people worked for federal, state, and local government as in all types of manufacturing combined. State and local employment doubled in only 18 years, from 6,387,000 in 1960 to 12,743,000 in 1978.

Public employees are the single most important determinant of the quality of our government. In the language of the economist, government is "labor-intensive." In other words, it is the people delivering the service—collecting the garbage, putting out the fires, processing the welfare checks, manning the health centers—who control the quality, the quantity, and the costs of what is delivered.

Nowhere in the entire management spectrum is the contrast between deficient public management and relatively successful private management greater than in the personnel area. The systems and procedures to recruit, to motivate, and to deploy people, systems that are highly developed in industry, are virtually nonexistent in government. This is a time of great ferment and change in the "people" area of government, and therefore a time of great opportunity for improvement. Three issues are at the heart of this change: civil service reform, the new collective bargaining, and tightly constrained public resources. These broad issues will define the agenda in the personnel area for at least the next decade.

In Part I these challenges to managing with people in the public sector are examined. Chapter 2 describes ways to move personnel policy and administration toward the post–civil service era. Chapter 3 considers practical approaches to cushion the impact of collective bargaining. Chapter 4 focuses on enhancing employee effectiveness within tight constraints on public resources.

2

Moving Personnel Management Toward the Post–Civil Service Era

Of the people who work for state and local government, most are covered under one or more variations of a civil service system. Civil service protection covers almost 75 percent of all municipal employees; 35 states have civil service systems.

The classic civil service system, which has dominated personnel concepts and practices at the state, local, and federal level for the last 75 years, is on the defensive. No aspect of the public sector has a greater sense of perceived failure than civil service. Once hailed as the main line of defense against the evil of patronage, it is now clearly associated with inefficiency, rigidity, and indifference to performance. Even in Great Britain, the once-proud civil service elite has become the target of public scorn. In America, the term "civil servant" has become a pejorative to the average supporter of Proposition 13.

Established in the 1890s, civil service has become a deeply embedded way of life in state and local government. Much as the spoils system began as a Jacksonian democratic reform in the 1830s, the merit system was the basis for the 1890s reform of the abuses of the spoils system. The first state to have a merit and fitness system was New York State. In 1884 this merit system was incorporated into the state constitution. It provided that "appointments and promotions in the civil service of the State and all its civil subdivisions shall be made according to merit and fitness, to be ascertained, as far as practicable, by competitive examination."[1] While the constitutional requirement for competitive examination remains unusual, most states followed suit in the adoption of the basic concepts of civil service. Thirty-five out of the 50 states have comprehensive merit systems.

The elements of civil service are familiar to most Americans: a selection process based on an examination, often a written multiple-choice examination; the person scoring highest on the test is selected first for a job. The civil servant has tenure and is difficult to discipline or remove. The mission was and is to protect the public against the appointment of people whose sole qualification is their political or family connection. As a reaction to patronage and nepotism, the merit system has been a rallying point for public service employees, government groups, and civic-minded journalists since the days of the muckrakers. A paradoxical consequence of this system is that the average personnel director in a city spends most of his or her time in the testing process and in developing and implementing a myriad of detailed rules and regulations which have accreted to protect the public against abuse. In a typical personnel department, 70–80 percent of the resources may be involved in developing and administering tests. The mission is to protect the holy grail of the merit system.

The contrast to the private sector could not be greater. The mission of the personnel system in a well-managed private company is to fit the best person to a job, to identify and nurture talent, to help and support the line manager to do a better job. In describing the personnel and budget system in New York City in the late 1960s a distinguished department head said, "Administrators, with the present overhead setup, if they want to get anything done, have to fight the system every minute of the time and try to beat the system. If you studied the time that went into jogging this guy, complaining to that person, trying to track something down, hearing the tales of woe of people who haven't gotten paid for six to eight weeks, you could count up a fairly significant number of hours every month. It is an incredible waste of time."[2]

Will the civil service system collapse or will it evolve? There are those who have argued that civil service is passé. States such as

[1] Constitution of the State of New York, Article V, Section 6.
[2] *Personnel* (New York: Mayor's Management Advisory Board, 1977), p. 20.

Minnesota and Oregon have recently abolished their civil service boards and given elected officials a strong role in hiring, firing, and promotions. For all practical purposes, one could say that they have eliminated civil service. On the other hand, there are those who have argued that it is better to salvage the good aspects of civil service and eliminate the bad.

Civil service does provide objectivity, some commitment to professionalism in the public service, and job security for individual workers. Patronage is as real today as it was in 1890. While it is unlikely that a purely appointive system would result in disappointed office seekers shooting elected officials (President Garfield's assassination by a disappointed office seeker was credited by many with giving impetus to civil service reform), a truly appointive system is likely to increase the pressures for political reward regardless of individual competence. A liberal state assemblyman opposed "liberalization" of hiring procedures on the grounds that the existing system protected him from dealing with hordes of job seekers all holding some political "voucher."

The problem with the classic civil service system is that objectivity and job security are bought at the price of a sacrifice of managerial control, thus making it difficult to improve performance. Completely abolishing civil service and maximizing flexibility decreases the opportunity to maintain standards of quality and objectivity, making it difficult to improve performance.

The workforce of government, like the workforce in industry, needs to be managed so that competence and performance become the essential criteria for appointment, promotion, and reward. Personnel decisions need to be made by managers held accountable for results within a framework of explicit policies and programs. This approach to civil service reform offers a useful way out of the classic conflict between flexibility and objectivity. Such a program to revamp public service management is likely to incorporate a complete overhaul in six key areas of personnel policy and administration:

1. Recruitment of professional and managerial personnel becomes active rather than passive.
2. Employees are selected essentially by the line manager who is held responsible for performance, rather than by a personnel examiner.

3. Jobs are defined not by rigid, often out-of-date personnel classification, but by individual position description.
4. Barriers to reassignment and deployment of personnel are replaced by flexibility in response to changing needs.
5. The current vacuum in the area of performance-oriented rewards and sanctions is filled, using performance appraisal systems as a base.
6. The elusive middle ground between centralized and decentralized personnel administration is found. Personnel policy planning and control is likely to be extensive and centralized. Personnel administration is likely to be decentralized to the line manager.

Each of these six areas is discussed below.

Recruitment: From Passive Response to Active Strategy

Good people are a scarce resource, and the best companies invest heavily in recruitment. Bloomingdale's has built part of its substantial success around the recruitment of an extremely high-caliber, high-status sales force. McKinsey & Company mounts a full-fledged campaign for its Harvard Business School recruitment, and another management consultant firm was considered to have outperformed McKinsey when it attracted more Harvard Business School graduates. Scientific and engineering companies mount elaborate advertising and recruiting campaigns at the good graduate schools and in the newspapers.

On any college campus the relative investment of effort by big companies and by government in recruitment activities makes it clear that government runs far behind in the area of recruitment. Industry has long since made the decision to invest heavily in recruitment. The remaining issues are where to recruit, how to recruit, and whom to recruit.

Cities and states historically do little recruitment, and the recruitment that is done is sporadic and often through word of mouth. In essence, recruitment in the private sector is active, whereas recruitment in the public sector tends to be passive. Occasionally, a charismatic political leader will attract a following. Mayor John Lindsay in

New York, particularly in his first administration, did send recruiters to the major law schools, but such efforts are not built into the very fabric of government the way they are in industry, and the next administration in New York did little or no college recruiting.

Many parts of the country are experiencing an urban management crisis brought on by the aging and retirement of a depression-recruited, middle management group and the problems of recruiting their successors. In the thirties cities and states were able to recruit very high-quality college graduates and young professionals for whom there were relatively few other opportunities. Many of those initially recruited stayed with government, because they found satisfaction in the work, were able to get ahead, and could reap substantial benefits such as pension accumulation. Someone recruited in 1930 at the age of twenty-two is likely to have retired in the mid-seventies.

Government, like industry, needs to attract the best and most qualified applicants for the available jobs. The shortage of resources makes it even more urgent that every single position be filled by the best-qualified available person. The top recruitment priority in government should be the same as that of industry: the bright, young, talented professionals and managers. Yet government suffers from a significant competitive disadvantage. What does government have to offer to attract such people? Even if entry-level salaries are made competitive, the ambitious young college graduate is looking down the road. Certainly the salaries of middle and upper levels in the corporate community far outweigh those of government. Government also carries little prestige, and increasingly, government employment doesn't even have much security. Moreover, because of the civil service testing system, it is difficult, if not impossible, to offer a college graduate a job. The best that can be offered is the opportunity to take an exam. Even such opportunities are limited, because most entry-level managerial positions in government are considered midway or "lateral-entry" in the civil service promotion sequence. That is, an earlier position is a prerequisite to taking the exam. It is no wonder that those public officials who have tried to introduce recruitment programs have been frustrated in their efforts.

There is a model, however, which could work in the public sector if pursued vigorously. Although government cannot offer the opportunity to compete for the money and status of senior business executive positions, it can often offer a quality of experience not easily duplicated in the private sector. Such a process works in at least one area of government: the offices of U.S. District Attorneys tend to be staffed by bright young law school graduates who seek these positions because of the quality of experience, the contacts, and the well-deserved reputation for excellence. If this strategy could be spread into other areas of government, if young people knew they could reach upper middle-level management positions within a relatively short period of time, then the quality of experience could be a substantial inducement to bright young people to join government service.

Such a strategy would be a radical shift in the philosophy of government employment. Rather than a workforce built around security and longevity, the managerial, technical, and professional public service could be characterized by high-quality experience, rapid mobility, and a relatively short average stay in government. Bright young people could move into government positions, work five to ten years, move rapidly to the top, and move out into industry. This is a long-run strategy. In the short run, cities and states can and should establish formal recruitment programs in their personnel departments.

The issue of recruitment is closely linked to the need for management development. In the best-managed private companies, managerial development is recognized as a crucial handmaiden to successful recruitment. The opportunity to learn under a series of good managers, which is implicit in any management development program, is itself a key element in a recruitment strategy. Good management development consists of a mixture of carefully selected training and education experiences and rotational assignment.[3]

Shifting from Examiner to Manager

Selecting the right person for a job is always somewhat mysterious, but the chances of success may be improved if the selector has a stake in the outcome. In the well-managed company, the choice of an employee is made by the manager who is responsible for the

[3]See Chapter 15 for a more complete treatment of management development in relation to training and building managerial capacity.

performance of the position being recruited for. The job of the personnel department is to help: to recruit and screen candidates and to advise. The choice itself is made by the person with the most to gain or lose by the new person's performance.

In government hiring, procedures are dominated by examiners—the personnel examiner who writes and administers an examination and the budget examiner who complicates and delays hiring in order to save money. Most of the time the choice of a person for a job is based on an examination score. The typical examination is a written, multiple-choice exam. The manager is then sent an employee with the highest score on the list of those who passed the test in rank order. Scoring of such exams is often to the nearest decimal point so that sometimes no more than a point or two separates the top candidates from those candidates who are so far down the list that they have practically no chance of getting hired. This type of testing is widely viewed as a relatively poor predictor of job performance. The written exams employed by the typical city or state have been virtually discarded by private industry, which, under pressure to demonstrate job relevance and objectivity of selection procedures, found it almost impossible to validate written exams.

The government personnel department is the watchdog of the system, not the helper or the facilitator of the manager. Its job is to prevent the manager from abusing the (civil service) system. Since the objective is to prevent abuse, the personnel department views the line manager not as a client for its work, but as a prime candidate for suspicion of abuse. Instead of a partnership between the personnel department and the line manager, there is essentially an adversary relationship.

The crucial change which is needed is to put the line manager into the central decision-making role in selection and hiring without eliminating objective processes. Ideally, each manager should be responsible for hiring and firing everyone who reports directly to him or her. Managers higher up in the hierarchy should have authority over promotion as well. At the same time, of course, managers must maintain rigorous standards of objectivity, or else government departments could begin to resemble a series of ethnic, racial, and socioeconomic feudal states.

To maintain objective hiring practices, some form of standardized testing is likely to be an element in public personnel selection and promotion processes for the foreseeable future. This is necessary for four reasons. First, there tends to be a large number of applicants for many city and state jobs. Particularly at nonmanagerial levels, public service jobs are still considered good jobs. In New York City, in the midst of a well-publicized fiscal crisis, 30,000 applicants signed up for a fireman's exam. Similar high numbers are typical of police, fire, and sometimes sanitation jobs in any large city. Completely individualized hiring procedures are simply not relevant in this environment. Second, there is a continuing need to insulate public hiring from political and familial pressures. There is no reason to suspect that patronage is any less a vital aspect of the democratic political process now than it was 50 or 70 years ago. Third, there are stringent federal requirements regarding job selection procedures and test relevance connected with affirmative action. Fourth, in some states strict constitutional requirements and judicial interpretation of these requirements mandate some form of testing in public hiring.

Advanced city and state governments tend to minimize their use of multiple-choice written examinations and utilize tests that simulate a job situation. Auto mechanics, lab technicians, computer programmers, bookkeepers, and typists—all involve occupations where a simulation of part or all of the job is possible in a standardized testing environment suitable for a large number of applicants.

Where large numbers of applicants are not a factor, there are techniques in use in private industry which should be suitable to the city. One such technique calls for different interviewers to ask each candidate the same questions and discuss the same topics. The interviewers' scores are then aggregated to produce an overall score for each candidate. This is a more controllable process than the oral exam by panel which is widely used in government. The objectivity of the latter tends to be muddied by intrapanel dynamics.

It is possible to develop a hiring method in the public service which allows the line manager to select the best person for a specific job while at the same time using large-scale testing to satisfy rigorous standards of objectivity. Such a system would work something like this:

Step 1: A competitive exam—a job simulation where possible and a written multiple-choice otherwise—functions as a screening device. To the extent possible such exams would be based on job relevance. The exam would be graded on an A,B,C,D basis rather than a percentage score. Examinations cannot possibly discriminate among different candidates' probable success in the job at the level of the third decimal place. Establishing groups according to grades (A group, B group, etc.) provides a set of graded pools of potential applicants who, within each group, are roughly equal in their knowledge of the basics of the subject or subjects most relevant to the job.

Step 2: Candidates for specific jobs would be drawn first from within the A group. A detailed job description should provide the basis for defining specific skill requirements relevant to the specific job. Each candidate would be evaluated in terms of the relevance of previous experience and education, performance evaluations in previous relevant jobs, and a structured interview. In order to ensure objectivity, multiple interviews such as described above might be necessary or useful.

Step 3: The person in the A group who best met the criteria established for the specific job would be hired. The actual hiring decision would be made by the line manager directly responsible for the performance of the unit within which the appointment is being made.

Such a process, if followed carefully, has a reasonable chance of balancing the competing needs of objectivity and mass testing on the one hand with a key role for the line manager on the other. This system will work only if the individual manager who is responsible for the hiring and firing of staff is at the same time held accountable for the performance of those employees. The manager who is going to be accountable for the performance of the person who is hired is likely to work harder at making a good selection. If the manager is not going to be held accountable for the performance of the person who is hired, then it might as well be done through the personnel department.

The actual hiring process used by the typical city or state similarly needs drastic overhauling. The process tends to be cumbersome and slow. Many months and sometimes a year can elapse between the time a job is advertised and the time the first person is hired. The consequences of such delay are catastrophic from the point of view of attracting quality workers. Such long periods mean that by the time a job is filled the best candidates are likely to have gone elsewhere. There are two components to the delay: the testing process itself, and the variety of checkpoints needed before a hiring decision can be implemented.

The process of preparing and administering exams tends to be very long and time-consuming. Grading exams, allowing time for protest, publishing the list, certifying the list—these are some of the steps in a long process. But even more important than the delay in the testing process are the delays in the actual appointment. Because of budget pressure, endless roadblocks are placed in the way of a hiring decision. Even though federal funds may be involved, the budget officer is likely to slow down an appointment to conserve cash; and even under a merit system, a political aide to a chief executive is likely to exercise some veto power over appointments, endlessly delaying the actual appointment of individuals who are regarded as political liabilities. Within the civil service system itself, elaborate checks are often made to ensure that a person meets a list of requirements many of which may have no particular relevance to the job for which the person is being hired (such as residence requirements). In a study of the appointment process in New York City for non-civil-service jobs, there were 15 separate steps involving 8 agency approvals before a person could actually be appointed to a specific job. Thus, the appointment processes of state and local government must be speeded up so that the process itself is no longer a serious impediment to obtaining the most qualified employee.

Defining Public Jobs

In a large complex organization a systematic approach is needed to define the jobs that need to be performed. There are two theories of job definition: (1) In the "top-down" approach the types or "classes" of jobs that need to be done to carry out the mission of the organization are listed, and each individual job is classified within the overall scheme. (2) In the "bottoms-up" approach, each job is described in terms of what it is expected to contribute to the overall organization. The building block is not a class or type of job (as it is in the first theory) but is a specific job or position description for the individual job. According to the second theory, the job classification is used merely to assure some consistency among different parts of the same organization with regard to salary and work content. The crucial difference between the two approaches is that under the first the appointment process is built around a class of job, and under the second the appointment process is built around a position description.

Industry has been moving away from a focus on job classification (theory 1), and increasingly uses the bottoms-up approach (theory 2). In the well-managed private company, the position description for the individual job is the key to the appointment process. The position description is part of the accountability of the individual line manager. The manager who is held accountable for the performance of an individual in a job has a strong incentive not only to recruit the best possible person but also to describe the job in such a way as to accurately reflect that job's contribution to the product or output of his entire unit. Such a manager has a powerful incentive to make the position description as accurate as possible and to set the skill requirements so as to get the most appropriate possible person for the job. The manager in a public agency has no control over who is hired and thus has no incentive to develop or maintain an accurate or relevant job description. Even companies that use a job classification system to hire nonmanagement workers typically base their hiring of managers on organization charts and explicit position descriptions.

In government theory 2 still predominates. A fundamental attribute of civil service is a job classification or title structure into which each job must fall. This job structure is the basis of the examination process. An exam is given for each title. It is difficult for a modern, private sector manager to appreciate the power, significance, rigidity, and complexity of civil service job classification systems. "The classification plan determines how work will be performed in an organization to a far greater extent than the wishes of its chief executive, its managers, or its employees."[4] The classification plan groups and labels similar positions by assigning a title to each position in the civil service system. This title defines the limits of the duties and responsibilities that an employee in that position may perform. The plan establishes the appropriate examination for each position and links titles in a sequence of promotions.

[4] Annual Report of the New York City Personnel Department, 1970, p. 2.

Civil service classification systems vary tremendously in their size and complexity. New York City in 1975 had over 3,900 titles organized in 243 occupational groups. In contrast, the federal government has only 22 occupational groups. In writing about New York's system we said, "The multiplicity of titles and the resultant mass of exams is bewildering to both workers and managers and obscures the options available to each. Most titles are so specialized that they allow only a relatively narrow range of duties to be performed, thus cutting down on flexibility of assignments."[5]

Most systems have too many titles. The vested rights of an individual worker in a position, earned by passing a particular exam, make it difficult to eliminate titles. So systems tend to add titles and rarely succeed in removing any. Large complex classification systems are expensive to administer and control. Interagency transfers are complicated. It is difficult to keep track of the titles that exist and there tends to be no logical or simple career path for people in government.

Civil service titles reflect a conception of a job and in many technical and professional areas those concepts rapidly become outdated. For example, in a third-generation computer era, computer titles in government frequently reflect first-generation concepts and organization of work.

Sometimes, however, the title structure is not detailed enough. For example, a forensic chemist with an international reputation was unable to pass the examination for senior chemists because so much of the exam content was based on general chemistry, whereas the specific requirements of the chemist job in the medical examiner's office were extremely sophisticated and specialized. As long as testing and hiring are aimed at matching a person with a class of jobs rather than a specific job, such mismatches will always occur.

Combining Titles

The traditional civil service title structure often brings a caste system approach to municipal services. For example, if the man who drives an asphalt crew to the site is called a motor vehicle operator, he cannot participate in the work at the site and sits idly until the

[5]*Personnel*, p. 24.

work is completed, when he drives the crew back. The simplest way to overcome this incredible subdivision of labor is to create a civil service title of highway repairer, with duties and responsibilities including driving and filling potholes. Where there are a large number of separate titles, title consolidation (horizontal) and broadbanding (vertical) represent a modest incremental approach to the large-scale problem of sensible job definition in the public sector.

It is difficult to envision such a process having a substantial impact within a reasonable period of time. The process is slow: jurisdictional disputes exist where the titles to be combined are covered by different unions, and extra personnel costs are likely when higher- and lower-salaried titles are combined into a single title.

In this situation, some attention must be given to the issue of whether the right jobs exist. In particular, there is no point in mounting a massive effort to recruit bright, talented college graduates unless there is a specific layer of jobs for them defined within the overall system. Logical entry positions for potential managers tend to not exist or not be clearly defined in the public sector. When six kinds of "analysts" were combined in New York City into a single "staff analyst" position, the initial reaction of the personnel department was to make the staff analyst position the prerequisite title for an "associate staff analyst" leading to a "senior staff analyst." It was with difficulty that personnel was made to understand that the critical need was to make the staff analyst title also a prerequisite to regular managerial titles in the civil service system so that bright young people could move from "assistant to" positions into line management responsibility at an entry level. Few governments that have established internship programs have enough positions, and few have clearly thought through the relationship between the internship job and the rest of the job structure. When recruitment is done on the basis of a career path, a career path should actually be defined in the government.

Basic Reform

A more radical but more rational solution to the operational problems caused by the rigidity and complexity of civil service classification systems is to simply eliminate the entire concept of a civil service title. Rather than a classification approach (theory 1), cities and states would use the more modern position description approach (theory 2). Like industry, government would tap the energy and intelligence of the individual line manager in the definition of the job and hold that manager accountable for that job's contribution to the total effort of the organization.

With this approach, recruitment, selection, and actual appointment of individuals to jobs is on the basis of a specific performance-relevant position description. Each department is required to maintain on file (with the personnel department) a table of organization with specific detailed job descriptions, appointment criteria, and salaries for each job. These could be updated and revised either at fixed annual intervals or as part of an overall agency reorganization plan, not normally at the time that a vacancy occurs. Individuals are appointed whose skills best match the specific job specifications for the job to be filled.

Similar jobs are grouped into one of a small number of occupational groups along the lines used in the federal government (20–25 groups). This system of groups is enough to provide the basis for the kinds of screening exams discussed above. Related occupational groups are defined in three to five major classes or services (managerial, technical and professional, service delivery and clerical blue collar). The general characteristics of each service are defined in law.

The approach to hiring, administration, and salary range should be designed to suit the specific characteristics of the particular service, but the process has to be very carefully controlled in order to work. Often government job descriptions are a joke—either ten years old and irrelevant to the real job, or written after the fact to fit a person who has already been selected because of non-job-related characteristics such as political connections or instant availability. Pressured top managers often do not have the time, energy, or institutions to recruit the best candidates and may take the first candidate who appears to be acceptable.

Such an approach is a part of the civil service reform package enacted in the state of Wisconsin in 1977. These revisions changed the practice of establishing training and personnel requirements for classes of positions. Managers can now establish such requirements for individual jobs and are also responsible for justifying those requirements.

Replacing Barriers with Flexibility

The ability to assign and reassign people as needed is practically a nonissue in private industry. In a multinational corporation, reassignment of the upwardly mobile manager can mean frequent transfers of an entire family from one region or state or even continent to another. It is probably easier to move a middle manager working for an oil company from the Middle East to corporate headquarters than it is to move a city engineer from the water bureau in one end of city hall to the public works department down the hall.

Redeployment and reassignment among different departments is tremendously difficult in most cities and states. Why? First, the civil service title structure may be specific to a particular agency with no established equivalence in another department. This restriction is most serious with regard to managers. Civil service rarely recognizes that "a manager is a manager is a manager." The title structure for managers tends to emphasize the technical side rather than the managerial side of the task. Titles like Supervising Engineer and Supervising Architect are more common than titles like Manager.

Second, there is little or no tradition of involuntary transfer for the public manager. More seriously, there is little or no incentive for a manager to accept transfer. Unlike a well-managed private company, government has no tradition of lateral transfer in order to increase the experience and learning of the individual manager. In government, moving from one bureau to another at about the same level in the organization has no material bearing on the prospects for later promotion. Learning different parts of the organization does not help the manager to move up the ladder as it does in private industry, because most of the high-level jobs are equally specialized up to the very top. There, of course, appointments are based essentially on political criteria.

Third, there is typically very poor information with regard to the skills of individual workers. Most governments do not have a skills bank, and it is not easy to identify people in one part of an organization who might be useful in another. In setting up the staff of the Citizens' Committee for Effective Government in Hartford, the Hartford Insurance Group with 19,000 employees was able to identify three qualified candidates for the position of executive secretary within a matter of days. The three candidates who were identified were all excellent. In most governments of even half that size such a process would be difficult to imagine.

Particularly during a period of declining resources it is crucial that individuals be placed in environments and in jobs where their talents and skills are used to the maximum. Applying an attrition policy (hiring freeze) is a typical response to the resource squeeze and it often means that one agency might experience very large staff reductions while another has very small reductions. The ability to reassign and redeploy easily and flexibly in response to changing needs and changing patterns of attrition is crucial.

Where more than attrition is required, the randomness of government policy is even more obvious. It is virtually impossible to manage the layoff process because of the rigid application of seniority rules. "Last hired, first fired" not only hurts in terms of affirmative action goals, it also reduces management's capacity to prune the least useful individuals and the least useful functions from an organization. While it is true that seniority is a zealously protected right among workers in industry as well as government, it virtually never applies to managers in the private sector. In the public sector seniority applies to everyone. Where layoffs must take place, the employee who was hired last must be fired first, even if he or she is obviously more competent than someone hired one day previously. While it is admittedly easier to measure length of service than it is to measure competence, this seniority policy prevents the public from protecting its best or most valuable employees.

It is easier to point out the shortcomings of the seniority principle than it is to suggest ways which would work to make this principle a more meaningful tool. One approach to this modification would retain seniority as the predominant criterion in layoffs for nonmanagers as it is in the private sector, with these exceptions: (1) The definition of seniority would be broadened so that employees with approximately the same amount of seniority in service could be treated as equivalents. This could be done, for example, by establishing successive ranges of two years each. (2) Within each group the following factors could be considered: the relative importance of the employee's job and the quantity and quality of the employee's past experience (rather than simply the amount of time in the specific civil service title). (3) Employee performance should be recognized as an additional factor. Where performance rating systems are not in effect (see discussion below), an approximate measure of past performance can be used, such as sustained high absenteeism. For managers, the primary criterion for layoff should be performance.

Cities and states need to develop procedures for retraining personnel, along with redeployment. For example, with some retraining, engineers who are underutilized because of a cutback in capital construction might be used more effectively in high-priority areas such as computer-related or productivity (industrial engineering) applications. This capability not only would benefit the government, but would open new opportunities that would benefit the employees themselves.

Flexible redeployment strategies are possible with these modifications. In industry, examples are legion. When the New York Telephone Company reduced its staff of operators by 25 percent over three years (without layoffs), a complete program of reassignment, reorganization, and retraining was carefully developed and implemented within the context of a general attrition program.

Designing and Using a Performance Appraisal System

Modern personnel administration places significant emphasis upon systematic processes to measure and evaluate individual performance. These processes and measurement systems are extremely difficult to design and implement in any organization, especially where the service or product delivery is not easily quantifiable. The problems in designing and using performance appraisal and evaluation systems in the public sector are substantial.

Performance evaluation is a long-established tradition in government. Unfortunately, many of the older systems are relatively meaningless today. Evaluations are often based on personal traits or characteristics, not really on performance. Criteria tend not to be explicit. Often there is no real application of the results of an evaluation because promotion is by exam or through political relationships. There is little incentive for the line manager to do an effective or realistic job of evaluation. In New York City, for example, the performance evaluation system was abandoned in the late 1960s because it had proved to be ineffective. The 1963 Brookings Institution study of the city's personnel system demonstrated that the rating system then in use had little impact. In 1960–61 over 95 percent of the service ratings given were standard ratings while only .004 percent were below standard.[6] An average rating required no justification, whereas an excellent or unsatisfactory rating required a written justification. In the case of an unsatisfactory rating, the manager might become involved in an elaborate defense of the rating. With imprecise standards for ratings, there were actual disincentives for managers to evaluate their employees rigorously.

Modern performance appraisal systems have a number of critical elements. First, specific areas in which performance is to be measured are identified within the job specification. Performance standards are defined for each job. Second, the criteria for measuring performance are explicit. The employee knows before the period when the evaluation is carried out what is expected of his or her performance and what criteria will be used. Third, a specific rank or score for each employee is estimated. The system should incorporate controls on the number of high and low scores, since a system in which everyone receives an average is not of use. For example, in one such process all workers who report to a single manager and perform approximately the same duties would be ranked from the best to the poorest. Fourth, it is important that the standards for evaluating individual performance be linked to the overall system for measuring and evaluating the performance of the unit and the organization. Systems in use in the private sector vary. There are those in which the individual's full range of accountability is defined by the objectives of the unit for which the individual manager is responsible. Other organizations have two separate systems but ensure that there is a link so that ultimately individual performance is evaluated in terms of the contribution that the individual is making toward organizational objectives.

Promotion and Performance[7]

In a well-managed company, the driving force making managers work hard and effectively is the desire for promotion. The competi-

---

[6]David T. Stanley et al., *Professional Personnel for New York City* (Washington, D.C.: The Brookings Institution, 1963), p. 177.
[7]See Chapter 8 for a parallel discussion of work-related rewards and sanctions.

tion for promotion motivates managers to be creative about getting workers to work harder and better. In government, on the other hand, promotion is only marginally related to performance, at best. At the lower level, promotion tends to depend on some combination of seniority and ability to pass examinations. At the higher levels, political relationships and contacts are likely to be the key levers. Thus, in the very environment in which it is urgent to improve performance, rewards for good performance and sanctions for poor performance are rare, and the most important potential reward is removed and obscured by the civil service system. At best, promotion by examination mirrors performance indirectly. In some departments, such as police or fire, the most effective managers tend to do well on exams because there is a well-established tradition of preparing for and studying hard to pass examinations.

The system works most poorly in those types of departments where such a tradition does not exist. There the best people are usually too busy to study for exams. The people who score well on examinations and get promoted tend to be the less effective managers, who have been given less responsibility and are able to concentrate their efforts on passing the examination.

Despite these differences, opportunities for rewarding good performance and particularly for using performance in the promotion decision do exist in the public sector. Cities and states should recognize that the best way to fill a vacancy above the entry level is by promoting an employee who is performing well. This provides a sense of opportunity and mobility within an organization and supplies motivation. This principle applies not only to managerial appointments, but to nonmanagerial positions as well. Even in the context of the civil service examination process it is possible to give people "points" based on a mix of years of experience and quality of performance. In effect, each year that an employee receives a superior performance evaluation would add additional points to the examination score. Of course, there are limitations in the value of promotion in the public sector. Because of relatively great salary compression, the lure of potentially enormous salaries and benefit packages, which is an effective force in the private sector, does not exist in the public sector and probably never will.

Even relatively sophisticated reformers of public management have not adequately appreciated the importance of filling higher positions through promotion. They have argued that cities and states need to bring in an infusion of technical, professional, and managerial talent from outside the government. During the Lindsay administration in New York, such a "lateral entry" strategy was attempted. Many of the managers recruited during this effort had little knowledge of the city's operations and no lasting commitment to their improvement. In effect, it became a band-aid approach postponing the inevitable need to change the city's civil service system and to develop a process for the city to grow and educate its own managers. To workers and lower-ranked managers in the city, unrestricted lateral entry severely limits promotional opportunities and has a negative impact on morale and incentive to perform well. While it is important to keep open the possibility of recruiting new talent, it is much more important in government, as it is in industry, to give insiders credit for their knowledge of the organization and for the value of an established track record within the organization.

It is better to have a promotion system based on performance without bonuses or merit increases than to have merit increases and bonuses with a promotion system based either on exam-taking or subjective favoritism. In an environment where promotions are few and far between, something may be needed to augment even the most thoroughly performance-based promotion system, and it is here that merit increases and bonuses are probably not a bad idea.

Salary and Performance

The precise relationship between salary administration and performance appraisal is a subject of debate within the private sector. There are those who argue that performance appraisal should be most closely linked to the process of individual training and development and only loosely linked to salary administration. Others believe that salary administration should be the essential outcome of performance appraisal. All observers agree that some form of connection between performance and salary is a useful element in any management system. In the public sector, attempts to create such a link have not been generally successful.

A well-established system of performance-linked pay which does seem to work has existed in the state of Vermont for ten years. One hundred percent of the state employees in Vermont are eligible for, and approximately 95 percent receive, some pay increase. These increases range up to 9.25 percent, depending on performance. The distribution of recipients among level of salary increase roughly approximates a bell-shaped (normal) curve. A percentage is established for each level of performance appraisal. Thus all "good" employees receive the same percentage increase while "outstanding" employees receive another, higher percentage. Here are some conclusions from the Vermont experience, summarized by the state's commissioner of personnel:

- It can function only when the compensation plan is competitive with the labor market.
- It can function only when the classification plan is in good condition and is perceived by employees as equitable.
- It must be based on valid standards of performance objectives or PPBS which has provided for employee input.
- It must be accompanied by intensive supervisory training.
- It must be reviewed by an objective third party who can tie the distribution of performance ratings to the overall accomplishments of the organization.
- It must have the support of the chief executive.
- It probably is advisable to change the performance categories or definitions periodically, because no matter how closely one guards against it, the distribution tends to creep upwards.[8]

Performance Appraisal and Managerial Development

It is most important that appraisal be linked to a process of training and development, so that evaluation of an employee's performance can lead to help in performing better. The developmental objective of performance appraisal is one crucial link between individual appraisal and the long-range goal of improving the performance of the organization.

Discipline and Termination

Performance evaluation involves not only rewards for good performance but sanctions for poor performance. Do such sanctions

[8]Jacquel-Anne Chouinard, *Summary of Proceedings: Conference on Personnel Management Reform*, remarks given Jan. 23, 1978 (Washington, D.C.: U.S. Office of Personnel Management).

exist, and if not, can they be developed? Many believe that the inability to discipline or fire the public employee is the key difficulty in the public personnel arena and the most important difference between public and private personnel management. It is argued that the civil service employee is protected by that system, and the political appointee is protected by the same political connection that got him or her the job in the first place. Thus it becomes an accepted part of the conventional wisdom of managing in government that there is no point in trying to fire someone for performing poorly because that is impossible, and one simply has to cope.

While there is no question that both the civil service and political system act to protect the tenure of their workers regardless of how poorly or how well they are performing, it is not true that it is impossible to discipline or fire the nonproductive employee. To some extent the myth creates a self-fulfilling prophecy. A more useful mythology would be based on a different set of assumptions. In the private sector, too, strong unions place substantial limits on the ability of managers to discipline or fire workers for poor performance. Public managers tend to document discipline cases very poorly. Often they operate without explicit standards of what constitutes grounds for discipline or how the process is to be pursued. The line manager typically has less access to legal advice in the pursuit of a discipline case than does the worker. There is often no incentive for the manager to discipline. In environments with a hiring freeze, managers who suspend or fire a nonproductive worker find themselves with a position that they cannot fill for a very long period of time or with some risks that they will not be able to fill the position at all. In such a case, every manager agrees that "half a loaf is better than none." Often the procedures for discipline are so complex and cumbersome and poorly understood that to suspend or terminate an employee who is not performing effectively generates costs in time and energy that exceed potential benefits.

Over the long run, the definition of civil service tenure needs to be changed so that poor performance by itself is considered grounds for discipline or termination. In the short run, however, more opportunities appear to exist within the system than are typically used. Manuals for supervisors which document procedures, standards, and criteria; a process of legal counsel and advice and training for the line manager; maintenance by top management of standards of documentation—using all these methods would go a long way toward improving performance. In addition, other problems often go hand in hand with performance problems. For example, high absenteeism and lateness often correlate with poor performance, and under almost any system, high absenteeism is grounds for discipline and ultimately dismissal.

Centralization versus Decentralization

Under the traditional civil service system, personnel operations in government are highly centralized. Since the objective of the total system is to protect the holy grail of civil service against the potential inroads of political forces, highly centralized control built into the civil service commission was considered to be absolutely essential. Many attempts to reform civil service argue for decentralization of most personnel functions to the individual operating agency.

This view, as developed, for example, in the New York City Charter of 1975, argues that responsibility for personnel administration should be with the department head. In practice, this strategy means many personnel departments instead of one, with each operating unit (fire, police, etc.) operating a small personnel department as a staff unit to the department head. From the point of view of the individual line manager responsible for a unit, there is really no material change. Instead of dealing with the city's personnel officer, now he has to deal with, for example, the health department's personnel officer.

The practical impact of this approach is to limit the possibility of maintaining consistent standards, to reduce the possibility of the interagency transfers so badly needed in the face of declining resources, and to reduce the capacity of the central executive to implement overall objectives and policy within individual departments. At the same time, this approach does not necessarily untangle the knots for the individual line manager—it merely brings them a little closer to home (into the same department).

The real issue is not *whether* to centralize or decentralize personnel management, but rather *what* should be centralized and what should be decentralized at the level of the responsible line manager operating a unit. In the largest cities and counties, it is useful to

Figure 1. Allocation of functions in a centralized-decentralized personnel system for a large government.

	Centralized Personnel Department	Intermediate Office of Commissioner	Decentralized Line Manager
Hiring, Firing, and Promotion	Policies and standards	Postaudit individual actions for consistency with citywide standards	Individual decisions
	Recruitment and preliminary screening	Advocate of specific needs to central recruiter	
Salaries	Salary plan	Budget control	Individual decisions
Performance Evaluation	System and general standards	Agency-specific criteria	Individual evaluations
Personnel Planning	Database Forecasts Overall priorities	Needs analyses	Prospective (short-term) openings

think of three levels: central, line department, and the individual line manager. Planning systems and policies and standards are centralized in the personnel department to ensure consistency. Individual hiring, firing, and promotion decisions and the actual definition of each job are decentralized to the line manager. The department head plays the role of the arbiter between overall governmentwide imperatives and the specific needs of the individual line managers. Through the liberal use of detailed postaudit procedures, the department manager is the guarantor of the activities of each line manager to the overall government. Figure 1 lists this allocation of functions. Such an approach makes sense only in the context of a commitment to change the civil service system in ways discussed earlier. In tandem with managerial accountability for performance, decentralization of hiring makes sense; without it chaos results.

A key element in the ability of a government to restructure its personnel management is a much stronger emphasis on centralized personnel planning. Relatively little emphasis has been placed in the public sector on personnel planning. So much effort goes into testing that the average personnel department does little else. The typical personnel department in industry is responsible for designing, implementing, maintaining, and administering a personnel planning and control system. Virtually none of these functions exist in the typical government environment. Beyond the reforms in personnel policy needed to move governments into the post-civil-service era, the typical city or state needs to develop the kind of personnel planning and control capacity that exists in any reasonably well-managed company.

Information systems, forecasts of future needs, and succession planning are central to the concerns of the personnel director. Over the long run, cities and states must develop the kind of centralized personnel record-keeping and information systems as well as the manpower forecasting and planning capacity typical of any modern, large-scale organization. Standardized personnel records should be maintained within each department. The information should flow into a central citywide database containing demographic and skills-related information on all employees in the government. This information, together with annual reviews of personnel needs in each department, should provide the basis for manpower forecasting and planning, including plans for the reallocation of existing personnel.

But comprehensive personnel information and planning systems are expensive to design and implement. In the immediate future, cities and states should concentrate their efforts on an inventory of existing technical and professional skills. For it is in this area—which includes computer programmers, systems analysts, accountants, engineers, and lawyers—that cities and states are most vulnerable to the gradual erosion in work quality that many fear will be a by-product of Proposition 13. A skills-oriented personnel data system for technical and professional personnel is in itself a large undertaking, but it is relatively manageable compared with the comprehensive effort required to develop a total database on all city personnel.

Conclusions

The historic rigidities of the civil service system have tended to make the process of matching people, positions, and titles a game in which the creative or innovative manager can operate only by devising complex strategies for defeating or bypassing the civil service system. If necessary, the job description is reworked to fit the best candidate. If an examination has recently been given for the title most relevant to the specific job, then some other civil service title can be made to fit the specific job that needs filling, depending on the political and bureaucratic clout of the department head. Thus, the practical approach for hiring a staff assistant involves finding a candidate, defining a position that fits that person's background and classification, and matching the position with a civil service title for which no civil service examination list of qualified candidates currently exists, so that the candidate can be appointed provisionally.

Ironically, this approach has been used both by the unprincipled political operative seeking to place the least qualified person because of a political deal and by the most creative and innovative managers seeking to bring the best talent into the system. What is needed is an approach to civil service reform that will separate these two situations, that will make it difficult to bring incompetent and unqualified people into the system, but that at the same time will not throw up foolish roadblocks in the path of those willing and anxious to bring talent and expertise into the public service.

3

Cushioning the Impact
of Collective Bargaining

If civil service reform were the whole agenda for improving public personnel management, the task would be difficult enough, but cities and states in the United States have not one but two personnel systems apiece. The two—a civil service system and a labor relations system—provide in many areas of the country total redundancy, constituting a kind of fail-safe arrangement that doubles the personnel management task. In some governments two different sets of agencies operating under two different sets of statutes govern the two systems, each acting almost as if the other did not exist.

The most fundamental area of overlap between the two systems is job security. A keystone of the civil service system is tenure: the employee's right to a job once the probationary period is over. Under this system it is virtually impossible to fire a civil servant for poor performance. Public service unions are also zealous in protecting their members. As in the private sector, union apparatus to protect workers against arbitrary and capricious actions by management, including firing without cause, is firmly in place. Many other areas of overlap exist. For example, although civil service systems typically include a compensation plan, salary scales and salaries are actually established at the bargaining table. Grievance, discipline, or absence policies are the subject matter of both systems.

It is difficult to find the justification for such a dual system; the only apparent reason is historical. In the 1950s the civil service system offered only limited opportunities for general adjustments in salary levels and working conditions. Labor organized to press its case; collective bargaining machinery was established so that management and labor could address the legitimate issues; and so a new personnel system grew up alongside the old.

The central role of labor relations in personnel administration is relatively new compared to the 75 years of civil service. The classic Brookings Personnel Study of 1963 does not even mention municipal labor unions. Yet only nine years later Brookings published a volume by the same author, David T. Stanley, entitled *Managing Local Government Under Union Pressure.* In only six years, between 1962 and 1968, membership in public employee unions increased by 136 percent, compared with only a 5 percent increase in the private sector. By 1976, over 50 percent of the public employees in the United States were members of organized labor, compared with only about 30 percent in the private sector.

Public sector collective bargaining—new, vigorous, and powerful—differs markedly from the long-established civil service system. Collective bargaining in the public sector is difficult for everyone; compared to the private sector, it is chaotic. The lack of continuity of management from one administration to another makes it difficult to negotiate in good faith and to make long-term commitments.

While different areas of the country vary greatly in the militancy, power, and effectiveness of labor unions, over the next decade a period of increasing labor unrest in the public sector can be expected. Public employee strikes, especially in essential services, were virtually unheard of 10 years ago, but the unthinkable has become the thinkable within a relatively short period of time: a police strike in New Orleans in 1979 ruined the Mardi Gras. Precisely when cities and states must reduce costs and decrease personnel, labor union leadership, to sustain itself, must secure greater salary increases and must protect its membership. To protect its interest, labor unions must maintain pressure on managerial prerogatives, thus making the task of improving performance that much more difficult.

Collective bargaining in the public sector has some unique characteristics compared to industry. In the private sector collective bargaining is an adversary proceeding between labor and management. In the public sector the adversary nature of the bargaining process is diluted by the electoral process of the democratic society. This distinction has often been recognized, but what has not often been recognized is the fact that the conflict between the electoral process and the bargaining process is generic, except where there is a strong city manager system.

Every mayor or governor has a dual and contradictory role: as the chief executive and as the primary representative of the interests of all constituents. As chief executive, a mayor or governor is an adversary of unions. He or she is ultimately responsible for the settlements that are reached and sets the parameters for management negotiators. As the representative of his constituents' interest, however, the mayor is required to be responsive to union demands since municipal workers are a legitimate and important group of the mayor's own constituents. Thus, there is a paradox which translates at the operating level into such exclamations as these:

"How can you negotiate with someone who elects you?"
"When he [the mayor] got up from the negotiating table and put his arm around the union leader and said, 'Don't forget, I'm a friend of labor,' the bargaining was all over."

It is inevitable that the mayor's ability to bargain strongly with municipal unions as chief manager of the city is sharply limited by their legitimate view of the mayor as an elected official. Unlike private employees, city workers have the ability to influence the selection of management. It is no wonder that unions heavily invest not only money but, more important, the time and energy of their members in campaigns for public office.

These characteristics of collective bargaining in the public sector do seriously constrain the ability of city and state to improve personnel management. But the impact of these constraints can be cushioned. First, cities and states must be alert to the need to create a managerial class outside collective bargaining. Second, cities and states can adapt the strategies for preparing for bargaining that have developed over a long period of time in the private sector. In general, the preparation for bargaining in the average city is very poor. Third, there are new opportunities for labor-management cooperation in the area of productivity. Enlightened labor leaders have recognized that in the long run management and labor have a common interest in improving productivity. These three opportunities for cushioning the impact of collective bargaining are the concern of this chapter.

Creating a Managerial Class Outside of Collective Bargaining

The single greatest negative consequence of collective bargaining in the public sector is the tendency, in a unionized government, for managers to be covered. In the typical unionized company, collective bargaining is an adversary procedure involving workers on the one hand and management on the other. The individual manager identifies with management. The manager, not a member of the union, perceives his or her interest as being more wrapped up with the future and well-being of the company than with the future and well-being of individual workers or the unions that represent them. When this process works poorly, the result is labor-management strife, protracted strikes, hostility, and lack of productivity. When the process works well, there is a healthy, creative tension which keeps the system going. Even in companies experimenting with participatory strategies which dilute the traditional manager-worker relationship, workers and managers tend to preserve a substantial portion of their separate identity.

In the public sector this traditional distinction between manager and worker is virtually absent. Most employees whose function involves management are included under union contract. Indeed, many public managers find themselves in the very same collective bargaining unit as the workers they are supposed to manage. Often, this ambiguity is compounded by the civil service title structure. For example, a "supervising" title is often used to signify a higher level of skill and higher level of pay rather than the fact that the employee actually supervises other workers. Thus, a "supervising stenographer" is unlikely to supervise anyone.

The identity problem is further complicated by the fact that managers in the public sector often do not share a common civil service status. In the typical government, managers fall into two groups: political managers and professional managers. Political managers tend to come and leave with each administration. Professional managers tend to be long-term civil servants who have come up through the ranks. Not only do the political managers and the professional managers not view each other as part of a common group, they are often antagonistic. The political appointee is likely to view the civil servant as overly cautious and unresponsive to the policies of elected officials; the civil servant is likely to view the political appointee as transient and poorly informed about a department and its problems. Civil service managers are much more likely to identify with the people and processes that accompanied their rise through the ranks of competitive titles. Political managers are more likely to identify with the political processes and people that accompanied their progress. They are more likely to identify with the staff of elected officials at the state, federal, and local level than with the civil service managers whom they rub elbows with each week.

The public sector organization, unlike the typical private company, does not have a cadre of people in critical executive positions who are motivated to perform because they perceive their identity and interests as being wrapped up with those of their peer managers and those of the company that employs them. The public sector needs such a concept of managerial identity. Success will be attained when a manager chosen at random from a government organization, awakened in the middle of the night and asked, "What are you?" answers, "A manager," rather than "an engineer," "a civil servant," "a parks department employee," or "an officer of the American Federation of State, County, and Municipal Employees."

The absence of strong managerial identity in the public sector is expressed in the basic legislative framework. For the private sector a supervisor or manager is usually defined as anyone who supervises two or more people and who spends the majority of his or her time in supervision. While there is some variation from one state to another, a typical statute might define a manager (for the purpose of exclusion from collective bargaining) as someone who has a "policy-making or confidential role." Given this definition, it is not difficult to understand why, in a unionized environment, the percentage of people who are outside the union and are considered part of management tends to be very much higher in the private unionized company than in the public unionized department. In a typical company 10 to 20 percent of the employees are likely to be considered part of management. In a typical jurisdiction with a "policy-confidential" definition of manager written into the statute, fewer than 5 percent might be in this category.

The lack of managerial identity is deep and widespread. For example, a distinguished commissioner with a strong management track record publicly announced that he was turning in his union card because of a public conflict with the union, but his announcement came four years after his appointment as commissioner. A new police chief made a public statement expressing sympathy for the position of the union seeking salary increases for policemen precisely at the same time that the management team was sitting down to begin negotiations. It is difficult to imagine the chief executive officer of a company either keeping a union card or taking a public position in support of labor on the eve of labor-management negotiations.

Why did the system evolve this way and what sustains it? First, managers themselves who are outside the union often seek to join the union precisely because of their inability to get pay increases. Whereas in the private sector top management takes care of lower-middle and upper-level managers in the salary arena out of a sense of self-preservation—remember, they are identified with the company and its success—in the public sector raises for managers are often politically embarrassing to the chief executive and his top advisors. High salaries in the public sector are a political liability: the salaries of managers are high in comparison with the salary of the average voter.

Second, the existing system is sustained by the unions themselves. While union leadership recognizes the adversary nature of collective bargaining and the philosophical inappropriateness of having managers bargaining collectively, as pragmatists they must support anything which expands union membership. Union leaders believe that they can provide a genuine service to managers who are "getting the short end of the stick" on matters of compensation. Even in states with a legislative framework in which a manager is defined more or less as in industry, there is often pressure to reverse the definition and allow managers to bargain collectively. The state of Connecticut, for example, recently amended its state civil service statute to allow managers to bargain, whereas previously they were forbidden.

The consequences of this state of affairs are far-reaching. One of the most obvious problems is that without a management cadre of adequate size, government cannot take a strike. Thus the whole debate over whether public service unions should be allowed to strike is rendered moot, because without enough managers to operate services, the government has no choice but to capitulate in any strike environment, legal or illegal. The private sector company that can take a strike is that company which has a management force of adequate size.

Since improving public management requires a managerial class outside of collective bargaining, all employees in a state or local government who spend the majority of their time on supervisory or managerial tasks should be recognized as managerial for the purposes of exclusion from collective bargaining, as well as for the purposes of training, development, and a unique method of selection and advancement. Regulations prohibiting union membership for individual managers should be strengthened and penalties imposed. All managers in a jurisdiction should be explicitly identified as having a common status (for example, appointed through the same method), at least on paper eliminating the distinction between political managers and professional civil service managers.

A basic goal of the managerial class—a goal which transcends the collective bargaining/labor relations issue—should be *to maintain the delicate balance between professional management skill and commitment on the one hand and a capacity to respond to the policy perspective of elected officials and their appointees on the other hand.* Various proposals to achieve this balance have been advanced, and to some extent the struggle between civil service proponents and those who would destroy civil service as a system is precisely this struggle between political policy imperatives on the one hand and professional management skill on the other. Those who stress the professional management side of the argument tend to argue for a variation of the historical British model, in which all managers are professional and a permanent undersecretary actually administers a department. The proponents of the political policy perspective argue that a department head should be allowed to appoint all managers through unlimited lateral entry.

Neither of these two extremes seems viable. In searching for a useful middle ground, governments should experiment with the use of three- to five-year employment contracts for managers, explicit criteria for filling jobs in relation to detailed job descriptions, and an independent body to verify that individual managers who are appointed actually meet the standards and qualifications established for each specific job.

Strategies for Preparation for Bargaining

Even in those unusual environments in the public sector where there is a substantial managerial service outside of collective bargaining, labor relations can significantly constrain management's ability to implement improvement programs. A key constraint is the relative weakness of public sector management at the bargaining table.

In the private sector labor and management face each other across the bargaining table like two Japanese wrestlers—powerful, massive, evenly matched. Seasoned negotiators on both sides are backed up by mountains of data. Each side approaches the bargaining table after many months of preparation, equipped with a variety of arguments and alternatives. In the public sector collective bargaining is a relatively new, less sophisticated process. Government management often comes to the bargaining table outgunned, outmanned, and outmaneuvered by the union. Organized labor is likely to present seasoned negotiators backed by comprehensive and sophisticated analysis, clear policy directives, and a sense of where the leadership must come out, whereas management is likely to be represented by relatively inexperienced negotiators, who have been given no clear marching orders and who may be operating with some hastily scribbled numbers on the back of an envelope. Cities and states will not be able to implement programs for management improvement if organized labor in the pursuit of legitimate worker interests can undo these programs at the bargaining table.

The best private sector experience tells us that there are three key ingredients to a successful management negotiating posture: (1) a working process for reconciling conflicting views within management well before coming to the table; (2) adequate resources and time to develop information to define and support management positions; and (3) a clear negotiation strategy, including roles of people and scenarios.

Process for Reconciling Views

In any organization, different managers are likely to have different views of an appropriate posture on work rules and economic benefits for workers. The line manager wants maximum control over work conditions which affect output and would be willing to exchange these for higher economic benefits if that will mean more effective workers. The fiscal officer wants minimum costs. The "front office" is likely to want harmony and good public image.

In government, too, different actors have different views and interests. A department head may even support the salary demands of workers but is likely to be much more concerned about work rules which limit managerial prerogatives. Personnel officials are likely to be concerned about the impact of negotiations on existing established merit procedures. The budget agency is likely to be deeply concerned about the costs of any settlements. The difference between the typical city and the typical private company is in the time, energy, and procedures to reconcile these differences in an orderly fashion. Companies do it, and cities and states tend not to do it. The private sector pattern can be easily adapted by government (see Figure 2). At present, department heads either are not involved at all or mistakenly believe that they should be involved in the actual negotiation process. Systematic options are rarely developed, and participants in the process do not have access to a useful digest of the relevant background information.

Resources and Time to Develop Information

Most private companies devote substantial time and personnel resources to develop comprehensive information as part of the presentation of their case at the bargaining table. This is not the pattern in government in general. Even basic factual information regarding a city's own labor force—the number of employees by type of position and their current salaries—may not be completely accurate and up to date. Information on city wages and benefits compared to those of the federal government, other comparable governments in the same region, or similar positions in private industries in the region is rarely available in a useful form. Information on increases and changes in the cost of living and facts relating to the actual financial position of the city are typically available only in partial form. In some areas, an effort has been made to develop a management information system for labor negotiations. In Connecticut, for example, the Conference of Municipalities has developed such a system, and the data are fairly comprehensive. But in order for raw data to be usable in the intense environment of negotiations, they need to be

Figure 2. Recommended process for preparing for bargaining.

Step	Responsible Manager	Elements
1. Policy overview	Personnel Director Budget Director	Key negotiation issues
		Fiscal and economic condition of government
		Regional trends: wage and benefit levels (public, private)
2. Department proposals	Department Heads	Key work rule changes
		Relative salary scale of groups of workers within each department
3. Synthesis of policy overview and department proposals	Labor Relations Manager	Common concerns
		Conflicts between different departments
		Conflicts between departmental perspective and central policy overview
4. Options and associated costs	Labor Relations Manager	
5. Negotiation guidelines	Chief Executive	
6. Specific scenarios	Labor Relations Manager (negotiator)	"If . . . then. . . ." alternatives

thoroughly analyzed and carefully packaged. In many public environments management is unable or unwilling to devote the resources and time to assemble, organize, verify, analyze, and package this type of information. Very often the municipal unions put far more resources into preparing for bargaining than do managers. Such imbalances will have to be overcome or municipal unions will continue to outperform management at the bargaining table.

Preparing Clear Negotiation Strategies

In a typical private company environment, the information collected on the views of various managers and the overall guidelines developed by the chief executive are reworked into a set of alternative scenarios and strategies. These scenarios—in the form of "if they say 'x' we'll say 'y,' and if they propose 'z' we'll counter with 'a' "—are in the hands of a seasoned professional negotiating team. There is little or no ambiguity about who represents management at the table.

The public sector bargaining environment is very much more chaotic. First, the negotiating team often is not equipped with alternatives. They may in fact be somewhat in the dark about the chief executive's ultimate intentions as to what constitutes an acceptable settlement. Often negotiators are not given clear authority to represent management. It is characteristic of municipal and state bargaining processes that negotiators' positions are weakened by an end-run. When a senior public official (like a mayor) meets privately with union leadership to make the real deal and makes concessions after those self-same demands were rejected at the bargaining table by the negotiator, the impact on the credibility of the city's professional staff is devastating.

Second, public sector negotiators are often relatively inexperienced nonprofessionals. A wise observer of this scene once commented, "Labor relations is like sex. Everyone thinks they're good at it." Appointed officials newly arrived in the public sector at a high level suddenly find themselves thrust into leadership roles in labor negotiations. They are pitted against labor representatives who not only have years of negotiating experience but are, increasingly, professional negotiators. It is crucial that public sector manager-negotiators be of the same professional caliber as those representing the unions in the public sector, and that they be characteristic of private industry negotiators on both sides of the table. In the typical private sector pattern, a single professional company negotiator, armed with marching orders from the chief executive clearly defining the parameters of an acceptable settlement, actually carries out the negotiations and completes them with a handshake.

The relative weakness of management preparation in the public sector has a long-term negative impact on labor as well. This is illustrated by an incident which is supposed to have taken place during the Lindsay administration in New York. A key union official extremely active in the bargaining process is said to have called a Lindsay official not involved in the bargaining process. The message was, "For God's sake, please get someone down here who knows what they're doing—we are taking the city to the cleaners." In the long run, it is in the interest of labor and management for their representatives at the bargaining table to be approximately equal in the level of preparation, the quality of information, and in professionalism. In such an environment bargaining in good faith can take place, and the adversary process can work to develop an approximately equitable outcome.

Labor-Management Cooperation

The best way to cushion the adverse impact of collective bargaining is for management and labor to work together where common interests exist. A number of attempts have been made to involve labor and management in joint efforts to improve performance and productivity in the public sector. The theory is simple and appears compelling. If labor and management cooperate to save money or increase efficiency, then labor and management can share in the benefits that result from such savings. This gives labor a stake in the managerial agenda of improving service or reducing costs. While the prescription sounds simple, it is actually fairly complex.

First, the classic method for improving productivity is to mechanize, but substituting machines for people reduces the number of jobs and reduces union membership. In this area there is not in fact commonality of interest between union leadership and management. Second, many productivity improvements in the public sector are not easily translated into dollars.[1] In a typical industrial setting, increasing the number of widgets per hour is likely not only to decrease costs but to increase revenue, since widgets typically carry a pricetag. Increasing the output of trees pruned per hour in a public park may reduce costs but is not going to increase revenue unless we start charging tree viewers in the parks. Thus, it is possible to increase productivity, thereby increasing the quality and the quantity of service, without any dollar benefit to management. In a tight fiscal environment, this places a substantial strain on labor-management relations instead of improving them. Labor believes that because it has worked harder and produced more service it should be rewarded

[1]This discussion is amplified in Chapter 8, in the section headed "A Note on Productivity."

with higher pay. Management, on the other hand, is baffled as to where the higher pay is to come from if there is no reduction in cost. The most significant impediment in the way of labor-management cooperation to improve productivity is the traditional mutual suspicion that dominates labor-management relations in the public sector. If labor believes that management is out to exploit the worker, and management believes that labor is out to avoid work, the groundwork for cooperation and trust is not very substantial. Despite these difficulties, a number of interesting and significant experiments in labor-management cooperation have been undertaken.

Among the oldest examples of labor-management cooperation are the Tennessee Valley Authority's Union Management Cooperative Committees, operating since the 1940s. Joint committees involve construction, plant, and office workers in plans for increasing productivity and improving the workplace. A more recent example involves the fire department in Tacoma, Washington. As a result of a joint management-labor effort, the firemen's work week was reduced by two hours (without hiring additional men to make up the difference) by closing one stationhouse entirely and using the men and equipment from the closed facility as a roving batallion.

The most ambitious of the recent efforts in labor-management productivity developed in New York City during the fiscal crisis. The experiment attracted substantial national attention both because of its scope—all municipal departments and programs were involved—and because productivity was linked to a cost-of-living adjustment (COLA) and so had a direct impact on the salaries of all workers. As a case study it neatly captures most of the pitfalls and opportunities inherent in this area.

Case Study in Labor-Management Cooperation:
New York City's Productivity Program

The overall climate for labor-management cooperation in New York City was actually improved by the onset of the fiscal crisis in 1975. The union leaders in their roles as members of pension boards decided that they would prefer to risk the resources of the pension fund in an attempt to save New York City from bankruptcy than to risk the uncertainties of federal judicial receivership. Through the loan of $2 billion in pension funds that they effectively controlled, the leadership of municipal unions in New York bound the fate of municipal unions to the fate of New York City and the management of its government. This view affected cooperation in other areas as well. In the spring of 1975, a joint labor-management productivity council was organized. James Cavanagh, then first deputy mayor, was chairman. The key labor figures participated. Robert Schrank from the Ford Foundation was recruited as the senior consultant.

The council staff produced a report which documented some accomplishments and outlined a series of possible areas for further cooperation. As a prototype for cooperative projects, the report cited an agreement worked out between the teamsters' union representing bridge tenders and the city's transportation administration. The agreement followed a period of several years during which bridge-tender manpower was gradually reduced by attrition. As the force shrank, the men remaining were assigned to longer and often double shifts. The workers protested, while the city was paying $1.5 million in overtime. The union, the transportation administration, the fire department, and the coast guard reached an agreement whereby canal traffic would be scheduled on an 8 to 4 shift, with tenders on call during other hours. The workers no longer needed as bridge tenders were retrained and transferred to other city agencies, for example, as school security guards. "The outcome provided a satisfactory alternative for all parties; the city was spared the extra expense of overtime. The workers were relieved of overly long shifts; departments in need of personnel profited. Unnecessary jobs were eliminated and nobody was laid off."[2]

The staff of the productivity council recommended that a series of such discrete projects be undertaken. One involved an experiment in a sanitationmen's cooperative in one district. This experiment was never carried out because of opposition from national union leaders whose locals were involved in private carting. A second experiment involved the decentralization of substantial management authority to the district manager in three parks department districts. Although members of the union, they were being recognized as managers, given some responsibility for and authority over their own budget, and given increased capacity to deploy and redeploy personnel as needed. This project was implemented. A third project

[2]*Improving Productivity in Municipal Agencies: A Labor-Management Approach* (New York City Productivity Council, 1975), p. 14.

involved the concept of "contracting in." Parks department employees working in teams were given targets and cost standards for doing bench repairs that were comparable to those typically required of outside contractors, but this time they were given the opportunity to compete rather than having the work taken away from city employees. This project, too, was implemented with modest success. In the main, teams of parks department employees were able to produce at about the level of the private contractor, effecting cost savings and productivity increases over past efforts within the department.

In the early spring of 1976, labor and management were faced with the same dilemma. Labor contracts were expiring and the process of collective bargaining was expected to begin. Yet both sides were convinced that the municipal government had little or no resources to put on the table to meet demands of labor. Almost as a strategy of desperation, labor and management agreed to a productivity concept for pay increases. Under the provisions of the Financial Emergency Act of 1975, there was a salary freeze. Thus, technically no pay increases were possible. So a system was evolved whereby workers would receive a cost-of-living increase to be funded essentially by savings from productivity.

An elaborate network of labor-management working committees was set up, with one in each department. At the top of the pyramid was the labor-management productivity committee (reconstituted from the previous labor-management productivity council), which was to oversee and supervise the total efforts.

It did not take long for the basic issues to emerge. What is productivity? How should service improvements that did not yield increased costs be viewed? How and by whom should productivity be measured? Who will ensure that it really is taking place? Should all the gains from the different unions be pooled or should each local and department be on its own? Pooling savings would take away the incentives from any individual unit or manager or try harder. Not pooling meant that departments that had little opportunity for measurable productivity improvement because of the nature of their work (such as the personnel department or planning department) were at a disadvantage vis-à-vis "hard service" departments where some measurable function was being performed (number of checks processed, number of potholes filled).

Substantial differences also existed among departments with regard to the efforts already made to improve productivity. For example, it was widely believed that the fire department had managed to maintain service in the face of sharply decreased staffing levels, that is, a productivity increase, over the three years prior to the fiscal crisis. It was widely believed that other uniformed forces had not done so. The fire department was being penalized because it had "used up" the bulk of its potential productivity improvements, whereas the other departments would benefit from the fact that they had not been aggressive in improving their management.

These dilemmas became very real points of contention between the Emergency Financial Control Board and Special Deputy Controller Schwartz on the one hand and city management and unions on the other. The control board staff and Special Deputy Controller Schwartz demanded increasingly more detailed justification and documentation of actual productivity gains before authorizing the cost-of-living adjustment (COLA) payment. The unions, particularly the rank and file, became increasingly disillusioned with the entire process, because they viewed the COLA payment as a matter of right which was being withheld unfairly. City management, somewhat more sophisticated about the real complexity of productivity measurements than the control board staff or the special deputy controller, was constantly involved in trying to invent explanations to bridge basic conceptual gaps. The actual effort varied greatly by department, some departments putting forward a good effort to find and implement productivity projects; in other departments the effort became a mechanical or paper exercise.

The effort to link specific dollar payments to specific productivity or performance improvements on a citywide basis turned out to be counterproductive and less effective than the individual project efforts of the preceding labor-management council. By the end of the contract period, the whole effort had deteriorated to such a degree that neither labor nor management had any interest in continuing it in the next round of negotiations. It is difficult to allocate blame for this outcome. There were those who blamed the special deputy controller for "nitpicking" the effort to death. Others blamed the unions and management for turning the effort into a "Mickey Mouse" operation.

Conclusions

This effort suggests that labor-management cooperation is best based on specific projects rather than on any all-encompassing mechanism or process. The overall committee structure as a device to break down historical suspicion and hostility can be useful if there is something useful to put on the table. In the absence of projects which seem to meet the specific interests of management and labor, the overall process is likely to deteriorate into debating sessions or simply to go out of existence because of competing time pressures.

Collective bargaining in the public sector is here to stay. Management improvement programs need to include efforts to create a strong (nonunion) managerial class, to develop better management approaches to preparing for bargaining, and with some care, to build labor-management cooperation around specific projects.

4

Enhancing Employee Effectiveness

The contraction of public resources affects all areas of government, but it has a special impact on the people who work in government. Particularly in the older areas of the Midwest and the Northeast, city and state governments are struggling to close substantial gaps between projected revenues and estimated expenditures. The largest portion of government expenditure is for personnel—that is, salaries and fringe benefits for workers. Thus, personnel costs must be reduced or at least held relatively constant. This cannot mean a long-term salary freeze, for governments would soon find themselves unable to compete for skilled labor with the private sector. The increasing power and militancy of public labor unions would make a long-term salary freeze impossible in any event.

This situation suggests that the basic tool for cost reduction in most environments is reduction in the size of the workforce. The ability to manage such a reduction in an orderly and humane way without destroying public services is a key element of the public management challenge. This can be done the right way—without impairing and, hopefully, while improving the quality and quantity of services—or it can be done the wrong way, which will hurt services. The obvious approach is to replace fewer and fewer employees when they leave, that is, to take increasingly large levels of net attrition. Clearly this is the course of action that has the least harmful impact on individual workers and on the local economy. If that is not enough, then the inclination is to turn to layoff.

In order to minimize the political impact on any particular constituency, the tendency in government is to apply such policies across the board. If a hiring freeze is in place, it typically affects all departments equally. If there is a policy of replacing every two or three employees who leave with one new employee, such a policy again is typically applied evenly across the whole government. In some instances, no distinction is made between those who retire and those who are dismissed for disciplinary reasons. In such a case, there is an obvious disincentive for any manager to terminate a nonproductive employee, on the general theory that some help is better than none. Where rehiring is done selectively, it tends to be in those areas that are the most visible and politically sensitive (such as police and teachers). Cuts in personnel level tend to hit the least visible functions. "Backroom" workers such as computer specialists, payroll clerks, or finance auditors are likely to be the most heavily affected by traditional responses to the need to reduce labor costs, despite their obvious importance.

This conventional approach to reducing the cost of labor under the pressure of declining resources is essentially a strategy of gradual bleeding. Services become eroded, and morale is set back as more work seems to accumulate with fewer hands to do it. Some units may have more than enough staff while other, comparable units are completely unable to cope with a workload because of the way that retirement and other attrition is distributed. One unit may lose half its workers in a year while a comparable function in another part of the government may not lose any of its workers. Highly qualified professionals with other job opportunities are particularly likely to leave public service, so that in time the overall quality of this workforce is bound to decline.

Most significant of all is the impact of gradual retrenchment on morale and motivation. If government is on the defensive and the resources are declining while the needs and demands on government are not, a decline in morale and a loss of sense of opportunity are almost inevitable. This will make it increasingly difficult for government to retain, let alone attract, good young professionals and managers. It is a truism that where worker morale is high, productivity is high. Ironically, precisely at the time when government productivity increases are most urgent, contraction and retrenchment have brought public service morale and motivation to their lowest point.

The talented individual in government does not experience the financial rewards that are possible in industry or the sense of satisfaction at carrying out public service, or even the sense of being appreciated. At least since the depression, government has been particularly attractive to workers placing a high value on both short- and long-term security. With declining resources and fiscal uncertainty, even this security is no longer guaranteed. In New York City, for example, it became difficult to recruit qualified accountants even though the installation of new accounting systems and drastic improvement in financial management made the opportunities for rewarding professional work outstanding. The main reason given for this difficulty was not the pay scale but rather the sense that government employment was no longer secure. Particularly in an environment in which layoffs occur in seniority order (last in, first out), young accountants were reluctant to take risks.

In the effort to improve management, the most difficult challenge of all may be to find workable strategies to maintain the morale and quality of the public workforce.

The long-range strategy that appears most viable is to build a workforce much smaller in numbers and more highly skilled, supported by maximum possible automation and mechanization. With such a workforce, cities and states should be able to pay the individual worker higher wages, attract effective workers and managers, and provide good service at reasonable cost without exceeding expenditure limits.

The best mid-range strategy is a systematic program of redeployment and reassignment to fill critical needs, as well as a process of setting priorities and reassessing basic functions to eliminate programs no longer critical. It includes retraining of personnel in conjunction with the redeploying of people from less crucial to more important occupational areas. Both the long-range and mid-range strategies depend on the successful implementation of civil service reform as described in Chapter 2.

This chapter examines short-run strategies that enable cities and states to go beyond simple attrition (hiring freeze) programs: efforts to manage employee time more effectively, streamline organization structure, and increase employee accountability and participation to combat declining morale.

Managing Employee Time

The least painful response to declining resources is to manage the time of existing personnel more effectively. Losses of manpower due to attrition without replacement can be at least partially made up by increasing the available time or, conversely, reducing the amount of lost time and the amount of nonproductive time of city and state employees. All the available evidence seems to indicate that absence rates are substantially higher in government than they are in industry. In a sample of six typical companies in comparison with eight city departments in the municipal government in Hartford, it was found that whereas the city's average absence rate was twenty days per year from all causes, private companies ranged from eight to ten days lost. There is no reason to suspect that public employees tend to be less healthy than those employed in the private sector, but there are some who argue that there is a greater distribution of hazardous occupations in government than in industry. In order to test this assertion, departments with primarily white collar occupations were compared to private companies that were similarly heavily white collar, and departments dominated by blue collar jobs were compared to manufacturing companies. (See Figure 3.)

In both government and industry higher absence rates were associated with blue collar than with white collar jobs, but in both cases the absence rates in government were substantially higher. While no comparable body of national data exists, the few studies which have been done seem to indicate that the Hartford data are not unusual, that the Hartford municipal government is comparable to other governments and Hartford industry is reasonably representative of absence data in industry in general. There are those who would argue that this finding simply supports the more general view that government workers have excessive benefits. Many public sector labor contracts do allow for up to 12 or 15 days of illness and are often liberal in their interpretation of an allowable absence up to and including illness of a member of the extended family (aunt or grandmother). Others point to the difference in attitude between employees in the public sector and those in the private sector. In the private sector, typically, an employee who is sick a reasonable amount of time is entitled to be paid but must account for and verify illness. In the public sector the typical employee believes that he or she is "entitled to" a specific number of days (12 or 15) and that any questioning of the amount of sick leave begins after those days are used up. Sick leave is considered analogous to and sometimes combined with vacation pay. Still others point out that in many private companies, absenteeism impacts pay levels. However, there is some

Figure 3. Comparison of lost-time rates (sick time and workers' compensation only) between city and private industry employees in Hartford, 1978.

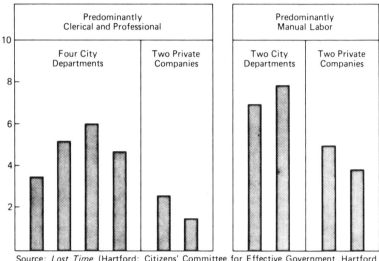

Source: *Lost Time* (Hartford: Citizens' Committee for Effective Government, Hartford Management Study, 1979), p. 9.

evidence that these collective bargaining and attitudinal differences are not the controlling factor in explaining variation in sick leave. The Hartford study on loss of time showed that the amount and level of absence varied greatly not only among departments with roughly similar functions, but also among different units within the same department.

The important determinant of the level of absence seems to be quite simply the extent to which absenteeism is managed. In the same study, through interviews with personnel managers in private companies in the Hartford area, it became obvious that different companies had quite different approaches to the management of absence. In one company the system was built around very intensive data collection and reporting, and a complex scoring system to measure and evaluate the level of absence. In another company the records were relatively sparse, but supervisors had been highly trained in the art of managing absence and were deeply and personally involved in helping each employee maintain the maximum well-being. In other words, the choice of a particular model for

Figure 4. Lost-time rates in Hartford and proposed initial targets for their reduction, 1978.

	Current Lost-Time Rates (Sick time and workers' compensation)		City Proposed Initial Targets
	City	Private	
Predominantly Clerical and Professional	5.0%	2.5%	3.5%
Predominantly Manual Labor	7.5%	4.5%	5.5%
Predominantly Hazardous	7.4% 12.5%		7.0%
Value of decreased lost time: $800,000			

Source: *Lost Time* (Hartford: Citizens' Committee for Effective Government, Hartford Management Study, 1979), p. 9.

managing lost time was not as important as the commitment to *have* a system for managing lost time.

In general, two elements seem crucial in the design of an approach to managing lost time. The first is to recognize the first-line supervisor as the central actor. A simple supervisor's manual based on a sequence of increasingly intense intervention seems to be the critical element. The second element is to develop a formal process for measuring lost time, reporting information on absenteeism up through the management system, and establishing a set of targets for lost-time reduction. Managers at every level of the organization know and are held accountable for the level of absence within their own units.

Such a program was partially implemented in Hartford. In Figure 4, the left column shows the average lost-time rate for the three main categories of city employees in 1978. The middle column shows the two comparable rates found in the private sector. Finally, the right column shows initial proposed targets for the city's new process for managing lost time. These performance measures were developed by comparing city rates with private sector rates and by comparing work units within departments. Through this program Hartford did succeed in reducing absenteeism by about 10 percent.

A closely related problem is nonproductive time, which is the time the employee spends on the job during which the employee is not working. Relatively few cities have working systems for keeping track of nonproductive time. At a minimum such a system is required for any serious effort to manage the work process more effectively. This is discussed further in Chapter 8.

To cut absenteeism from 10 percent to 5 percent and nonproductive time from 30 percent to 15 percent is the equivalent of a 20 percent increase in the number of employees. An attrition program coupled with a program to increase productive time and decrease absenteeism has rather different consequences from the typical attrition program which is not coupled with any attempt to increase the working time of existing employees.

Streamlining Organization Structure

A second significant way to reduce labor costs without disrupting services is by systematic examination of organization. Many managers believe that formal organization charts are essentially meaningless, yet organization structure still continues to turn up on a variety of lists of the key ingredients in well-managed companies. In the public sector a great deal of public administration literature is devoted to organization and organization structure, discussed not only in terms of internal structure but also in relation to technology and environment. The analysis of internal structure, much more situational than the "old organization theory," is epitomized by Harvey Sherman's excellent little book, *It All Depends*.

Yet the conventional, real-world approach to reorganization in the public sector remains quite simplistic. It is typified by "super-agency" reorganizations, such as were undertaken by the Connecticut and Massachusetts state governments and Lindsay's New York City administration. These efforts tend to respond to two specific issues: (1) the perception of overlap and the duplication of functions among different agencies or bureaus, and (2) the perception that there are too many separate departments reporting to the chief executive. In Connecticut's case, 96 separate departments were combined into 17 departments. The criterion for creating these units was functional, that is, activities that appeared to be related were grouped. The approach is top-down, starting with the broad functions of government and the key related constituencies. Reorganization of the superagency variety tends to be costly, as a new layer of people and positions is added.

The approach outlined below takes a completely different stance from the assumptions of the classical top-down functional reorganization. According to this approach, streamlining the organization in an environment of contracting resources requires more attention to the bottom and middle than to the top of the organization; it therefore starts the organization structure with a bottom-up rather than a top-down approach, and focuses on reducing positions wherever possible. Reorganization is seen primarily as an instrument of cost reduction. This approach is illustrated with reference to two classical issues in organization analysis: (1) increasing span of control, and (2) reducing the number of levels of management.

Span of Control

The new organization theory has virtually demolished the rule of thumb of five to seven workers per manager, developed under the old organization theory. However, in practical terms, even the old rules of thumb are still fairly useful as a starting point.

Government is dominated by a pattern of one-on-one reporting relationships. Virtually every important position on a government table of organization has a deputy. There are several reasons for this. First, it is a status symbol. Having a deputy implies that the manager is a person of consequence and importance. Second, much high-level governmental activity is outward-looking, involving legislatures, the media, constituent groups, and the like. However, there is often no clear distinction between jobs. Number 2 is someone who accompanies number 1 to all those meetings where the projection of high status becomes desirable. The pattern is inefficient and wasteful. In effect, number 2 is an understudy. This pattern may make sense at the level of the President of the United States, where it is essential to have a high-level understudy waiting in the wings. It is not at all obvious that this pattern is useful in the typical state or city organization.

At the other extreme there are often horrendously high spans of control of large forces, where expenditures for supervision compete with expenditures for additional jobs for the available scarce resources. In one large northeastern city, people ceased to wonder why the beaches were dirty when it was discovered that CETA personnel were "supervised" in a ratio of one supervisor to 50 or 100 CETA workers.

In addition to bizarre extremes one also finds odd patterns. Through gradual attrition and historical accident, six units may all be performing roughly the same function with the same responsibility and workload and with widely varying ratios of span of control. In the New York City Parks Department, for example, it was found that area managers could have anywhere from 10 to 60 people reporting to them. There is usually a reason for the pattern. For example, given the difficulty of firing weak supervisors, there is a tendency to take people away from the individual supervisor who is performing poorly and assign them to the supervisor who is doing well. Even if this were reasonable, it is possible for the pattern to persist for several years after both people are replaced. Sometimes the reason is more subtle. Two parks districts may appear to be similar, but one may in fact contain a much more complex and difficult mix of population groups, whereas another, more homogeneous area is relatively easier to manage. The point is not to impose a rigid set of rules, but rather to insist that there be some reason for significant variation in the spans of control of people apparently performing the same or similar functions.

One would expect that field workers in scattered decentralized locations would require greater supervision and therefore a lower span of control than a group of clerks working in a single room. Within a division where one unit has demonstrably more complex work than another, greater supervision would appear to be required in the first group than in the second. Very often, however, none of these relationships holds true, and it is not unusual to find one supervisor supervising 15 or 20 people working independently in scattered locations, on the one hand, and a supervising clerk with only 4 or 5 people sitting in an office, on the other hand.

Span of control standards vary from the top to the bottom of an organization. In government, very often managers at the top of the organization (like the mayor) have very high ratios of span of control, that is, many people report to a single manager. This is because of the perceived need for many visible managers, each identified with an important constituency. At the bottom of the pyramid the ratios of span of control tend to be low, with relatively large numbers of first-line supervisors. This is because during periods of difficulty in getting pay increases for workers, the only way to give an increase is to create "supervisory" jobs and to "promote" workers into them. These positions are not really supervisory, but are simply a way to get pay increases for workers. From a management point of view the inverse should be true. At higher levels in an organization the work tends to be more complex, and more is at stake for the total organization in the work of each manager. This would argue for having relatively few people reporting to the top manager and relatively few people reporting to each of the second highest managers. At the bottom of the organization, where the work tends to be more routine and more defined, from a management perspective one would expect to find the highest spans of control, that is, relatively large numbers of people reporting to the first-level supervisor or manager. While the traditional pattern responds to real pressures, it has serious drawbacks in efficiency in public organizations.

Levels of Management

The issues relating to levels of management in an organization have not been as widely discussed in the organization literature as the issues of span of control, but they are probably as important from a practical point of view. Most public organizations have too many levels of management, that is, too many different managers in a reporting relationship between the top of the organization and the worker in the field. Deputies at the higher levels and supervisors who do not really supervise at the lower level add several levels more than necessary. It is not unusual to find six, seven, or even eight levels of management in a large government. However, a well-managed organization, even if large, probably can function perfectly well with four or five.

    The consequences of too many levels of management are serious. The more levels between the top and bottom of the organization, the more complicated do communications become, as mayoral policy is transmitted through both political managers and civil service managers to departments and then to workers. Some of the distortions in the structure of levels of management are the result of deeply rooted tradition, particularly within the uniformed forces, and very often the distinctions are really not functional. For example, most police departments have sergeants, lieutenants, captains, and inspectors. It is often difficult to discriminate between the functions of a sergeant and a lieutenant or between a lieutenant and a captain or between a captain and an inspector. This pattern, particularly in a small department, results in small spans of control and extra levels of management.

In the context of tight resources, the imperatives move in the same direction, that is, to maximize span of control and minimize the levels within an organization. The objective in both cases is to save money by reducing unnecessary positions. The best way to accomplish this objective is to eliminate a level in the organization. Almost automatically, this increases the span of control. An interesting application of this approach was reported on as the basic rationale behind the improved performance of Kaiser Industry.[1]

In the same department, it is not unusual to find an imbalance of responsibilities within the same management level. For example, the bureau of operating services within the public works department in Hartford, one of three bureaus in the department, accounts for 70 percent of the personnel and 65 percent of the expenditure of that department. This indicates that the other two bureau chiefs in that department, who earn approximately the same salary and have roughly the same status as the chief of operating services, have lesser responsibilities. A manager responsible for a portion of the operating services division (such as street cleaning) could be earning significantly less and have much less status than one of the bureau chiefs who has much less to do and far less of the city's activities under his or her direction.

In a "rational" organization managers at the same level of the organization (those with roughly equivalent salaries and status) are responsible for roughly equal amounts of the organization's activities, however measured. This approach assures that executive energy and status are allocated roughly in proportion to the organization's needs to produce, and that more managerial energy goes into those areas of activity that are more important, as measured by the number of personnel, budget, or workload. But the common tendency in the public sector is to establish a department when

[1] *The New York Times,* March 30, 1979.

pressures, demand, and constituency reach a critical mass. The results of this pattern of historical accretion are often quite peculiar. Thus, in New York City, for example, one commissioner might be responsible for 30,000 people and a budget of $1 billion, while another commissioner might be responsible for 100 people and a budget of $200,000. Each reports to the mayor; each has roughly the same status and the same salary. In effect, this means that within larger agencies there are individuals who, although responsible for enormously important functions, very large budgets, and large numbers of personnel are treated as if they were supervisors of a small unit. Agencies, boards, and commissions become multiplied in order to maximize visibility for important constituencies. It is difficult to close or eliminate departments. There is always pressure to form new departments. Questions of the efficient size of an operation tend to be ignored in such conflicts.

Increasing span of control and/or reducing management levels, particularly in smaller jurisdictions, is likely to require a single manager to supervise a variety of functions. In the public sector, where the professional and technical dimensions of a manager's job tend to dominate the managerial dimension, such a result is likely to be viewed with great hostility and alarm, and in fact is grossly unorthodox. But in principle there is nothing wrong with having a single manager responsible for a variety of different functions or activities as long as the subordinates are adequately skilled in the professional and technical aspects of the job and the manager can be trained or is already skilled in general management. Mixing apples and oranges is not always a problem.

The foregoing discussion applies primarily to line jobs (those involving operating authority and control), as opposed to staff (who are supporters and advisors to decision makers). It is useful to reduce the confusion over the relative importance of the two roles. There is a recent unfortunate tendency in government for staff positions to become more important than line ones, but in the last analysis only the line manager can directly produce improvement in quality or reduction in costs.

In industry, staff are seen as enablers. The organizational spotlight is on those who have the responsibility to produce for the organization, that is, managers in the line. Since the well-managed company typically rotates its managers through line and staff positions, no real rivalry develops, because today's staff person is yesterday's line manager, and vice versa. In some governments, however, staff positions have become predominant. It is not unusual for a twenty-eight-year-old budget examiner earning $25,000 a year to ride roughshod over a fifty-year-old parks department line manager who might be responsible for the work of 150 people and a substantial part of a city's park and recreation program and who is earning only $16,000 or $18,000. Staff tend to be higher paid and better educated and to have little respect for the line manager, who is likely to have progressed slowly through a civil service process and to have little formal orientation to management or new policy initiatives.

Implementing Organization Analysis and Change

To capitalize on the opportunities to reduce costs and improve service through better organization, it is useful to have a formal program of analysis incorporating three basic steps: (1) documenting the existing organization; (2) evaluating it, and (3) redesigning it.

Step 1: documenting the existing organization. In the well-managed corporate environment, the organization chart is viewed as an instrument of management control. Most public organizations have either very primitive or minimally useful organization charts, something that you pull out of the bottom drawer to show visitors.

Each department should maintain its own organization chart documented in the same way. The chart should document organization structure down to the first level of supervision, because this will show critical ratios such as the span of control and the ratio of staff to line. Substantial effort should go into keeping the charts reasonably up to date.

Documentation itself, however, does not necessarily suggest what if anything needs to be done to improve the existing organization.

Step 2: evaluating the existing organization. Each government should have a set of standards that can be applied system-wide to evaluate each unit in the organization. Standards are helpful for span of control and for levels of management. For example, instances of control spans that are too high, too low (such as one-on-one), or inconsistent among similar operations can be identified easily through standards. Similarly, reporting relationships can be analyzed to find instances where there are too many levels of management. Other relationships need to be assessed as well. For example, are there too many staff positions relative to the number carrying line responsibilities?

Step 3: redesigning the organization. In most jurisdictions such an analysis will reveal serious deficiencies in the existing organization. In attempting to redesign an organization, most people intuitively reach for the top of the page—the top of the organization. The best place to start, however, is at the bottom. The first decision is to determine the size and number of the basic work units as a function of the size and nature of the workload. Once the number of work units is established, the base of the pyramid is in effect determined. The foreman or supervisor leads one work unit or crew. The first level of management is established by a standard for span of control—how many work crew supervisors it is sensible or reasonable to have managed by a single manager. The same logical process repeats itself at the second, third, and successive levels.

Obviously this approach requires powerful support, for all manner of sacred cows are involved. Only in the context of sharply declining resources are such reorganizations as changing police rank structure even thinkable. Much of the opposition to reorganization comes from the apprehension that substantial numbers of people will lose their jobs, but reorganization can eliminate excess positions without necessarily firing or laying off anyone. It is an intelligent way to implement an attrition program. In an environment sadly deficient in planning and control staff and typically lacking ongoing operations analysis or in-house management consulting groups, excess managers become an excellent resource for such activities.[2]

Strategies for Improving Morale and Motivation

One of the major consequences of the gradual and constant decline in public resources is the loss of morale of the existing workforce and the long-range impact on the overall quality of the workforce. There is little doubt that Proposition 13 has been widely interpreted by public employees as an attack not only on their jobs but on the

[2] The need for operations improvement staff is discussed in Chapter 15.

value of what they do. The link between morale, job satisfaction, and productivity may not be precisely measurable, but it is difficult to deny that poor morale and low motivation help to lower output. Although there are still those who view productivity and performance as essentially a mathematical relationship between inputs and outputs, at least since Douglas McGregor's seminal work, *The Human Side of Enterprise,* most analysts have recognized the significance of the intervening human variable in improving job performance. Cities and states faced with declining resources and increasing public pressure to perform need explicit programs to improve public employee morale and motivation, increase job satisfaction, and develop incentives. The productivity report issued in the context of the early hopeful days of the labor-management cooperation effort in New York City makes this point clearly and cogently:

> Motivating employees means giving them incentives. The process of building worker morale has been given less attention than technology or measurement; it is far more complex, much more abstract, and requires a great deal of planning and patience. In the long run, however, the payoff may be far greater. . . . In the face of New York City's multiple crises—lack of money, lack of management, and lack of morale—the first question is why should public employees work harder? What incentives do they have? Lack of accountability usually means that no one is blamed for doing a bad job, and lack of appropriate recognition means that there are few rewards for jobs well done. Moreover, without clear, realistic Departmental objectives and performance standards to aim for, accomplishment is hard to come by. In short, there is no motivation to put forth one's best efforts. On the contrary, there are organizational obstacles at every turn—budgetary, bureaucratic, political.[3]

The seeds of a positive program to turn around employee morale and motivation in the public sector lie precisely within the current set of problems.

Accountability Strategies

Research indicates that very frequently people do not know what is expected of them in their jobs. According to one study, when super-

---

[3] *Improving Productivity in Municipal Agencies: A Labor-Management Approach* (New York City Productivity Council, 1975), p. 10.

visors and supervisees were asked to list what was expected of the workers in their jobs, there was an overlap of only 30 percent between the lists of the workers and the lists of the supervisors. A clear job definition, a meaningful organization chart, and explicit and clear performance standards and criteria for each job would go far toward establishing a reasonable structure for work. A clear set of objectives, and explicit feedback as to how one is doing in terms of those objectives, becomes a useful focal point for the worker.

A comprehensive survey of productivity and job satisfaction in the public sector found that these same factors were the most important:

> There is a strong set of correlations between a feeling of satisfaction and dimensions of the job such as autonomy or feedback from those who receive one's services. . . . In the area of job performance the most important positive variable was information and feedback [i.e., frequent communication with workers about the quality of their work]. . . . Feedback appears necessary to assure production improvement. This seems to say something about the need to establish clear and constant connections between a worker, his or her efforts, and the quality of the product or performance.[4]

Recognition

Another key strategy for improving morale and motivation is simply recognizing good performance. It is difficult for someone outside of the public sector to conceive of how little recognition there is for the individual employee who does well. It is not uncommon to walk into a small office in a government department and to find one person working very hard, a second person working moderately hard, and a third person sitting at a desk and reading a newspaper. The system does not in any way distinguish among these three employees whose duties might be identical. If the third employee eventually puts down the newspaper and begins to study for the next civil service exam, it is perfectly likely that that employee will advance while the one who is working very hard will not.

It is not surprising that most government departments have at least a sprinkling of angry or indifferent employees who came in like

[4] W. Patrick Dolan, *Work in the Public Sector* (Washington, D.C.: National Training and Development Service, 1977), pp. 14–15, 20–21.

"gang busters" and several years later are indistinguishable from their fellows. On the other hand, even in the typical public agency in which absenteeism is extremely high, there are still individual people doing dangerous or hazardous work who may not have missed a day's work in years.[5] The system does nothing to recognize let alone reward such individuals. While American workers are probably somewhat cynical about such rewards or recognition as the U.S.S.R.'s Medal—Hero of the Soviet Union, the public sector has an overwhelming need to try to develop meaningful ways to recognize good performance.

Reducing Frustration

Among the critical causes of poor morale in any work environment are roadblocks that impede the worker from doing his or her job. A schedule that is not ready, a truck that runs out of gas because another employee forgot to do his or her job, a set of guidelines or instructions from the manager that are internally inconsistent and impossible to carry out—these exist in industry as well as government. Working in government, however, imposes on the worker a very high level of frustration as part of the day-to-day work.

The political and bureaucratic environment constantly generates delay, indecision, and apparently arbitrary rules or changes in rules. Particularly in the beginning of a new administration, it is not unusual for three or four different representatives of a newly elected official to be articulating different guidelines or policies. To some extent the elimination of roadblocks in government, as in the private sector, is one of the most important contributions that management improvement programs can make. Equipment and equipment maintenance can be provided, schedules and procedures can be made more realistic and more workable.

But to a significant extent, much of the frustration of the public service is generic. The electoral process in a democratic society does generate uncertainty every two or four years. The system of checks and balances built into our democratic society does cause delay. The need to satisfy various constituencies and concerns in any important program also causes delay. A reasonably high thresh-

---

[5] See Chapter 8 for a discussion of work-related rewards.

old of frustration tolerance is simply one of the characteristics needed to work effectively in the public service, much as working in a submarine requires the capacity to operate within a confined environment without developing claustrophobia.

Participatory Strategies

The most complex and ambitious strategy for combating declining morale and motivation in the public sector involves increasing participative management. There is some evidence that where there is increased participation in decision making by individual workers, absenteeism is reduced and job satisfaction rises. New York City's productivity report pointed out, "Those who do the work, know the work best. There is no way to increase productivity without some participation by the workers, regardless of whether the work is a line, supervisory, or management function. Employee knowledge is often underestimated and underutilized."[6] Increasing the opportunity for employee input into decision making through such means as consulting with workers about what reforms make sense to them is one way to build a sense of teamwork. Giving workers and junior managers an opportunity to negotiate their objectives rather than having objectives handed down to them is another way to accomplish the same result.

Several major corporations are involving their employees in decision making through quality circles—committees of five to thirteen employees who devise plans for increased productivity. General Motors, Ford, 3M, Martin Marietta, and Westinghouse are using quality circles to generate greater output. This specific approach to increase worker participation in the design of work content and context seems eminently adaptable to the public sector.

While not in the same formal mode as the quality circle, specific examples of involvement of workers do exist in the public sector. In Scottsdale, Arizona, for example, a team of parks department employees worked with an architect on plans for a new building. From the janitor to the recreation superintendent, all levels of employee participated in designing the structure. The result was a building that was attractive, relatively inexpensive, functional, and easy to main-

[6]*Improving Productivity*, p. 12.

tain. The parks personnel take pride in it; they regard it as theirs and treat it accordingly.

Memphis, Tennessee, experimented for almost three years with joint labor-management health and safety committees prompted by union concern about the high rate of accidents. Three union representatives and three city officials collaborated on improved maintenance plans and the purchase of modern equipment.

Conclusions

From the measurable actions, like better management of lost time, to the more qualitative ones, like participatory strategies, these are some of the possible actions to maintain employee morale and effectiveness in the face of cuts in public budgets and workforce. Together with the earlier proposals for civil service reform and more balanced public collective bargaining, these ideas represent an approach to improving public management which recognizes the primacy of managing *with* people. Especially in the environment of stress so characteristic of many of today's governments, personnel management is not just another support service, but rather the heart of the enterprise to do more with less.

Part II

Conserving the Public Dollar

The financial arena is the first line of defense for public—or for that matter for private—management. It is in the financial arena that the first signs of a managerial crisis appear: budget deficits and difficulty in marketing credit instruments at reasonable rates.

Of all aspects of government, financial management bears the first impact of the cost-revenue squeeze. The tax revolt cuts public revenue and generates pressure to reduce spending. Particularly in an inflationary economy, these new demands represent a heavy burden for financial management systems to handle.

Because of this vulnerability, it is crucial to make management improvements in the basic processes related to spending and raising dollars. A critical challenge to state and local governments over the next decade is to develop better methods for planning and controlling public revenues and expenditures. The purpose of the next three chapters is to present the new concepts and tools of public financial management that are just now evolving.

City and state governments historically have had notoriously weak capacity for planning future revenues and for deciding how to allocate those revenues. In Chapter 5 the elements of a financial planning system that makes sense in the context of the political nature of public budgeting is outlined.

Public agencies have also used rather primitive methods for keeping track of actual expenditures and revenues and for ensuring that such spending is controlled. Public sector accounting, in theory and practice, is only now beginning to catch up with private sector accounting in its sophistication as a management tool. Chapter 6 considers the state of the art of public financial reporting and control.

Within the financial arena itself there are substantial opportunities to increase revenue or reduce costs via the operation of financial systems. In particular, better cash and debt management can have a substantial impact on the public financial equation. These opportunities are the subject of Chapter 7.

5

Financial Planning and Budgeting

The budget—a one-year projection of anticipated revenues and ex-penditures—is usually a key instrument of planning in every level of management in the well-managed private company. In the public sector, too, budgets are important but they are rarely useful as management planning tools. The public budget is a political document—a record of the outcome of combat among important groups for a slice of the public pie. Giving out money is a political reward. With-holding resources is a political punishment. The legislature and the chief executive compete for the use of resources to reward their favorite constituency or program. The different actors in public pol-icy making compete for relevant political points by appearing to gain resources; but money that appears in a budget might never really be meant to be spent. As a result, budgets have become useless for planning purposes.

Fiscal crisis places new emphasis on the need to plan in order to carefully husband scarce resources. At the same time, a diminishing pot often means intensified political competition. To some extent systematic budgeting in the face of serious fiscal pressure offers political leaders a way out of the dilemma of which important consti-tuency's favorite program to axe: one can always blame the plan.

There are four substantial areas of opportunity for improving public financial planning: (1) Governments can develop effective devices for setting priorities, especially for strengthening the link between operational performance and dollar allocations. (2) Govern-ments can lengthen their perspectives from a single year to a multi-year framework. It usually takes more than one year for fiscal problems to develop and it takes more than a one-year plan to get out of difficulty. (3) A better capacity to deal with risk and uncertainty is needed by most governments, including systematic contingency planning. (4) Capital budgeting needs to become an instrument of reducing operating costs and improving service rather than a collection of all things for all people.

Each of these areas is discussed in this chapter.

Setting Financial Priorities

Establishing budget priorities is one of the most difficult tasks to accomplish in a political environment. By nature, government is almost antipriority. Since political pressures for action come from a bewildering variety of interests, the tendency is to spread resources thinly in buckshot fashion, with the objective of touching as many bases as possible, that is, responding with some action or resource to as many of the political pressures as possible. The result is a government program which tends to do many things poorly rather than a few things well. It is only in a crisis environment that there is a political mandate to set priorities. In New York City, for example, it was only under the impact of potential bankruptcy that the city was forced to actually set priorities.

Much of the literature on budget reform over the last ten or fifteen years has pointed out the apparent irrationality of a budget process which is essentially incremental vis-à-vis last year's budget and in which the flow of information is from the bottom of the organization to the top. In this classical process top management rarely if ever identifies its own priorities. Rather, top management enters the budgeting process at the margin with each important actor in the process representing powerful constituencies and with executive management negotiating out these marginal conflicts.

In the well-managed private company the budget process is top-down. Executive management sets the overall priorities within a strategic planning multiyear framework. In the private sector the allocation of resources in a budget is closely linked to planning for operations or performance. In other words, a manager supposed to produce 100 widgets at a cost of $1,000 might well be allocated additional resources if he can demonstrate the ability to bring output up to 200 widgets for $1,500. This performance/operation-resource planning process goes on within an overall structure of bottom-line control. The controller projects overall costs and revenues for the company. Within this framework the allocation of resources is a function of a series of judgments about relative potential performance of different divisions or units within the company.

In the public sector there is typically no systematic process for linking projected performance to the way dollars are budgeted. Each budget officer is usually responsible for assigning resources to a particular program in response to fiscal and sometimes political concerns rather than to operational performance mandates. The overall framework of possible expenditure is set by a judgment about "what the traffic will bear," in other words, what level of taxation is politically feasible within a context of intergovernmental funding. Thus, the projection of the bottom line—overall expected revenues and expenditures—like the allocation of resources within that framework, is a political act. Generally this allocation is only marginally related to the question of relative performance. The issue of what additional results could be expected with additional expenditure is rarely seriously considered.

The literature on public budgeting shows a sharp split between those who have focused on the political necessity to budget in the current incremental marginal way and those who have focused on the rational costs of budgeting in this manner. There is relatively little literature on how to add strategic planning within the real-world political process. City and state governments have been struggling to add a front-end planning component to the budgeting process for decades. Performance budgeting in the 1950s, program budgeting in the early 1960s, and planning-programming-budgeting systems (PPBSs) in the late 1960s were all aimed broadly at the same overall objective: improving the capacity of government to use the budget as a planning tool.[1]

The most recent of these efforts, zero-base budgeting (ZBB), has been widely touted in the private sector and probably has been used fairly effectively. ZBB received substantial emphasis in the public sector because of a reasonably successful experiment in the state of

---

[1] For a very helpful comparative analysis of these three approaches, see Allen Schick, "The Road to PPB: The Stages of Budget Reform," *Public Administration Review*, Dec. 1966, pp. 243–258.

Georgia under the then Governor Carter, and because budget cut-ters like the basic idea.[2] The theory of zero-base budgeting rests on the assumption that in most budgeting processes, new program pro-posals receive detailed scrutiny as to whether or not they should be funded at all, whereas existing programs are usually assured of more funding than they had in the previous year. In zero-base budgeting all programs are supposed to justify their existence as if they were brand new. ZBB requires four analytic steps:

1. The budget is divided into programs or budget units.
2. For each budget unit a series of alternative decision packages is identified involving alternative levels of service (quantity and quality) and associated costs—including the option of eliminat-ing the program.
3. Decision packages are evaluated on the basis of potential cost and effectiveness.
4. Decision packages are ranked and the highest-ranking decision packages are funded within projected resources.

This system is a marginal improvement over its predecessor—planning-programming-budgeting system (PPBS)—as it more di-rectly focuses on setting priorities.

Yet those who have used ZBB in the private sector and who are familiar with the public sector situation, guffaw at the notion of using ZBB in government. For ZBB, like its predecessor, PPBS, fails to deal with the two central problems of strategic planning in the public sector: the political costs of explicit resource allocation, and limited knowledge or measurement capacity. In an environment in which every potential program elimination affects at least one powerful and articulate constituency, actually applying ZBB could have very negative consequences for someone who has to face those constituencies in an election. The limited data, difficulties of mea-surement, and lack of understanding about cause and effect make it extremely difficult to comprehensively evaluate the relative costs and benefits of alternative public investments.

[2]For a description of an application of ZBB in government, see David W. Sin-gleton, Bruce A. Smith, and James R. Cleaveland, "Zero Base Budgeting in Wilming-ton," in Frederick S. Lane, ed., *Managing State and Local Government: Cases and Readings* (New York: St. Martin's Press, 1980), pp. 223–240.

In short, ZBB is too ambitious. To take one example of the gap between data needed to run ZBB and what is typically available, consider the following. ZBB analysis is dependent on precise unit cost information. Most governments do not know precisely how much it truly costs to deliver each service to a user. For example, to compute the actual cost of providing sanitation services twice a week requires not only the basic wages of workers, but a loaded hourly wage rate—including an allocation of fringe benefits, the value of lost or nonproductive time, as well as a measure of the complete cost of operating vehicles including a factor for depreciation or replacement cost. Such data are rarely available on an across-the-board current basis. In the absence of accurate estimates of the cost of twice-weekly service, how can one estimate the savings of once-weekly service or the additional costs of thrice-weekly service? Of course, these data can be generated, but the cost in time and energy is very great.

Strategic budgeting works best in the public sector if it is used to supplement rather than to supplant incremental political decision making. Strategic budgeting does not have to be zero-based. It can be incremental.

A simpler version of ZBB, called priority-choice analysis, offers an opportunity to sidestep some of the knowledge and data problems and avoids the potential confrontation of considering all programs as candidates for elimination.[3] This method is summarized below.

Step 1: Establish overall priorities; for example:
    Priority One—protect life and limb
    Priority One—revenue raising activity
    Priority Two—maintain economy
    Priority Two—protect residential tax base
    Priority Three—all other programs

Step 2: Establish budget units or programs.

Step 3: Assign each budget unit or program to a priority category (based on probable impact of service or program).

Step 4: Estimate the baseline cost of each program or budget unit (last year's cost plus inflation).

[3] Jacob B. Ukeles and Allen Brawer, "Priority Analysis and Resource Allocation in New York City's Budgeting Process," *Urban Analysis*, Spring 1978, pp. 182–186.

Step 5: Project future revenues; sum baseline costs of all programs; and estimate the average percentage reduction
required to balance budget.

Step 6: Assign average reduction to second priority programs, a
higher percentage cut to the third priority programs and a
lesser percentage cut to the first priority programs; iter-
ate and adjust to balance revenues and expenditures.

This process leaves room for negotiation (the precise difference
between the percentages applied to each priority level); it leaves the
department manager some discretion as to how to allocate cuts
within his or her own departments; and the analysis can be operated
with relatively rough information.

Additional refinements are possible. For example, the first priority cut could be objectified by estimating possible savings through
operational improvements for "productivity." Thus a large "life and
limb" department such as police might make a substantial dollar
contribution to cutting the budget, if cost-saving management improvements are possible.

The same approach can be applied to the management of an attrition program. Instead of a hiring freeze which could be counterproductive or an arbitrary or time-consuming hire-by-hire review,
priority standards can be set. High-priority programs can hire two
replacements for every three people who leave, second priority programs one for every two, and low priority programs one for every
three. Here, too, a department head has some discretion over which
positions are the most critical.

Multiyear Financial Planning

Strategic financial planning implies not only breadth but length of
time as well. The problem of a comprehensive front-end approach is
closely linked to multiyear financial planning.

Multiyear financial planning is difficult to undertake in cities and
states for all the reasons discussed in Chapter 1. The two- or four-
year electoral cycle places finite limits on the concept of long-range.
If two or four years is the outer limit of an administration, then one
year becomes middle-range, and short-range becomes days and

weeks. Contrast this with a typical corporate environment in which long-range is five to ten years, middle-range three to five years, and short-range one year. When one adds the lack of agreement about ends or objectives and the uncertainties of intergovernmental financial relations, it is not surprising that multiyear financial planning is rare in the public sector. Politicians in general, out of long and bitter experience, are notoriously uninterested in being pinned down with regard to decisions they may take affecting the next several months, let alone two, three, or four years in the future. Yet even companies that do not have a highly developed long-range strategic plan of the five- to ten-year variety do have a financial plan in the mid-range time frame of three to five years. Cities and states also need to look ahead in order to manage effectively today.

Slowly but surely, more cities and states are beginning to view financial plans in a three- to five-year time frame. Washington, D.C., and Detroit each publish a five-year forecast of revenues and expenditures in a multiyear financial plan. San Diego also publishes a multiyear forecast which appears as a separate report from the annual budget. Projecting six years of revenues, expenditures, and capital needs, the report is generated by a special unit within the city's financial management department.

The city which invested the most time and energy in multiyear financial planning is in many ways the city that one would think of last for this exercise. Both in the complexity of its politics and the complexity of its finances, New York City would not have been anyone's candidate for leadership in this area. Under the impact of near financial collapse, the city has developed an elaborate and highly structured process for multiyear planning required by law under the State Financial Emergency Act. The substantial effort invested in making this system work provides rich raw materials for other cities and for states contemplating movement in this direction. The following discussion of New York City's first four-year plan illustrates a number of the difficult issues involved in actually carrying out multiyear financial planning in the public sector.

Case Study: New York City's Four-Year Financial Plan

The first official plan included four elements: (1) a revenue and expenditure plan, (2) a cash flow and borrowing plan, (3) a capital commitments and capital expenditures plan, and (4) covered agency plans.[4]

Revenue and expenditure plan. The most important element of any financial plan is the forecast of anticipated revenue and expenditure. In New York City's case there were specific legislative mandates which required a balanced budget by the end of the four-year period. In most state and local government environments a balanced budget is either an implicit or explicit objective; increasingly, "gimmicks" which redefine what a balanced budget means are less and less acceptable. If New York City's near-collapse accomplishes nothing else, it underlines the necessity for honest financial information in the public sector.

In New York City's plan the revenue-expenditure plan had two elements or levels. The first part of the plan incorporated basic assumptions about the state of the economy and probable tax yields, projected inflation, and the impact of legislative fiscal mandates such as the phase-out of the use of capital resources to fund operating expenses. It also incorporated basic policy and program commitments to deliver a specified set of services with a specific set of taxes. The net impact of these basic assumptions was an increasingly large budget gap expected to peak at $1 billion in 1982. The second part of the plan consisted of a series of programs aimed at closing the gap. This part of the plan incorporated a number of cost reduction and revenue enhancement programs as well as more optimistic assumptions about federal and state aid that would be forthcoming to help New York City close its gap. This two-level plan is shown in Figure 5.

Any revenue plan is a mixture of policy judgments and predictions of uncontrolled events. A plan is more than a forecast of trends. This interdependence of policy and forecast pervaded each of the four categories of revenue in the plan: taxes, miscellaneous (local) revenues, categorical intergovernmental aid, and unrestricted intergovernmental aid. In the tax area, for example, the plan included a policy about the future property tax rate—that the property tax would continue to be capped at its 1978 level for the duration of the plan. At the same time, the plan also incorporates an assumption about the (uncontrolled) state of the economy. Seven taxes were

---

[4]Covered agencies are semi-independent bodies, such as the Housing Authority, which were not directly under the municipal government but which were covered by the Financial Emergency Act.

Figure 5. New York City four-year financial plan for revenues and expenditures, in millions.

Description	FY1979	FY1980	FY1981	FY1982
REVENUES				
Taxes				
General Property Taxes	$ 3,133	$ 3,089	$ 3,081	$ 3,124
Other Taxes	3,220	3,287	3,388	3,496
Miscellaneous Revenues	1,393	1,250	1,277	1,308
Grants				
Federal	2,411	1,952	1,925	1,930
State	2,177	1,968	1,993	2,021
Disallowances	(100)	(100)	(100)	(100)
Unrestricted Intergovernmental Aid	1,037	922	925	975
	13,271	12,368	12,489	12,754
Transfers from Capital Budget for Capitalized Expenses	445	300	150	—
Transfers from Capital Budget for Inter-Fund Agreements	79	79	101	109
	13,795	12,747	12,740	12,863
Less: Intra-City Revenues	(413)	(422)	(430)	(439)
Total Revenues	13,382	12,325	12,310	12,424
EXPENDITURES				
Personal Service	5,724	5,873	6,202	6,378
OTPS	5,938	5,379	5,527	5,661
Debt Service	1,486	1,314	1,227	1,186
MAC Debt Service Funding	483	520	563	566
	13,631	13,086	13,519	13,791
General Reserve	164	100	100	100
	13,795	13,186	13,619	13,891
Less: Intra-City Expenditures	(413)	(422)	(430)	(439)
Total Expenditures	13,382	12,764	13,189	13,452
Gap to be Closed	$ —	$ (439)	$ (879)	$ (1,028)
City Program to Close Gap		139	303	427
Remaining Gap to be Closed by Federal and State Actions		300	576	601
Supplemental and Additional City Programs to provide for shortfalls in Federal and State Actions		111	375	482
Remaining Gap to be Closed by Federal and State Actions		189	201	119

Source: *A Review of the New York City Financial Plan FY1979–FY1982: Projections of Revenues and Expenditures* (New York: Financial Control Board, 1978), p. 3.

identified by control board staff as being sensitive to the state of the economy. A relatively modest fluctuation in the depth and timing of a projected recession could have shifted the revenue estimates anywhere from $50 to $100 million for economy-sensitive taxes.

The revenue picture increasingly depends not only on local effort but on intergovernmental aid. In New York City's case of a $13 billion basic revenue budget, over $5 billion was expected to come from the federal and state governments. From the point of view of a municipal government, federal and state aid policies are as uncontrollable as the state of the economy or the influence of the stars and foreign wars.

On the expenditure side as well, the plan is a mixture of policy judgments and a projection of the consequences of the policies of others as well as future uncontrollable events, such as inflation. Sometimes, inclusion of a policy judgment is itself an issue. For example, future collective bargaining wage settlements are likely to have a major impact on future costs. There were two wage settlements at issue: the recently completed negotiations (for FY1979) projected forward onto the plan for FY1981 and FY1982, and the prospective negotiations for FY1981.

Part of the 1979 settlement was what the mayor and the unions agreed would be a one-shot payment, framed variously as a cost-of-living adjustment or a bonus. The mayor initially argued that since this was a one-time payment it would be renegotiated for 1981. The control board argued that although it was framed as a one-shot payment, it was not realistic to argue that wages, however packaged, could go down. The plan was ultimately adjusted to take account of the $300 million implications of this initial omission.

The second aspect of the future labor settlement was any new increases that could be won. The mayor argued that for management to project a future labor cost settlement in its financial plan would in effect provide a floor from which negotiation would proceed. In this instance, the control board agreed, and the financial plan did not include, in fact, any additional estimate for future labor settlements. Personal service, including wages and such fringe benefits as pensions, accounted for slightly less than half of the city's projected expenditure.

A good deal of discussion revolved around the question of what constitutes an adequate reserve. The basic $100 million figure, which was the general reserve agreed upon for the city's financial plan, reflected a compromise between a city budgeting tradition under which all reserves had gradually been eliminated, and a private sector tradition of reserves anywhere from 1 percent to 3 percent. The $100 million figure seemed a reasonable compromise.

Cash flow and borrowing plan. While the revenue and expenditure projection formed the backbone of the financial plan, there were several other critical issues that the cash forecast did not deal with. The first and most important of these was the cash flow projection, a complex set of judgments about the timing of revenues and expenditures many of which are outside the city's control and are difficult to predict. Particularly in the case of intergovernmental revenue flows, the city is completely at the mercy of the cash schedules of the state and federal governments.

A systematic effort to predict cash flow provides the basis for better prediction of the magnitude and timing of the city's short-term borrowing needs. To the extent that the timing of disbursements can be adjusted by the city, this can be translated into a slowing down or speeding up of the need to borrow. These relationships, though simple in concept, are complex in actuality, but the exercise helped the city improve its cash management. The cash flow and borrowing plan provided the financial community and the city and other levels of government with some assurance that the city's cash needs would be in reasonable balance with the city's ability to borrow, thus introducing the beginnings of some stability in what had been the most chaotic and day-to-day, hand-to-mouth aspect of the city's fiscal existence since the spring of 1975.

Capital commitments and expenditures plan. The third element of the four-year financial plan, the capital commitments and expenditures program, was the subject of fierce debate between control board staff on the one hand and city officials on the other. City managers feared interference with the mayor's legitimate prerogatives to allocate resources. Yet the traditional instruments for planning and controlling capital expenditures in New York, as in many cities, are woefully inadequate. The capital budget tends to be a wish list of prospective possible projects, and the fiscal implications of this wish list are completely unclear. A project might be listed in the capital budget and built or not built. If it is actually built, it could be in any one of two, three, or even four years. The financial requirements generated to borrow money to build facilities are virtually unpredictable from a capital budget. At the other extreme, in terms of specificity, the operating budget records debt service requirements. These are the city's obligations under financial commitments made in the past. As such, the debt service figure is the least controllable of any dimension of the budget and is therefore not useful for planning purposes.

After a long period of discussion it was concluded that the city actually needed two additional planning documents: a capital commitments plan to record when the city actually expected to commit capital funds, and a capital expenditures plan to record the anticipated consequences of capital commitments in the actual flow of funds. The capital expenditures plan becomes the basis for the city's long-term borrowing and should be consistent with the cash flow and borrowing plan.

This structure of multiyear planning elements in the capital arena represented a novel component, which should find its way into the practice of state and local governments. The capital budget is the basis for the capital commitments plan. The capital commitments plan is the basis for the capital expenditures plan, and the capital expenditures plan becomes the basis for the borrowing plan. Solutions to questions hitherto impossible to answer with any confidence would come within reach. For example, what are the future borrowing implications of current capital commitments, and are these sustainable? Cities and states would have the capacity to carefully assess the consequences of their own capital actions on future levels of expenditure for debt service through the operating budget.

Covered agency plans. The fourth element of the plan was necessitated by the large number of local governments drawing resources from New York City's municipal government but not under control of its chief executive. The Health and Hospital Corporation, Transit Authority, and Housing Authority all drew resources from the city in the form of subsidies, but yet they were not subject to the city's limited capacity to increase revenue. Covered agency plans, in effect, were miniature plans for revenue and expenditure, cash flow and borrowing, and capital expenditures and commitments for those governments or departments which received funds from New York City but were not part of the city government apparatus. Most cities

in the United States similarly have semi-independent local governments with financial links to the municipality. To be realistic, any
multiyear financial planning program should incorporate these other
quasi-governmental entities.

Overall, the process of reaching agreement on this four-year
financial plan was complex, difficult, and time-consuming. The plan
shown in Figure 5 above was actually submitted to the Financial
Control Board on November 8, 1978. It represented the eighth revision of an initial draft plan appended to the mayor's budget on April
26, 1978. The protracted nature of this process was not the result of
ineptitude on the part of the city staff involved in preparing the plan,
nor was it the result of changing whims on the part of the approving
agencies. Rather, it was the result of the rapidity with which events
shifted even during this four-month period; the lack of any clear
guidelines or precedents as to what should and should not be included in a public sector financial plan; and the complexity of a
negotiation process in which the federal government, state government, Emergency Financial Control Board, Municipal Assistance
Corporation, city executives, elected officials of the City Council
and Board of Estimate, and municipal labor unions all had substantial stakes.

A brief capsule of the highlights of this process was presented in
the control board's staff report evaluating the city's financial plan.
After summarizing changes between April 26 and June 21, 1978, the
staff went on to say:

> On June 22, 1978, the City transmitted to the Board an adjustment
> to its FY1979 financial plan making it consistent with the budget as
> adopted by the City Council and the Board of Estimate. This
> change was approved by the Control Board on June 28, 1978. On
> August 24, 1978, the city revised its proposed four-year financial
> plan to reflect the projected costs of the actual labor settlement as
> reflected in the Coalition Economic Agreement as well as changes
> in the prospect for federal countercyclical aid. Subsequent discus-
> sions between City, U.S. Treasury, Office of Special Deputy Con-
> troller (OSDC) and Control Board officials and staff resulted in
> revised submissions on September 25th, October 6th, and Novem-
> ber 6th.[5]

[5]*A Review of the New York City Financial Plan FY1979–FY1982: Projections of
Revenues and Expenditures* (New York: Financial Control Board, 1978), pp. 1–2.

Advantages of Multiyear Planning

Multiyear financial planning is possible in cities and states even in the face of substantial political and informational uncertainties. In fact, in the face of declining resources, a longer-range look at a city's finances is not only a necessity but an urgency.

Looking ahead three to five years gives a state or local government some significant advantages. It forces a process of explicating assumptions (often otherwise implicit) about the state of the local economy. State and local governments are just as dependent on the overall economy as industry; forecasting government revenues and expenditures forces attention on the nature of the public's relationship to and dependence on the local economy. This process in turn forces a systematic effort to think through the trends in the city's revenue base and a long-term revenue strategy including the nature of the case for intergovernmental aid. A simple projection of expenditures for most jurisdictions clearly and dramatically establishes the need for immediate expenditure control, and the process of explicating trends in public makes it harder to sell temporary political or symbolic solutions to basic fiscal problems.

A three- to five-year financial plan establishes a framework for decision and action. Once trends are set in motion it is likely to take more than one year to reverse them. A program of cost control and revenue expansion almost by definition should be looked at over more than one year. One may need to spend in one year (especially capital spending) in order to save in the next. Jurisdictions need lead time to plan for future problems. For example, the impact of tax reduction plans is most usefully looked at in a multiyear framework. The multiyear financial plan is a useful place to record and test strategies for economic development and stimulus.

The Analysis of Risk and Uncertainty

Multiyear planning in the public sector is most useful if it is married to a process of contingency planning to deal with the substantial levels of uncertainty characteristic of the environment. Even in the most highly structured business environment, it is difficult to predict key financial outcomes in the future accurately. Hundreds if not thousands of variables interact to shape the future, ranging from relatively controllable factors such as worker productivity to shifts in consumer taste and new product activities of competitors. The prediction of even a single variable influencing financial outcomes can be extremely difficult. Predicting interest rates one or two years into the future is viewed by the experts as an extremely hazardous operation. Even relatively short-term projections of inflation rates have often turned out to be wrong. Since there are thousands of such variables which influence future sales and profits, it is no wonder that long-range financial planning is considered the most precarious aspect of all business planning and analysis.

In government the future is even more murky by several orders of magnitude. Not only must such factors as future interest rates be projected, but implicit or explicit judgments must be made about the future policies of governments whose leaders have not yet been elected. Because of the "fishbowl" nature of management in the public sector, planning information cannot be kept confidential. For example, to predict a future labor settlement in public virtually establishes the baseline for negotiation rather than the final outcome. Telegraphing future tax policy may have a negative impact on a whole series of economic development decisions by potential entrepreneurs. It is no accident that crucial planning data in the private sector are always treated with the greatest confidentiality. In government this is not possible.

Closely related to the concept of uncertainty is the concept of risk. Risk can be defined simply as some chance that revenue will be lower than projected or expenditures higher. Because of the unpredictability of political, social, and economic factors bearing on financial projections in the public arena, any budget or financial plan estimate in a city or state carries with it substantial uncertainty, that is, reasonable probability that individual revenue and expenditures will be different from what was originally anticipated. Obviously this uncertainty increases over time, and what appears relatively solid six months or a year hence becomes almost a wild guess two, three, or four years hence, particularly if an election or two intervenes.

In the financial planning environment there are four important uncertainties: There is some chance that the revenues will be lower than anticipated, that the revenues will be higher than anticipated, that expenditures will be higher than anticipated; or that expenditures will be lower than anticipated. Two out of these four possibilities involve risk—the possibility that the financial plan will not be met and that future budgets will be unbalanced.

In reviewing a budget or (multiyear) financial plan from the point of view of risk and uncertainty, three judgments are crucial: (1) How much risk and uncertainty is there in the budget or plan? (2) What constitutes an acceptable level of risk? (3) Has the city or state adequately provided for risk in its plan? A great deal of experimental work needs to be done in this area before it will be apparent how cities should analyze their risk, how the risk should be described to potential investors, and how cities should ensure, with some reasonable probability, that their financial plans will not fly apart under the impact of substantial uncertainty.

In the short run, a number of principles seem applicable:

1. Governments should present—and typically do not present—an explicit analysis of uncertainty and risk as part of their annual budgets and (multiyear) financial plans.

2. Obviously it is important to project conservatively; revenue estimates should be on the low side of what is expected, and expenditure estimates should be on the high side. Cities and states have historically been under pressure to do exactly the opposite in order to maximize the political executive's ability to make spending commitments to different political constituencies.

3. The conventional response to risk in any organization is to provide adequate reserves. The issue of reserves, hotly debated during the New York City financial crisis, was a complex one, particularly in an environment in which all reserves had gradually eroded over time. How much is enough? Should reserves be specialized—against specific risk areas—or general? How big should the government reserves be compared with industry?

4. Governments should develop contingency plans, that is, cost-reduction or revenue-raising programs to be triggered if and when needed. This concept is particularly important as a way of covering against relatively large identifiable risk areas such as those involving a decision by a higher level of government.

5. States and localities should systematically monitor risk areas. Major risk areas should be identified and placed in a time frame so that crucial milestones on the road to losing revenue or increasing expenditure are identified. For example, when a critical revenue in

New York City's plan involved a projected $80 million state revenue resulting from the purchase of the Westway right-of-way—a highly controversial project—it was recognized that unless a crucial court decision was forthcoming by the end of December, there was no way that that revenue could be counted in the fiscal year for which it was identified in the plan. Placing risk areas in a time frame sets up the potential for triggering specific contingency programs.

6. Governments should experiment with a variety of tools to express in public the real uncertainty which surrounds budget and financial plan estimates of revenue and expenditure. At a minimum, a range of likely outcomes should be provided with some rationale as to why the financial plan figure was chosen. Cities and states should experiment with the use of explicit measures of subjective probability or simple classifications of risk areas into high, medium, and low probability. Over time it should even be possible to build risk analysis simulation models. In this approach, the first step is to identify major risk areas and to assess, at least subjectively, the probability that each risk could materialize with lost revenue or increased expenditure.

7. A useful criterion for assessing the adequacy of a plan's protection against risk is that *the amount of reserves plus the amount that would be yielded in revenue increases or cost reductions from implementing the contingency program is equal to or greater than the sum of all the potential risks that are reasonably probable.* This would include risk areas whose probability was moderate or high and would exclude those identified as being of low probability. In this approach those areas in which there is some reasonable probability that revenues could be higher or expenditures lower than initially projected become protection against unanticipated risks or problems.

The Special Role of the Capital Budget

In the well-managed private company, some of the most important budget decisions revolve around the use of capital resources. The purchase of new equipment and the building of new facilities often involve the company, or the government, in borrowing money. In this environment capital investment decisions are rigorously analyzed to maximize performance. Whether measured as return on investment or in some other way, capital resource budgeting is typically closely integrated with operating decisions. In government, capital budgets are usually rigidly separate from operating budgets. This may be necessary in order to ensure that borrowing is not done for operating purposes but rather for facilities and equipment. Yet maintaining the separation in decision-making processes, documents, and departments—as when city planning commissions are involved in capital budgets but not in operating budgets—has some serious negative consequences.

In the private sector the key tool for increasing productivity—outputs in relation to inputs—is not a generalized effort to make workers work harder but is a systematic and careful capital investment to reduce operating costs, as in the substitution of machines for labor. Upgrading the quality of machines and equipment is a key strategy for reducing cost and improving results. This strategy, so crucial to the long-term improvement and upgrading in the quality of public services, is virtually never employed by government. The failure to systematically develop capital investment strategies which would have this objective in the public sector as well is one of the key reasons that public sector productivity programs have had so little impact overall. Yet this failure to use capital investments to reduce operating costs is perfectly understandable and completely consistent with the nature of public sector budgeting described earlier.

In the public sector the capital budget is almost invariably viewed as anything but a systematic program for improving government. Capital spending in the public sector is considered a tool for increasing construction jobs in the local community. As an internal bureaucratic strategy, a new building or facility is often seen as the only device for getting more staff for operating programs; in a tight-budget environment the only way to increase staff is to open a new facility.

In the political arena, capital investment is viewed as a reward to "good" neighborhoods, and the withholding of capital spending is viewed as a punishment of neighborhoods that were not cooperative or that did not vote appropriately. Neighborhoods vary sharply in their ability to pressure the system for new school buildings or more parks. A city's capital program—be it for one year or for five—tends to be a shopping list of the favored projects and pet facilities of a variety of decision makers and interest groups.

Even if there were the capacity to develop and implement explicit strategies for guiding capital investment in the public arena, the operating cost reduction strategy has at least two valid competitors: (1) The capital program is the essential source of funding for the local infrastructure. The network of roads, sewerlines, and waterlines is one of the most important determinants of physical development. Both for jurisdictions wishing to control or minimize development as well as for those seeking to encourage it, the capital program is one of the few tools available to carry out either objective. (2) A second capital strategy, particularly in older areas, is the use of the capital program as an economic development tool. Governments which can target their capital spending effectively to focus on land improvements, buildings, and infrastructure in selected areas of high market potential are likely to have a substantial advantage in the competition for good taxpaying economic activity.

Even though these alternative important needs do exist, well-managed governments will not ignore the potential contribution to increased productivity which could be made by careful capital spending. The well-managed government will attempt to develop orchestrated strategies which would be aimed at productivity, economic, and physical development objectives.

Moreover, even if governments develop explicit capital investment strategies there is no widely accepted criterion to evaluate capital investment choices which would indicate which projects were more likely to achieve any of the objectives discussed above. Unlike the private sector, which has seen substantial development over the last decade in increasingly sophisticated applications of return-on-investment (ROI) criteria in the capital arena, the public sector has not developed general measures of project viability. The classic ROI criterion is relevant only in an environment in which both the return and the investment can be expressed in dollars. Clearly, in the public sector social benefits, economic benefits, and even physical benefits are not easily expressed in dollars. In the case of multiple objectives—where the units of measurement used in relation to highways are different from the units used for police service—it's extremely difficult if not impossible to even compare the relative value of projects in different areas. Thus return on investment criteria are not useful in helping to make the decision as to whether it makes sense to buy more police cars or spend more money on paving streets. Faced with the political realities of how projects are selected and the substantial measurement difficulties, most governments have done even less than they could do to develop and use investment criteria to evaluate proposed individual projects or to array a set of projects in a capital program.

Cities and states can improve their capital investment planning through systematic effort to fully measure all dollar costs of capital projects and to measure dollar benefits for those projects where they exist. Measuring dollar benefits includes reductions in future operating costs resulting from proposed capital investment and increases in revenue (if any). Fully measuring all costs includes the cost of borrowing money (future debt service), the lost property taxes and charges if land is removed from the tax rolls, and future increases in operating costs (if any) resulting from proposed capital investments. Projects can be ranked by the net dollar impact (dollar benefits minus dollar costs). Such an analysis cannot provide the basis for choosing capital projects, but it does provide an interesting baseline for more qualitative analyses and judgments.

There are several specific advantages to this exercise. First, projects aimed at reducing operating costs (for example, automation) would be highly ranked and their value demonstrated. This would reinforce those who were seeking to use the capital budget as an instrument for productivity improvement. Second, public managers would know the true costs of projects with substantial difficult-to-quantify economic and social benefits. Approximate, often subjective, judgments about social and economic benefits would be more meaningful in the context of relatively specific judgments about total net costs. Difficult tradeoffs do exist between high-cost, high-socioeconomic-benefit projects and those which are low in cost but are relatively lower in their socioeconomic benefits. The advantage of such a structure of thinking, however, is that it does provide the basis for questioning projects whose social and economic benefits are difficult to pin down and whose costs are quite high.

An example of a deliberate strategy for using capital investment to reduce costs (and in some cases to expand revenue) is the State of New Jersey Productivity Investment Account. Funded initially in FY1979 with $400,000 of state funds, the account provides seed money to state departments to implement cost-saving programs. A portion of the savings is transferred back into the account to be used for new projects, and the remainder is available for use by the individual department. Priority was given to provide equipment or facilities (over noncapital projects); of the initial 16 projects, 13 involved capital investment. The investment of $400,000 was expected to yield $2,500,000 in savings over a three-year period.

Conclusions

The political environment has always placed substantial constraints on the ability and willingness of American governments to plan. As cities and states increasingly confront the problem of limited resources, classic political imperatives are beginning to give way in the face of the need to more carefully and skillfully manage resources. In this new environment of constraint, better financial planning and budgeting—using new tools of analysis and decision making—can make a substantial difference in the ability of a government to cope. Systematic methods for setting and carrying out priorities in the budget process, the addition of a multiyear planning component, capacity to cope with risk and uncertainty through contingency planning, and more sophisticated use of the capital investment tool—all these can make a substantial difference in the ability of cities and states to respond.

6

Financial Reporting
and Control

Two financial systems are important in controlling public expenditure. The first, the budgeting system, incorporates decision making about groups of expenditures and revenues and monitors actual spending and revenue in relation to the budget plan. The second important financial system is the accounting system, which measures and records individual financial transactions. Major changes are taking place currently in the whole pattern of public financial reporting and control which affect these two systems and the relationships between them.

Four areas are particularly important: (1) Glaring weaknesses in traditional concepts and techniques of budget control have been exposed by urban fiscal crises, and new approaches are coming into use. (2) The theory of municipal accounting, which has lagged far behind private sector accounting, is beginning to catch up. (3) There is increasing pressure to use the new accounting to increase public accountability, and new interest in finding better ways to measure state and municipal financial health. (4) There have been some important and far-reaching efforts to integrate not only accounting and budgeting systems, but payroll and purchasing (payment) systems as well. These four frontier areas of municipal financial management are examined in this chapter.

Controlling the Budget

Much of the literature of public budgeting has focused on budget planning. Yet most of those who have practiced in government are convinced that the budgeting process—despite decades of experimentation—is still essentially a control process and that implementing the budget is far more important than planning the budget. How have cities and states traditionally controlled their budgets?

In most cities and states the budget is controlled by the individual budget examiner. The examiner, who is one of many actors in budget planning, takes center stage when it comes to actual spending. Department heads are literally at the mercy of their budget examiner, and stories are legion in all governments of major department heads with powerful constituencies and established reputations being reduced virtually to tears by a relatively junior budget analyst who refuses to approve a key expenditure of funds already in a budget. The last point is important. Unless one has been a participant in government, it is difficult to understand that the examiner controls the actual expenditure of funds to a remarkable degree even after funds are budgeted. The mechanisms for accomplishing this control may vary, but the thrust is the same. In Philadelphia, for example, the budget bureau's seven senior analysts can forestall or pass funding appropriation items back through the chain of command to the deputy director of finance. The deputy director has the power to kill the expenditure. All salary increases, promotions, and appointments for exempt personnel must be approved by the budget bureau. While the city council must authorize transfers and appropriations between city departments, the budget bureau generates the proposed transfer.

In many line budget environments, money cannot be moved from one line to another without preaudit approval by a budget examiner. The tiniest budget modification—changing a code number for example—may not be possible without prior approval by the examiner. Ironically, what appears to be a very tight system of control is riddled with loopholes. The examiner often operates with primitive data systems. Each examiner keeps his or her own numbers on actual spending. Since top management typically does not get reports on actual versus planned spending on a periodic basis, the examiner controls the information and its use. By and large, he or she operates without explicit criteria for the decision to allow spending or withhold funds. The examiner doesn't have to really justify decisions. A department head is unlikely to press too hard on a specific decision lest he lose a battle on half a dozen other things that might be more important.

The examiner often acts by delaying paperwork rather than by explicit denial of an approval to hire or purchase. There are so many actors in the approval process—auditors, legal staff, and people at various levels within the budget bureau, purchasing department, legal department, and mayor's office—that there are many opportunities for passing the buck. The baffled department head attempting to find out why a key appointment has been held up has no way of knowing whether the issues raised were political, personnel-related, or budgetary and may search in vain for days at a time to locate relevant pieces of paper in a convoluted pipeline. The general tendency to delay approvals of expenditures is part of a general cash conservation strategy, usually implicit and not clearly articulated, with severe management frustration consequences. Often there are genuine citywide policy concerns embedded in the overall arbitrary framework, such as general revenue shortfalls requiring general spending cutbacks, or the need to balance shortfalls in one area with surpluses in another, or new mayoral priorities.

In most public environments there are no monthly spending plans and no regular reporting of actual versus planned expenditure on a monthly or bimonthly basis. Therefore, there is no formal way to identify when a department is on or off target in its spending. The examiner usually has some data and some experience as to what constitutes typical or reasonable patterns of spending and bases the judgment as to where spending has to be slowed down essentially on experience and hunch.

As in the personnel area, the line manager has little or no accountability and little or no control over budget. Below the level of the department head, the line manager is likely to not even know his or her budget. A revenue-raising agency is not likely to have explicit targets for revenue which they are held accountable for.

The contrast with private industry is startling. Private managers drawn into the public service are appalled to learn that their counterparts neither are held accountable for overall spending nor have any flexibility in how the money is spent. In the private sector revenue and expenditure are at the heart of most managers' accountability, whereas in government social and political objectives are paramount, and the manager who alienates an important and vocal citizens' group is not an effective manager. However, handling of public monies is also an important area.

The budget structure itself historically does not encourage pinpointing accountability below the department head. The line budget encourages a preaudit mode with the examiner monitoring the actual expenditure on a line basis in conformance with the line budget plan. Spending is restricted to specific codes for specific purposes. A manager cannot move money around—the manager is unable to trade equipment money for asphalt unless he or she can convince the budget examiner that that is an appropriate thing to do. Many months of poor operations can go by before the necessary transfer is approved.

In short, this historical pattern of examiner-centered, preaudit, line-by-line control without monthly reporting of actual versus planned expenditure leaves the line manager with no incentive to save or even to monitor costs effectively and with no flexibility to organize spending in a way that will increase or improve performance. In no area of government is the lack of responsibility and accountability more sorely felt than this one.

The new approach to budget reporting and control reallocates responsibilities between central staff (budget examiner) and the line manager. In this approach, the chief executive's staff (budget examiner) is no less important than in the traditional system but the roles are different. While some naive reformers (such as those who formulated New York City's 1975 charter) see the problem of reforming budget control as one of "how to break the power of the budget bureau," more sophisticated analysis of budget process recognizes that complete decentralization of financial accountability is likely to be counterproductive in the short run and lead to fiscal chaos in the long run. There will always be a need to adjust actual spending overall so that it conforms to actual revenues, to make midyear programmatic corrections that respond to new program needs and priorities, and to reduce one department's spending to cover unanticipated "blameless" shortfalls in another department. A number of elements in this new approach to public budget control are discussed below.

Line managers at all levels, not just department heads, have a specific budget which they are responsible for. The line manager is accountable for keeping spending within budget limits and for achieving revenue targets if revenue is associated with the function being managed. The budget is structured around organizational units, or responsibility centers, corresponding to the level of management within the organization where budget accountability will be placed.

Along with the budget there is an allocation or allotment of funds to a department on a quarterly or bimonthly basis. The department head has flexibility to spend money for various purposes within the overall budget and subject to citywide policy constraints (for example, one cannot spend a little now that commits a great deal of funds later). Managers are responsible for a monthly or bimonthly expenditure plan and report of actual spending that is the basis for citywide and departmental monitoring. The plan should reflect seasonal variations and is everyone's benchmark of a given manager's adherence to the budget. Obviously, these plans should be consistent with a quarterly or bimonthly allocation.

The review of individual items of expenditures (such as a specific purchase or hiring of an individual) is on a postaudit basis for adherence to citywide policy. Particularly in policy-sensitive areas, such as office furniture or vehicles for executives, the policy concerns are not necessarily fiscal, and individual expenditures could be highly inappropriate even if not a great deal of money is involved. Rewards for savings and extra revenue are built into the system. Such incentives are crucial to achieve savings and/or to increase revenue.[1]

The New Public Accounting: Evolving Theory and Practice

The objectives of accounting systems are common and basic to any organization of any size: to record financial transactions accurately; to apply consistent and widely used principles in defining when a transaction takes place and to use common definitions/categories of transactions; to provide a clear documentation trail for verification and audit purposes; to provide raw data for financial controls and timely financial reports; and to provide the basis for financial statements showing the balance between revenues and expenditures.

Public accounting for many years has been a stepchild of general accounting theory. The issues are complex, and there has been little external interest in the development of the field. Over the last several years the consequences of sloppy accounting concepts and

[1]The specifics of the use of incentives in a management system are discussed in Chapter 12.

practices have proved to be nearly disastrous, and major strides are now being made to overcome past deficiencies. Many cities, such as New York City until recently, did not even have outside auditors. Of those that do have outside auditors, over 40 percent of the outside auditors in a sample gave a "qualified" opinion. In other words, they were unwilling to attest to the appropriateness of all the financial information and accounting judgments. The audit committee, increasingly common in private industry, is practically unknown in government.

Eighteen thousand governments are eligible for the Municipal Finance Officers Association (MFOA) Certificate of Conformance for adherence to generally accepted accounting principles (GAAP), but only 400 such certificates have been awarded during the past 30 years. By 1980 only one state, Tennessee, had received an MFOA Certificate of Conformance.

Two issues dominate current efforts at municipal accounting reform: fund structure and accounting recognition principles. Since the complex character of government operations precludes a single unified set of accounts, municipal accounting has developed the use of fund classes. A fund class is a complete set of self-balancing accounts. Typically, a fund is established for discrete purposes or operations. The establishment of funds or fund classes forms the broadest set of categories in the chart of accounts.[2] Thus, the decision as to which fund classes to establish and how to establish them affects all subsequent, more detailed classification decisions.

In many municipalities the fund structure is a potpourri of historical accidents. Often money is moved among funds in ways that are difficult to track. New York City's case prior to the accounting reforms of 1975 and 1976 is illustrative:

> While the City maintains over sixty separate fund classes, expense budget activity is primarily recorded in one of four fund classes. Virtually all expenses are charged against one fund class while most revenues are received in one of three fund classes. However, balances often miraculously appear in other funds and are then used to finance operating expenses. . . . The general fund does not control general governmental expenses. . . . From an informational view, the City's fund accounting structure has little relevance. . . .

[2] A classification system within which financial transactions are recorded and reported is called the chart of accounts.

Accounts which should be listed as assets or liabilities within a fund class—budget notes, unexpended balances of appropriations, balance of authorizations—are set up as separate funds. . . . Many accounts are maintained on a *net* rather than *gross* basis. . . . Rather than establishing one account for revenues and another for expenses, the City nets out both in a single account.[3]

While the MFOA has published guidelines for the establishment of funds as part of a general chart of accounts for cities, there is no single best chart of accounts. In general, reporting is simplified if there are relatively few funds and if the criterion for the definition of a fund is clear. For example, it is sensible to maintain special funds for enterprise activities, that is, where there are revenues such as user charges associated directly with the operation of a facility or group of facilities. Sometimes funds are established to simplify the accounting for major intergovernmental programs, such as community development block grants. This principle should be followed consistently. In some cities, older federal and state aid programs flow into the general fund, whereas newer programs tend to have separate funds identified for them. Interdepartmental service activity (in which one department carries out functions for another department and is "reimbursed" for the activity) is a logical candidate for a separate fund. Debt service, particularly long-term debt activity, lends itself to the establishment of a separate fund.

Beyond the issues involved in the establishment of a fund structure, many cities are struggling with the overall definition or redefinition of a chart of accounts. While it is impossible to generalize about the best way to categorize expenditures and revenues for accounting purposes, one crucial generalization is possible and is often violated. Since the ultimate purpose of a chart of accounts is to classify financial transactions in a way which will lead to meaningful summaries in financial reports, the process of establishing a chart of accounts should begin with the definition of reporting needs. Too often the process is reversed. The chart of accounts is established on the basis of what appears to be rational without any clear explication first as to what reports will be needed. There is no way to test the deficiency of a chart of accounts except by trying to lay out what a financial management report should look like.

[3] Steven Clifford, "Revising the Accounting and Control Systems of the City of New York," unpublished memorandum, 1975, pp. 6–8.

Another important issue in municipal accounting reform revolves around accounting recognition principles. Two basic theories exist in general accounting. (1) Recognition is on the basis of cash, that is, a revenue or expenditure is said to occur when there is a physical receipt or transfer of funds. (2) Recognition is on the basis of accrual, that is, a revenue or expense is said to occur when there has been a decision, action, or event which commits the revenue or expenditure with virtual certainty. These theories have extremely pragmatic implications. Historically many cities and states tried to have the best of both worlds: expenses were recognized at the last possible minute, on a cash basis, and revenues were recognized as soon as possible, on an accrual basis. Very loose definitions were used to decide when an event had taken place that indicates a revenue is forthcoming.

These loose or conflicting practices can cause substantial difficulties, particularly where the underlying financial condition of a government is under stress. A loose definition of accrual on the revenue side means that accounting principles will not be applied consistently from one year to the next. In fact, a revenue can be made to appear in whatever year it is convenient. In a tight budget situation the use of a cash approach on the expense side and accrual on the revenue side will obscure the dimensions of a budgetary imbalance until it is virtually too late to do anything about it. This approach is at variance with generally accepted accounting principles and generates inconsistency within and among different reporting units, making evaluation, such as that needed by bondholders and their counselors, all but impossible.

The new municipal accounting is evolving slowly, with a number of extremely complex determinations not yet widely agreed upon. In general, the movement is away from cash recognition and toward accrual or a modified accrual approach. Expenses should be recognized on an accrual basis, that is, as soon as the expenditure is specifically committed or incurred. Revenues should be recognized on an accrual basis only when they are "measureable and available," that is, when the amounts and timing of the actual receipt of funds are known quite precisely. Otherwise, revenues should be recognized only when actually received. Thus real estate taxes, for example, should be accrued, with adequate provision made for uncollectible taxes.

The application of these accounting principles can have a powerful impact on the balancing or unbalancing of a budget in a single year. The decision as to how to treat a federal reimbursement for previously disallowed federal Medicaid funds was one of the single, most important variables affecting whether or not New York City would have a balanced budget in fiscal year 1977. If the accountants decided that that revenue belonged to the year in which the initial disallowance took place, that is, before 1975, then the receipt of $20 million would have no material impact on the 1977 budget. If, however, they decided to count that receipt of funds as a legitimate 1977 revenue, then the city's budget would be balanced.

While the term "generally accepted accounting principles" has been widely used in connection with municipal accounting reforms, it is important to recognize that these principles are still evolving. Different major accounting firms involved in New York City's fiscal crisis often disagreed on key judgments. Issues such as how to account for outstanding judgments and claims against a city government are still basically unresolved. Challenges to the real estate tax law, in particular, constitute a substantial cloud on the horizon of future city revenues and are part of many an auditor's "qualified" opinion.

Financial Reporting and Public Accountability

One of the consequences of the fiscal crises in New York City, Cleveland, and elsewhere has been a new concern, fueled by investors and their counselors, about the quality of public financial reporting. A closely related concern is the quality of available measures to assess the financial health of local and state governments. Historically, published financial data on cities are poor, public reports tend to be confused and confusing, and criteria for determining financial health are not clearly established. Most investors in private sector securities can pick up an annual report and glean at least the basic data for an assessment of the overall financial condition of an organization. The signals may be confusing—profits may be up but the share of the market might be down—but the signals are there to be analyzed

In the municipal environment, however, basic questions remain difficult to answer: Which are more important, measures of the basic economy or measures of the specific fiscal condition of the municipality? Even when specific measures of fiscal condition are examined, the signs are not clear. For example, how much debt should a city have, and when is it reasonable to say that a city has too much debt? Or, while most would agree that cities should strive for a balanced budget, if a city runs a surplus is that a sign of fiscal health or poor planning or neither? Is a surplus a sign of good and prudent fiscal management or should it be construed as an abuse of the public interest because more tax revenues were raised than were actually needed?

A prerequisite to sophisticated analysis of financial health is a set of simple and understandable financial reports. The public at large ought to be able to see virtually at a glance on an annual basis, at least, how the government in a locality fared with regard to planned versus actual expenditures and revenues during a year. Developing such statements may require reform of basic accounting systems. A number of cities and states have begun to compile consolidated financial reports on the results of various funds into a single format that the average, intelligent layman can understand.

On June 4, 1979, the Hartford *Courant* reported a survey that highlighted the progress made in both state and city financial reporting. Dallas, Texas; Portland, Oregon; San Diego, California; King County, Washington; and the states of Colorado and Tennessee issued legible and accessible financial disclosures. Tennessee, for instance, developed an accounting system that produced financial statements giving readers an opportunity to form opinions as to the fairness of the financial statements. The Council on Municipal Performance has been very active in the effort to improve the quality of public financial accountability and reporting.

Integrated Financial Management Systems

The frontier of municipal finance is the integrated computerized financial management system. Such systems combine two or more separate systems: payroll, checkwriting (disbursements), banking, accounting, financial control, budget planning and control, debt management, and cash management. The most ambitious efforts to construct a large-scale municipal integrated financial management system have been those undertaken in New York City and Detroit. Because these cities are at the frontier of state and local efforts to improve financial management, it is useful to examine in some detail the experience with at least one of these efforts, to illustrate the substantial complexity and potential pitfalls of such comprehensive systems.

Case Study: New York City's Integrated Financial Management System (IFMS)

By now it is no secret that New York City operated in the 1960s and early 1970s with an extremely chaotic and sometimes nonexistent financial management system. The key actors in the financial management arena are defined by charter and state law as adversaries: the independently elected city comptroller and the mayor are traditional rivals. In such a polarized structure, there are no incentives to develop a common approach to revealing the city's finances. The comptroller, budget bureau, and city departments each maintained their own partial financial records. The city's financial documents—the city comptroller's annual report and the mayor's budget—agreed neither on the basic structure for reporting financial information nor on what the actual financial status of the city was. The chart of accounts was a historical accretion of funds and accounts that bore little relationship either to each other or to any rational overview.

When the city entered near-default, its bankers were aghast to learn that no one could agree how much New York City owed, how much had been spent as of a given date during the year, or even how many people worked for the city. In almost every area of finance there was no consistency of definition or procedure; and very poor links existed between the budget system under the control of the mayor and the accounting system under the control of the comptroller. Thus, at the onset of the fiscal crisis there was an early commitment to rebuild the city's accounting system in a modern framework and quite remarkably, in the midst of cutbacks, economies, and reductions in spending, the city allocated over $17 million to build a modern financial management system.

Because of the unprecedented complexity and size of the effort, three outside firms were recruited—two accounting firms and one computer systems firm. A small central staff was organized under the deputy mayor for finance, and an intricate implementation plan was laid out to bring the first phase of the Integrated Financial Management System (IFMS) on line by July 1, 1978. From the beginning, the project was conceived of and directed as a joint effort of the mayor and the comptroller with oversight of the state comptroller and from the Treasury Department in Washington. The single-minded focus of getting the accounting system in shape involved retraining thousands of workers, recoding hundreds of thousands of entries, and developing massive new computer systems; it was probably one of the largest, if not the largest, domestic governmental systems effort ever undertaken. Quite remarkably, phase one was completed on time and the budget and accounting phases of IFMS were operational on July 1, 1978.

Was the project a success? The project met the deadline, created a single set of concepts and data for the budget bureau and the comptroller to work with, and, for the first time, gave the city the kind of financial concepts and data that made an outside audit even possible. On the other hand, many months after the system was installed, there was still substantial uneasiness about the accuracy and usability of the data and, from the departments' point of view, real uneasiness about the ability of the system to make budget modifications as rapidly as needed. To some extent, paperwork continued to be backlogged months after the IFMS was on line. Many of these problems were subsequently ironed out; to some extent, the problem of the IFMS is the same as that of any large-scale computer-based system—GIGO, or garbage in, garbage out. If there is no incentive to produce accurate input information and if the front-end management controls are inadequate, there is no way to tell whether fraudulent or mistaken entries are being fed into the computer. The computer cannot tell the difference between inaccurate and true information.

From a much more fundamental point of view there were a number of flaws in the design of the IFMS. The most basic of these stemmed from the lack of a management orientation at the outset. In the early stages of the design of the system a great deal of time and energy went into the conceptual framework for the budget and accounting systems. Yet relatively little thought was given to the use of IFMS output in managing the city. In one early meeting with system designers, when the question was raised as to what financial management reports the system would generate, the answer was, "The system can do anything. It will generate whatever reports are needed." To some extent, however, the system was designed backward: the accounting system was produced before any thought was given to the design of reports by the financial managers who would use accounting data. A more systematic effort should have been made to design reports responding to the needs of decision makers for information. For example, IFMS designers neglected to link (crosswalk) revenue and expenditure so as to show how positions were funded when that funding was clearly from federal or state sources. Decision makers needed this information, and the system was not designed to provide it.

There was also a problem with the budget structure. From the beginning, there was a commitment to set up the budget in organizational terms. While this made a good deal of sense from a control point of view, it did not make much sense from a planning point of view. For example, a health department might very well be organized around a dozen district health centers. For control purposes, it is useful to know how much each health center director is spending compared to what he was expected to spend. However, all those health centers are likely to be delivering parallel sets of programs. For planning purposes it is important to diffentiate between spending for maternal and child care and spending for care for the elderly. In order to accommodate to such needs the IFMS had to be partially redesigned to allow for "program coding"—the capacity to budget and control expenditures in relation to a department's missions or programs. Because this feature was added later, it proved to be cumbersome to apply and to use.

One of the crucial design decisions in any such system is how many levels of detail to build into the basic financial structure. The IFMS was designed on a three-level system: unit of appropriation, responsibility center, and budget code. The lack of a management orientation in the whole IFMS arena was exacerbated by the failure to design and implement useful citywide criteria for identifying a decision-making level with a level of detail in the budget. Rather, the actual structure of the budget was the result of a series of separate negotiations. The city council wanted many units of appropriation because it was at that level that the new charter indicated the mayor had to come to the city council for permission to modify the budget and move money. The budget bureau wanted many responsibility centers with few units of appropriation so that the mayor's need to go to the city council would be minimized and its ability to control what the departments did was maximized. The departments wanted as few units of appropriation and as few responsibility centers as possible so as to maximize their own flexibility.

The negotiations resulted in a crazy quilt pattern of outcomes in which departments of similar size and complexity could have few or many responsibility centers depending on the success of their ability to negotiate. For many department heads the responsibility center was too detailed a level of financial reporting and the unit of appropriation was too general. One department created an intermediate level of reporting called a responsibility area, in order to meaningfully structure its own internal planning and control.

These three problems experienced in the New York City IFMS situation—the failure to link the budget structure explicitly to the structure of decision making, failure to think through in advance what kinds of reports and information would be needed in order to manage effectively, and the clumsiness of program coding—are typical of the kinds of problems most governments can expect in installing large, computer-based financial systems.

Conclusions

As cities and states move toward more sophisticated financial management systems, it is important to remember that the key word is still management. Modernizing budget and accounting control systems, raising the standards of public financial accountability and reporting, and installing computerized integrated systems are all tools for improving the ability of city and state governments to manage their financial affairs. The dazzling new computerized technology needs to be, and can be, harnessed to support more accountability and better information.

7

Fiscal Strategies
for Reducing Cost
and Expanding Revenue

Achieving a balanced budget requires extensive struggles to increase revenue and reduce expenditure. Given political pressures for more spending, it has never been easy to reduce public expenditures. Increasing revenue used to depend on increasing taxes, which was once relatively easy to do, but no longer is. Four fiscal strategies for reducing cost and expanding revenue are discussed in this chapter: (1) expanding revenue without increasing taxes, (2) managing expenditure reductions, (3) managing debt, and (4) managing cash. (Operational strategies are discussed in Chapter 8.)

Expanding Revenue Without Increasing Taxes

In the current environment, increasing the rate of taxation is difficult, and the natural increases due to economic growth occur in only some regions in the country. Even in the growth regions there is great pressure to convert increases in the tax base into reductions in the tax rate. Intergovernmental revenue is an increasingly unstable source of funding as the federal government cuts domestic nonmilitary spending. Expanding revenue in this climate requires creativity and energy, but it is possible. Increases in revenue need to come from better management of existing revenue sources together with some modest expansion of local nontax sources. The first of the revenue management options to be considered are reducing tax delinquency and improving tax collections.

Reducing Tax Delinquencies

Delinquency is an increasingly expensive problem in many cities, often linked to increasing levels of abandonment of residential property. The overall strategy for dealing with this problem transcends financial management and involves developing strong links between tax collection and the housing system. A first tax delinquency should be viewed as an early warning that something may not be right in the housing. Intervention may be needed to smooth a tenant-landlord problem, such as nonpayment of rent, or some public involvement may be called for to sponsor a maintenance expenditure.

Beyond the housing interventions, there are a number of financial system actions to consider. Very often, the penalties involved in delaying tax payment are too low to offer any major disincentive to withhold taxes. When the penalty rates for late tax payments are below current market interest rates for short-term investment, there is a positive financial incentive to delay tax payment. Some cities have experimented with the use of collection agencies in this area. While the costs are high, the returns also appear to be worthwhile.

Most cities do not maintain very good data on who the delinquents are. Without a useful database, it is difficult to identify trends and spot problems early, and early intervention either in a particular building or a particular type of building becomes difficult if not impossible. Many cities do not systematically purge their records of noncollectibles, so they cannot efficiently assess the true impact of their housing situation.

It is also important to maintain adequate legal staff so that the option of recourse to the courts is available. In some cities tax appeals represent a significant portion of delinquents. If the amount that the person appealing can hold back pending the outcome of the appeal is reduced (for example, in Connecticut from 25% to 10%), this will improve the actual cash flow and the collection.

Those states that still maintain general rather than real property taxes often experience very poor collection rates in the motor vehicle and other nonreal property tax collection. Wherever possible, motor vehicle taxes should be collected as part of the registration procedure, which is typically at the state level.

The time between an initial delinquency and public foreclosure varies under different state and municipal laws. In New York City, when that period was reduced from three years to one year, there appear to have been two contradictory trends. First, the overall level of tax delinquency was reduced; second, the volume of abandonment increased. This dual reaction underlies the necessity for a sensitive approach to the whole question of enforcing property tax collection. Too aggressive a policy and program of tax collection aimed at reducing delinquency can have the opposite effect by driving marginal landlords out of the real estate market, often while abandoning their property. At the same time, too weak an approach can encourage delinquency and reduce actual collections.

Improving Tax Collection Procedures

Another approach to increasing revenue from existing taxes without increasing the tax rate or revaluation is to improve tax collection procedures. Three issues are important: (1) decreasing the frequency of tax payments; (2) using auditors to improve collections and reduce delinquency rates; and (3) improving operating procedures in the collection process. Reducing the frequency of tax collection can result in improved cash flow and greater revenue through investment income (discussed in the context of overall cash management below).

In almost every instance, tax auditors more than pay for themselves, especially in the area of sales tax evasion, which is a growing and serious problem. Moreover, many states and localities that have an income tax have used supplementary auditing staffs effectively, particularly in relation to unincorporated businesses and self-employed professionals.

Collection agencies have been used successfully by some organizations to improve operating procedures. For others, simply maintaining good records can be helpful.

Miscellaneous Local Revenue

Most cities and states derive a relatively small portion of their overall revenue from a miscellaneous collection of fees, fines, and user charges. Compared to taxes and intergovernmental aid, the "miscellaneous local revenue" category is small potatoes. In absolute dollar terms, however, the revenue involved can be substantial; in New York City by 1979, miscellaneous revenue had a billion-dollar impact on the budget. Given the virtual lid for political and fiscal reasons on taxes and intergovernmental aid, these small items offer one of the few opportunities to increase revenue.

Since the fees for various permits tend to affect different groups, the overall impact on any individual is small. For example, if golf and tennis players tend to be different folk, the burden on any individual of an increase in fee for both permits is likely to be small. Although nuisance levies are unpopular politically, their relatively small magnitude makes them more palatable than increases in the basic property and sales tax. Historically, fees and fines have been considered as regulatory rather than revenue-raising functions. Advanced cities and states are reexamining this attitude and are beginning to think about fees and fines as a revenue source.

The largest and most important potential revenue in this area comes from local responsibility to regulate municipal parking. Most localities do a relatively poor job of their parking business. Fines tend to be too low to really discourage illegal parking; collection procedures are lackadaisical so that backlogs of millions of dollars of unpaid tickets are not uncommon in even a medium-size city; enforcement tends to be underfunded; the systems for recording and processing ticket information are often poor. The solutions are not complicated in principle, although they require some attention and often some political stamina. Parking fines should be high enough so that it is not economical for the wayward parker to risk a fine rather than pay off-street parking fees; tickets should be redesigned so that they are legible, and they should be processed in a timely fashion. Special parking enforcement staff almost invariably make money for the state or local government, and so enforcement could be at a reasonable level without diluting police resources. Regulations should be up to date so that they are enforceable. For example, some cities forbid all overnight on-street parking in residential areas. In older multifamily areas such a provision is virtually meaningless.

Other, more ambitious solutions exist. If an individual cannot complete vehicle registration without paying outstanding parking fines, the incentive to pay is substantial. Reciprocal interstate agreements to monitor and honor tickets are helpful. Some jurisdictions have experimented with strong antiscofflaw programs, such as putting a "french boot" (restraining device) on scofflaw cars that are identified by their license plates. Towing programs tend to be quite lucrative. The strategy is to view parking as a business. In New York City a mathematical model has been used to adjust parking meter charges to the demand so that revenue is maximized. The overall impact on revenue of these approaches can be substantial. In New York City, over a four-year period, parking revenue quadrupled.

Water and sewer charges offer another opportunity for relatively significant revenue increases. Vigorous programs to pursue delinquents and frequent analyses to remove uncollectibles and to locate the most flagrant violators can have a substantial impact. More frequent inspections of property to identify increases in value and utilization and better coordination between property tax, land records, and water and sewage charge records can also mean substantial additional revenue.

Other opportunities exist in every jurisdiction to increase nontax revenue. The key step is to develop an ongoing process to review fees on a periodic basis. Such a program of periodic review and analysis will reveal opportunities for increasing fees. Two criteria are relevant and have to be balanced: administrative costs, and what the market will bear. In most local governments, by either statute or tradition, regulatory fees are supposed to be set at a level to cover administrative costs. Since administrative costs are rising all the time, periodic review is crucial. In addition, cities and states are not notorious for extremely sophisticated cost-accounting procedures. Thus fees rarely reflect the full cost (including indirect and overhead costs) of administering regulations.

As for "what the market will bear," this calls for some ongoing analysis of what other, nearby jurisdictions are charging for similar functions. Clearly, in an environment where a jurisdiction wants to encourage an activity and has a fee requirement merely as a method of control and oversight, it is futile to raise the fees to the point where they will discourage the activity that the locality wants to encourage. On the other hand, where fees represent a very small portion of the stakes in a project, such as a fee for review of building plans, there is no reason not to charge the maximum possible. No multimillion-dollar shopping center is going to be held up or redirected because the fee schedule has been changed from a quarter to a half of a percent of the value of the project.

If fees are adjusted at the same time as a streamlining of the administrative procedures for getting permits and paying fees, the public outcry is not likely to be very great. One approach is to establish a consolidated permit application center so that someone constructing a new building, for example, does not have to go to four separate locations to get the relevant fire, building, health, and other permits required to begin activity.

Nontax revenues also offer the only opportunities for *new* kinds of revenues, and all permit and licensing activity for which a fee is not now charged should be considered for such a charge. Sometimes the analysis of the cost and revenues associated with licensing will identify situations where there is no possibility of recouping all the costs through the licensing fee. Golf courses, for example, are often more expensive to operate than the revenue in fees which they return. In "normal" times it is not unusual to take the view that golf courses are a public service and that a locality should no more expect to recoup full costs from operating golf courses than from operating municipal parks. In times of fiscal constraint, however, it is appropriate to reexamine such views.

Another area of untapped potential for nontax revenue often is in franchises and concessions. Cities tend to be relatively unsophisticated, sometimes deliberately because of political relationships, about how much to charge for concessions and franchises often associated with lucrative recreation or sports events. Not only open bidding but active marketing as well should take place and rarely does. Often concessions are renewed year after year without any serious reexamination of the actual profits being earned by concessionaires as a clue to potential additional revenue.

User Charges in Lieu of Taxes

Metropolitan cities have historically been the center for government and nonprofit service activity. As a consequence, such cities tend to have substantial portions of their real estate in the tax-exempt category. This is especially serious for those cities that are also state capitals and/or federal regional headquarters. Such government centers are also often the center for "third sector" activity—the universities, cultural and religious centers, and other nonprofit organizations that can use substantial amounts of land without paying any taxes. In some cities, such as New York, these functions do not pay for water or sewer use either.

There has been some limited movement toward user charges for direct services for all property, including currently tax-exempt property. Under this model, water, sewer, street cleaning, and perhaps fire and police services would be charged to all property in the city regardless of current tax status. The difficulty with this approach is that nonprofit organizations such as colleges, churches, or cultural institutions are often operating under great financial strain, and the additional costs of paying for municipal services could put them out of business with substantial loss to the public interest. The most innovative approach to this problem was developed in Connecticut with a program called Pilot—Payments in Lieu of Taxes. The state provides the city of Hartford with extra revenue for nine categories of currently tax-exempt property. Under this program, the state government recognizes the broader contribution provided by the city of Hartford as a cultural and government center for a large part of the state. Particularly in cities like Hartford where a substantial portion of the revenue continues to come from the property tax, such an approach can make a great deal of difference.

Intergovernmental Financial Management

Local governments often have relatively undeveloped grants management functions. For example, a dozen or more different grant proposals may each be funded by different federal departments without any overview as to consistency in policy and program content or how the budgets are drawn—the extent to which all direct and indirect costs are included within grant proposals. Federal reimbursement of all indirect costs requires the local government to have relatively sophisticated accounting systems and the will and expertise to use them.

The policy problem is most complex where indirect (overhead) costs compete with program use. In such programs a conflict is set up between the program manager, who wants to maximize direct expenditure, and budget and accounting personnel, who want to make sure that all costs are reimbursed. Under federal manpower grants, for example, expenditure for supervisory personnel, fringe benefits, and overhead competes with expenditure to fund job placement. In some instances, however, such as welfare programs, careful cost accounting will generate larger grants. In these instances, indirect costs are not competitive with program costs, but actually supplement direct expenditures.

Many cities and states lack formal policies and procedures for developing grants and administering them once received. To overcome this problem it is important to establish formal policies and procedures for grants financial management. Such a program can avoid the loss of revenue resulting from inadequate consideration of matching requirements and insufficient recoupment of indirect costs and fringe benefits. Congressional disillusionment with urban aid programs is as much a result of sloppy accounting and reporting procedures as it is the result of any inherent antiurban bias on the part of rural legislators.

Often federal grants have been subcontracted to neighborhood-based, nonprofit organizations where the experience with financial management is sharply limited. In the absence of heavy technical assistance and strong, central fiscal controls, fiscal mismanagement is almost inevitable. Even where the money is not misused, auditing trails are woefully inadequately. Unfortunately, creative program people struggling with difficult problems ranging from illiteracy to alcoholism often are impatient with detailed record keeping or with such mundane matters as the proper conditions for charging expenses to the project.

Managing Expenditure Reductions

The simplest way to spend less is to do less, that is, to provide fewer services or a lower level of service. A second simple way to reduce expenditures is to operate more efficiently, that is, to deliver the same services with fewer staff or less costly materials and equipment. In contrast to the revenue area, there are relatively few purely fiscal strategies, compared to these operational or policy strategies, for reducing or controlling expenditures. Of the available fiscal strategies for reducing expenditures, the most important relates to expenditures for salaries and fringe benefits.

Average Salary Controls

Under pressure of reduced resources, the typical response is to reduce or freeze hiring and to maintain tight control over the number of filled positions. This approach leaves a significant loophole. In New York City, for example, "crisis-fighters" were aghast to learn that despite the reduction of the city's payroll by over 80,000 people and the existence of a salary freeze, overall expenditure for personnel had actually *increased* modestly during the fiscal crisis. A key variable in this increase was found to be a gradual upward creep in average salary. Even with the salary freeze in place, a detailed unpublished analysis by the controller's office found a 9 percent increase in the average salary. This resulted from a whole series of "circumventions" of the salary freeze which line managers were forced to resort to in order to continue to operate. Positions were upgraded, that is, a clerk's position was redefined as a senior clerk's position; and promotions were made with the lower position remaining unfilled.

A helpful response to this problem is an average salary control system that monitors and controls the average salary which must be maintained for each group of positions. With a formal control system in place, it should not be difficult to maintain average salaries at approximately the same level. In the normal course of events, retiring personnel tend to be replaced by entry-level people, usually with a substantial salary differential. This control system includes control over promotion policy, so that the city or state does not end up with all supervisors and no workers. Obviously, a financial system is required to compute and monitor the actual average salary by unit and department, but such systems are feasible and should be effective in maintaining the lid on expenditure.

Reducing Use of Overtime

Another area of slippage which, in New York, contributed to increased personnel costs, even while the number of people working for the government was declining sharply, was an increase in the use of overtime. In many environments, control over the level and use of overtime falls to the workers or lower-level supervisors responding to a set of needs that may not have too much to do with the tasks to be performed. For example, on Monday, Mr. A, who fills a crucial position, calls in sick so that his buddy, Mr. B, who has completed his tour of duty, can be called in because B could use the extra cash from overtime. On Wednesday, B calls in sick so that A can get the overtime work (at time-and-a-half or double-time). Alternatively, Ms. A, Mr. B, Ms. C, and Mr. D all slow down a little during the day so that some extra overtime is needed to finish important work. Supervisory control over such abuses is very difficult, but in an environment in which there are very sharp limits and tight criteria on what constitutes acceptable overtime with specific dollar limits on the amount of allowable overtime, management at least has some tool for dealing with the problem.

Increased use of overtime is linked to increased municipal pension costs. In many cities and states, pensions are based on the earnings of the last year or two. Often there is passive or explicit agreement among supervisors and workers to ensure that Mr. X, who is in his last year, gets preference for overtime over Mr. Y, who has some years left to go, thus ballooning Mr. X's base salary and increasing the "hit" on the pension system.

Holding the Line on Pension Costs and Other Fringe Benefits

As the subject for collective bargaining, reductions in the cost of fringe benefits do not appear to lend themselves to managerial strategies. In some instances, however, substantial savings can result from a systematic analysis and reassessment of the funding of fringe benefits. For example, cities and states could do a better job of negotiating effective rates and good packages of service from private insurance carriers if they hired professionals in the insurance field to cost insurance coverage and to negotiate with the seasoned professionals of the insurance industry. As for pension systems, a review of the information base of the systems, including an updating of membership files, may yield an actual decline in the pension contribution required primarily because the system carries files of members who are no longer actually in the system. The point is that even in such highly political and sensitive areas as fringe benefits, there are opportunities to reduce costs through better financial management.

Managing Debt

Financial management usually does not begin with a clean slate at the beginning of a fiscal year. Reducing expenditure and increasing revenue in a budget sense only deals with a portion of the financial problem that many localities find themselves in. In addition to budget pressure and the need for explicit strategies to reduce costs and increase revenues, cities need strategies for managing their debt. Too many cities have been drawn into mortgaging the future in order to pay for present pressures.

Most cities and states, like most organizations, borrow money at some time. Borrowing is not necessarily a sign of financial trouble, as it may be for an individual or a family. On the other hand, city and state borrowing is rarely conceived of as it has been at the federal level, where borrowing decisions have been made in terms of the overall impact on the national economy. For state and local governments the situation is somewhere between the individual household model and the federal model. Up to a certain point, borrowing can be a reasonable adjunct to the public welfare. Beyond a certain point, it can be a sure sign of trouble.

The essential dilemma of debt management in state and local government is the separation in time between the decision to borrow and the impact of borrowing. The financial consequences of borrowing are reflected through debt service paid in the operating budget. By the time the debt service appears in the budget, it is too late to do anything about it. The crucial borrowing decisions were made long before. This situation creates a dilemma because in the political environment the decision to borrow is virtually costless. The mayor who borrows, particularly in the case of medium- or long-term borrowing, is not the mayor who pays. Particularly with the separation of capital and operating budgeting into two separate arenas, there is very little pressure to test the consequences of capital decisions on future interest and principal repayment costs. The political incentives are all in the direction of more borrowing to build more capital facilities; someone else will pay.

But the changes which are currently affecting the broader political climate, and which point in the direction of more efficient and more prudent financial management overall, also are having some impact in the debt area. In many areas, bond issues which were thought to be safe are no longer sure to be accepted at the polls.

What should be the criterion affecting municipal borrowing? If it is not to stimulate the economy (as the feds do), and if it is not to minimize borrowing (as the household does), what is it? The municipal borrowing criterion is to minimize the cost of borrowing consistent with the locality's need to borrow. Like any borrower, cities and states try to get the best possible deal, that is, the lowest possible interest rate for the needed maturity. This criterion is vague, but it can be clarified somewhat by examining the three basic issues in debt management: (1) What are the acceptable purposes for borrowing? Some purposes are legitimate and others are not. Many cities have gotten into trouble by gradually expanding the scope and nature of borrowing. (2) How much borrowing is too much? Unlike business, governments do not have generally useful rules of thumb to suggest when they are overcommitted in their debt. (3) What is the structure of the debt—the types of instrument used and, in particular, the mix between short- and long-term debt?

It is easier to point to the excesses of cities in financial trouble than it is to define the specific or precise point at which too much borrowing exists, the structure is unbalanced, or the purposes are inappropriate. Cities in financial trouble often have a large amount of debt and a rapidly rising debt with a shaky structure, that is, they have pyramided their debt, borrowed to repay previous loans; they use a wide range of questionable instruments, such as BANs,[1] that effectively mortgage their future; they borrow to cover gaps in current operating expenses and abuse the definition of capital spending to include items that are really for operating purposes. New York City in 1975 was the classic case of a local government whose debt was mismanaged and which suffered from general financial instability. It is not important whether excessive debt was a cause of New York City's problem or a symptom of deeper social and economic problems, as some argued. Clearly, there was a close association in New York between deepening fiscal problems, mounting debt, and the increasingly "creative" use of borrowing to paper over basic problems.

[1] BANs are bond anticipation notes: short-term notes sold in anticipation of a bond issue. BANs are retired by proceeds from the sale of bonds.

While the state of the art of local financial management is not at the point where a specific criterion can be suggested to specify the appropriate maximum level of debt or the minimally acceptable structure of debt, it is possible to point out some useful directions in thinking about these two issues. On the question of the purposes of debt, the ground is a great deal more solid, and there appears to be fairly general agreement as to what is a legitimate reason for borrowing and what is not.

Restricting the Purposes of Borrowing

There really are only two legitimate categories for state and local borrowing. The first is short-term borrowing to deal with (downside) seasonal variation in cash flow. Short-term borrowing is by definition a temporary tide-over. Better cash flow management can reduce, minimize, or even eliminate the need for short-term borrowing (see cash management discussion below).

There may be special temporary situations requiring legitimate short-term borrowing, but these are likely to be rare. For example, a major revenue may be delayed for specific and knowable reasons; if such delays are frequent, this suggests poor cash flow planning. Short-term borrowing to tide one over until a miracle takes place is hardly a reasonable basis for borrowing.

The second major acceptable category of borrowing is long-term borrowing to fund large capital needs. The theory is simple. Capital facilities involve heavy expenditure over a very short period of time to pay for something which will be used over a long period of time. Funds are borrowed to spread out the impact of the large-scale, one-time, relatively infrequent capital expenditure and to put the payment for the facility in better rhythm with the use of the facility. Implicitly here is the myth that if a city or state goes bankrupt, it can sell land or facilities to pay back at least a portion of the funds borrowed.

New York City was infamous for its creativity in developing phony capital programs and putting more and more into the capital budget. Manpower training was justified as a capital expenditure through some tortuous reasoning process. Every possible rationale was used to add items to the capital budget. The effect was to borrow to cover operating deficits, which merely postponed dealing with the real gap between revenue and expenditure. The Lindsay administration—under internal and external social pressure for more spending and faced with level or declining revenues—reacted by borrowing to cover the difference.

Reducing the Level of Debt

Although it is difficult, if not impossible, to specify an explicit rule of thumb as to how much debt cities should have, a variety of possible principles have been suggested by various observers of the municipal financial scene. Some have suggested that debt service should not exceed 20 percent of the total revenues. The U.S. Chamber of Commerce suggested that long-term debt that approaches $1,000 per capita signals fiscal trouble ahead for a city or state.[2]

Another proposal is to look not at the amount of debt, but at the trend of debt accumulation. In this context, some have suggested that if a particular city's or state's debt is growing faster than the national aggregate local and state government debt, then there is cause for concern, and if it is growing at or below the national rate, this is acceptable. The problem with this criterion is that in areas of growth such as the Southwest, the national average is too low, and in areas that have already been developed where growth is slower, such a criterion may be too high.

Another relevant criterion for aggregate debt is the rate of increase in relation to the rate of increase in revenue collected. If a city or state increases its amount of borrowing more rapidly than the expansion of its basic revenue (that is, locally generated revenue), then it would appear that that government is headed for trouble. In many situations the two will in fact be in conflict. The older declining central cities of the Northeast and the Midwest may be experiencing stable or declining revenues precisely when they need major capital investment in order to upgrade their infrastructure and make their cities more attractive to new economic activity which will later generate additional taxes. Since there is no guarantee that spending the capital money now will generate the revenue later, whereas it is clear that borrowing now will create major increases in operating expenses (through debt service) later, analysis needs to be done

[2] *Improving Local Government Fiscal Management* (Washington, D.C.: Chamber of Commerce of the United States, 1979), p. 33.

very carefully. In effect, the criterion of using the revenue trend as the standard to evaluate the level and direction of borrowing is an assessment of risk.

Still another way to look at the same situation is to project the future debt service implications of past borrowing, adding in the impact of contemplated borrowing to assess the overall future budget impact of current debts. If debt service is projected to consume a significant and growing proportion of the budget dollar, this, too, is a sign of significant concern.

Restructuring Debt

Again, it is difficult to specify the precise nature of an optimal pattern or structure of debt. A well-managed debt program is likely to be heavily tilted toward long-term as opposed to short-term debt. It is likely to reduce borrowing during periods of high interest and increase borrowing during periods of low interest (all other things being equal). In practical terms, when interest terms are high, borrowing should be postponed as long as possible, and when interest terms are low, borrowing should be accelerated to the extent feasible.

A crucial aspect of debt structure has to do with the practice of pyramiding debt, that is, borrowing to repay former borrowing. Another practice that has obvious disastrous consequences is committing the same revenue to three different sources of borrowing by the use of three different types of instruments. Restructuring debt is often as important as reducing debt, and the elimination of short-term, high-interest borrowing through the consolidation of debts into a longer-term, lower-interest form can substantially reduce the costs of borrowing.

Managing Cash

The third leg of fiscal stress—along with unbalanced budgets and heavy debt—is cash availability. Governments in fiscal trouble consistently seem to be short of the cash needed to meet obligations. Historically, much more attention in public financial management has gone into budgeting than into the management of cash flow.

The responsibility for cash management is often diffused. In New York City, it tended to fall somewhere between the separately elected comptroller, the mayor's office of management and budget, and the mayor's department of finance. Responsibilities for cash forecasting, investment decisions, investment processing, and bank service analysis either tend to be shared by several departments with no one department really in charge, or tend to be carried out informally. Governments in general are not particularly sensitive to the value of money. In the cash management area this insensitivity can be quite costly. For example, a one-day delay in the deposit of tax collections during the peak period in a relatively small city involves the loss of thousands of dollars.

The Municipal Finance Officers Association (MFOA), through seminars and publications, has played an active role recently in heightening awareness of improved practice in the cash management area. Under the pressure of tightening fiscal pressure, city, county, and state governments are responding.

Analysis of Cash Flow

Local and state governments often do not have a formal cash management program. Written policies, objectives, procedures, and job descriptions all tend either to be out of date or not to exist at all. Most local governments do not have formal cash forecasting systems in place. Most companies handling substantial amounts of cash have relatively precise methods, at least for the short term, for predicting how much cash will be available (for potential investment) on any day during the year. With so much of the city's resources coming from other governments which control the timing of their own disbursements, it is somewhat more difficult to predict when money will be in hand in the local government setting than it is to predict this in the private sector. On the other hand, a substantial portion of both revenue and outlay is fairly regular from year to year. Very careful record keeping as to how much cash is available on each day over a yearly period provides a baseline for going forward. In Hartford, for example, a sample of transactions revealed that idle funds were maintained in bank accounts at a level of 48 percent to 1300 percent beyond balance and reserve requirements.

Another sign of unsophisticated cash forecasting is the number of investment rollovers. The Hartford Management Study of Cash and Revenue Management found 22 examples of unnecessary investment rollovers in a relatively short period of time.

The Timing of Disbursements and Collections

The theory of cash flow management is quite simple: to delay payments for disbursements as long as possible and to bring revenue in as quickly as possible. On the collection side, a good example of an important issue for many cities is the frequency of property tax collection. The Hartford study, for example, pointed out that if the city were to switch from a quarterly to a semiannual collection of taxes the saving in administrative costs and potential additional investment earnings would be over $1 million. And if the city were willing to go to an annual payment for the largest property tax payers (over $100,000), the potential benefits could reach $1.6 million. The Hartford study also pointed out that by changing motor vehicle tax collections from four times a year to once a year another $100,000 of additional investment earnings were possible.

Whether residents pay once a year or four times a year, the tax collector faces very sharp peaks and valleys in the arrival of tax payments. Thus, it is not unusual to find significant delays in the time it takes to get payments to the bank and earning interest. Some governments have employed a "lock box"—which is simply a mailed-check receipt location within the bank so that the checks get into the account virtually immediately. In many instances, simply improving the manual procedures (such as using temporary employees specifically assigned to remove and deposit checks during peak periods) can have substantial benefits.

The timing of intergovernmental payment is not usually under the control of local government. In some instances, however, the local government can negotiate a more favorable timing decision from the state or federal government. Even very small things can help, such as sending someone to pick up a check when it is available if the city is in the state capital, rather than waiting for it by mail.

Cash flow management also involves managing the timing of disbursements. Many local governments use the practice of delaying payments to vendors in order to conserve cash. This process is clearly counterproductive as there is no question that a vendor who is alert will add the cost of money to the base price in making a bid. And it is not unusual for a vendor to call his banker to find out the cost of money over a three- or six-month period before entering a bid on a public purchasing contract. But there are some practices which are appropriate—such as careful monitoring and negotiation of the timing of insurance premium payments or debt service payments.

Fairfax County, Virginia, showed dramatic improvement in interest revenue by changing collection methods. The county stopped covering all payroll checks on payday and now deposits enough funds to cover 60 percent of the payroll. The county deposits the remainder in interest-bearing accounts over the weekend and transfers the amount at the beginning of the week. The county also found that tax and revenue checks could be mailed directly to a post office box, picked up by bank officials, and immediately credited to the county's account. These checks are then sent over to county offices for processing. These two improvements were expected to bring the county more than $27 million in interest payments in 1980 alone. Broome County, New York, set up a bank competition for its demand deposits, consolidated checking accounts, and negotiated a better cash flow from federal and state assistance programs. The county realized more than $400,000 in additional interest income in 1978, when these improvements were implemented.

Investment Management

Most cities and states are sharply limited by statute as to what types of investment instruments they can use. This is understandable, in view of the fact that public funds are involved and minimum risk investments are appropriate.

In some instances, however, the strictures appear to be too narrow. Where investment instruments are restricted to direct government obligations, time deposits, and certificates of deposit, as is often the case, it is reasonable to amend statutes to add government agency obligations and, with careful definition, prime commercial paper. A survey of the nation's 18 largest counties revealed that the most popular investment instruments were certificates of deposit, U.S. government securities, and repurchase agreements.

It is important, too, that local governments be knowledgeable about the actual restrictions on investability of state and federal funds. Very often the assumption is made without verification that the funds from another government are not investable. Even if the money cannot be invested, it can be used at compensating balances to pay for banking services.

The tradeoff between the nature and quality of banking services, interest rate paid on accounts, and the size of required compensating or minimal balances is complex and difficult. This is another area, like collective bargaining and insurance services, where city and state officials must negotiate with individuals, in this case bankers, who are very much more sophisticated about the issues than the typical civil servant. If at all possible, cities should receive professional advice. One useful tactic is to use insurance companies, which are sophisticated about handling money and which must negotiate their own banking services, to advise cities on their banking problems, and to use the banks which must negotiate insurance services to advise cities on the negotiation of their insurance programs.

There are other aspects of banking that are often neglected. For example, many governments maintain too many bank accounts, often with inadequate controls. (In New York City during the fiscal crisis it was found that no one knew all the bank accounts being maintained by the city.) Another strategy is to establish a pooled investment program, such as the one established by Lehigh County, Pennsylvania, for municipalities within the county. These municipalities invest smaller amounts for shorter periods at higher interest rates. Funds are invested in 30-, 60-, and 90-day certificates of deposit. The county returns the principal and interest to the townships and boroughs within two working days from the date of maturity.

Investment management has always involved developing a tradeoff between maximum return and minimum risks. In recent years, public investment management has been complicated by a third criterion—maximizing social benefits. Social benefit in the public arena has been defined as investing public money in programs such as housing or redevelopment, investing in local banks as opposed to banks from outside the city, and in some cases not investing public funds in activities relating to foreign dictatorships or military spending. While it is difficult to generalize about the legitimacy of a social benefit criterion, it does appear that given the stringent financial pressure on cities, there is no alternative but to maximize the rate of return within a framework of acceptable risks. Once a sophisticated investment management system is developed and operating, it is possible to think of marginal adjustments in response to other criteria.

Conclusions

The underlying theme of most of the suggestions in Chapters 5, 6, and 7 is greater fiscal accountability. The concepts and methods to implement this heightened awareness that government, too, has a bottom line are adaptable from private industry. In some ways, the governmental task is easier: there are no taxes to pay and no need to show a profit. In some ways, the governmental task is harder: social, economic, and political accountability still remains as important as the fiscal, and those results don't necessarily show up on the balance sheet.

Part III

Streamlining the Operations of Public Programs

With deliberate and explicit effort, a city, county, or state can streamline the operations of its public services. The evidence from public and private experience is clear, although the examples from government are not as numerous and the evidence seems to consist more of isolated examples than of comprehensive efforts. The chapters in this part of the book focus on opportunities that are most likely to yield significant dollar savings and/or substantial improvements in service.

There are two ways to look at this problem: from the vantage point of an individual service system (such as health) or from the vantage point of a specific approach (such as using technology). Ten years ago, while designing a curriculum for public service graduate education at the New School for Social Research in New York City, I invited two distinguished public management experts to review preliminary proposals. As part of their review, I posed the following question: Are the different service delivery systems (health, education, police, and so on) more like each other or more unlike each other? One of the experts said they were more unlike each other, and the other replied that they were more like each other. After a spirited debate, I concluded then and conclude now: both are right. The different service systems are like each other in some ways, so Chapter 8 includes a review of the most promising operational improvement strategies regardless of type of service. The different service systems are also each unique, and Chapters 9 and 10 focus on specific types of government functions.

State and local governments in the United States have two kinds of essential jobs to perform for the public. One is to provide *basic public services*. Cities, counties, and states share responsibility for social services, fire, police, corrections, highway maintenance, refuse collection, parks and recreation, education, health services, water and sewer services, and libraries. The other major mission is to carry out *development programs,* that is, to help improve the community as a place to live and work and to stimulate social, economic, and physical growth and progress. While traditionally responsible for basic services, concern for improving the quality of life has led government into urban renewal, manpower training, industrial and commercial development, land redevelopment, cultural affairs, and human resources programs.

The goals of such functions—more jobs, greater neighborhood stability, improved housing, broader tax base, and increased revenue—are important objectives in many areas. Of course, in some places growth versus no growth is an important public policy issue. The opponents of growth see an important government function in controlling or limiting growth, and many supporters of growth believe government should stay out of the issue.

The line service delivery departments spend most of the dollars and provide the services that most citizens see and care about. This lends a certain obvious urgency to improving the operation of basic services. In the long run the development program may have as much to do with citizen satisfaction. However, there is some question as to the potential contribution that management improvement can make to the development process.

In Chapter 9 the emphasis is on identifying specific operational improvements in service delivery and development. Development programs and basic services are the line functions of a state or local government that parallel the lines of business of a manufacturing or service company. To make it possible to operate these lines, governments perform a number of internal or support functions. The client or consumer of the line functions—basic services and development—are the people who live and work in an area; the consumers of support services are the line departments themselves. Operations support services are required for the line departments to function, but are less visible to the public. They include, for example, vehicles, building operations and maintenance, architectural and engineering services, purchasing, data processing, telephones, and energy.

Improving basic services or development programs may require substantial investment of energy and resources in improving support functions, but the relationships are subtle. There are two crucial traps to avoid. On the one hand, from the point of the view of the public and elected officials, resources invested in operations support are "wasted" because they are not visible to the public. On the other hand, those who operate operations support tend to see management improvement in their own area as an end in itself. The fleet manager wants a bright and shiny fleet, and the data-processing manager wants powerful hardware. Each sees these improvements as valid for their own sake. The appropriate middle ground is to recognize that effective service delivery and development programs often require focused specific improvements to operations support. Data processing, for example, needs to be viewed as an instrument for improving service delivery or for getting better development programs. Opportunities to improve operations support and thereby the line programs are the focus of Chapter 10.

8

Operational Strategies for Reducing Cost and/or Improving Service

This chapter discusses those management methods for improving public service and/or reducing their cost that have wide application and that have had some success. Theoreticians are fond of pointing out that it is impossible to "optimize" both costs and service at the same time, that is, the least-cost solution cannot at the same time maximize service. However, in a surprising number of cases, improving service is perfectly consistent with reducing cost. For example, reducing an absence rate is likely to save money (by reducing dollars spent on overtime) while at the same time improving service because workers are available when needed. Of course, it may not be possible to do both.

If the fiscal pressure is severe enough, a government may have to simply cut services. Particularly under extreme and sudden fiscal pressure, radical surgery may be urgently needed and is sometimes accomplished in a heavy-handed way, as with a meat ax, rather than deftly, as with a scalpel. Reducing taxes and freezing hiring across the board are examples of the former, and shifting a function to a higher level of government is an example of the latter.

There often are opportunities for eliminating duplication in functions among different levels of government or different departments within the same goverment. If possible, radical surgery should be postponed until management improvement options are exhausted. The successful implementation of a management improvement program may even eliminate the need for such radical surgery.

The discussion in this chapter is in four parts: (1) concepts for improving government operations, (2) management methods for improving the work process, (3) using new technology, and (4) developing a customer service orientation.

Concepts for Improving Government Operations

Managing a government is much more complicated than most people realize. A modern state, county, or municipal government is a far more complex organization than the typical private company of similar size, because government performs two basic missions—service delivery and development—whereas the typical private company provides only a product or service. Moreover, a medium-size city or county or a small state performs more different *types* of service than all but the largest and most varied conglomerates. From police service to road construction, from health care to the construction of park facilities, its activities and outputs, its clients or consumers and markets cover a bewildering range. A government may sell some services (like water and sewer service) and provide other services without a direct charge to the user (like sanitation or parks). It serves both individuals and businesses, neighborhoods and entire areas.

This complexity of mission and activity makes the job of improving public management harder and more time-consuming than comparable improvements in industry, but the job can be done. Recent experience in improving such service industries as telephone, insurance, or banking is likely to be more relevant to government than experience in improving manufacturing industries; government is rarely and only incidentally involved in production. But management experience in the relatively more orderly world of the private sector becomes increasingly less applicable as the extent and purposes of government intervention become more obscure, the politics more intense, the intergovernmental environment more complex and the understanding of the impact of government's actions more tenuous. All these constraints are even more characteristic of the development programs, such as manpower training or neighborhood renewal, than of the more straightforward delivery of, for example, street maintenance or water supply.

Because of the heterogeneity of government activity, there are relatively few strategies for improving public service that are likely to be universally effective. What works for one function may not work for another. We had best be wary of solutions that are projected as having global or universal application—there is no universal solution to the improvement of public services. For example, there are those who believe that government should get out of the business of delivering service and should contract everything to the private sector. This view is based on the assumption that the reason for government's apparent lack of management effectiveness is that it is monopolistic. Yet there are many monopolistic service industries, notably the telephone company, which have made dramatic improvements in internal management in the last few years. A community that contracts out everything faces an even worse dilemma if its financial situation worsens. When its operations are performed by others, the government's own capacity to review and improve operations is severely limited. In a number of cases, governments have contracted out a service previously performed internally because analysis seemed to project substantial cost savings. For a variety of reasons, very often the prices rise dramatically once the transition has been completed. Contracting out is no panacea. It is one of many concepts that should be carefully examined in the search for opportunities for management improvement.

A Note on Productivity

Most people's favorite conceptual handle for thinking about improving government is "productivity." Unfortunately, the use of this term has created a great deal of confusion. The collapse of New York City's much publicized labor-management productivity effort resulted at least in part from the lack of clarity about the concept and from confusion about how it was being applied.

The term "productivity" is often used to mean performance or cost effectiveness (as in "we must all work to improve the productivity of government"), but it also has a rather precise and narrow meaning: the relationship between inputs measured in person-hours and outputs measured in number of widgets. Almost no one involved in productivity ever produces anything but widgets. Productivity improves where the ratio of outputs to inputs goes up.

Used in the narrow sense, productivity is a perfectly valid concept, but it has relatively limited applicability in the public sector. It also presupposes two fairly rigorous measurement systems, one for measuring inputs (productive time) and one for measuring outputs (the amount of work performed). The mischief begins when, without valid measurement systems, people attempt to make judgments about whether productivity is or is not increasing. The mischief is compounded when people begin to believe that somehow improving productivity will automatically result in better services. The mischief culminates when people believe that productivity means dollar savings. In New York City's productivity program all these errors were made, and endless arguments took place over whether productivity was or was not occurring in an environment where there were virtually no measurement systems. There was great consternation where productivity improvement appeared to take place with no measurable dollar gains.

There is an important difference between public and private productivity. In the classic widget manufacturing plant, widgets are sold. Thus, if one can make more widgets with the same number of person-hours or if one can make the same number of widgets with fewer person-hours, the result is the same: lower unit cost, more widgets sold, more net income for the company, and hence, better performance. In the public environment where the "widget" has no price, making more widgets per hour does not necessarily imply dollar gains. It may not even mean better performance in a service sense. For example, tons of garbage collected per hour, a classic productivity measure, is more a function of the number of tons of garbage generated and put out and the frequency of collection than it is necessarily a measure of how good a job anyone is doing. In fact, one could probably increase productivity by reducing the frequency of garbage collection. It is unlikely that a single citizen would regard that as an improvement in service. Productivity—in the narrow sense of outputs relative to inputs—*is* meaningful if it is recognized as only one dimension of one way to improve public performance.

Improving the Work Process

The average citizen or newly elected official is likely to define the public management performance problem in terms of the need to "get people to work harder." The roots of this view are undoubtedly ancient. The Bible tells us how Pharaoh characterized the Israelites as lazy and urged the taskmasters to use their whips to encourage the Jews to reach their quota of bricks without straw being provided (Exodus 5:13). This is a classic case of increasing productivity, that is, maintaining the same output with less input. In George Orwell's *Animal Farm*, a key figure, Boxer the horse, approaches every problem with the maxim "I will work harder." Inevitably he works himself to death and the problems don't necessarily get solved. No model could be less useful for thinking about improving public management. The tendency to identify improved work with working harder poisons labor-management relations. The sanitation worker confronted with the challenge to increase productivity is convinced that management intends to work him to death, like the horse in *Animal Farm*.

The modern approach to the management of the work process ("productivity") focuses on two areas: the use of technology, and changes in the content and process of the work itself. The discussion that follows deals with the second area first. There are five basic tools for improving the management of the work process: reducing work, increasing productive time, work measurement, work standards, and work incentives and sanctions.

Reducing Work

One way to reduce unnecessary work is to *reduce demand*. Government, unlike industry, does not always view increasing demand with favor. Sometimes it is viewed with alarm. Many government programs are aimed from the beginning at reducing or preventing conditions that later could turn into more "business." In fact, all preventive programs, from health maintenance through fire prevention, are in some sense aimed at reducing future demand for services. Sometimes the reduction of demands can be an explicit management strategy, for example:

- Because of fiscal constraint, reductions in parks maintenance forces, and increasing vandalism, many older cities find themselves with park facilities in very poor condition. Part of the solution involves reducing the amount of work. In Hartford 64 examples were found where redesign could make parks easier and less costly to maintain, such as paving grassy areas which were difficult to seed and water.

- A welfare department with a declining number of caseworkers and an increasing number of welfare cases faces union action because the agreed-upon maximum of cases per worker is being regularly exceeded. The appropriate response is to try to reduce the number of clients by installing a quality control program and stronger employment referral. After ineligible and employable clients leave the rolls, the caseload ratio comes into line.
- Firemen respond to an increasing number of alarms. Analysis indicates that the component which is most rapidly increasing is the number of fires in vacant buildings. One appropriate response is to accelerate the demolition of abandoned structures, which will reduce the number of vacant building fires and reduce the amount of work that firemen have to perform.

Another way to reduce work is through *work simplification*. Particularly in clerical areas of service industries, substantial management improvement resources are being devoted to the general subject of work simplification or reducing the content of the work performed. Systematic charting of workflow very often reveals substantial amounts of useless work. Two or more people may be duplicating each other's efforts. The same information may be recorded on several different forms. The same form may travel back and forth between the same two offices. In government, opportunities for work simplification exist in almost all areas; for example:

- A police department discovers that it can reduce the number of forms with no loss, and in fact with an improvement, in the amount of information captured.
- A routine inspection is carried out four times a year, one each season. A review of the inspector's logs indicates a strong seasonal bias in the field being inspected: only two out of the four inspections (spring and fall) regularly turn up significant numbers of violations. Inspections are reduced from four times to two times a year.
- A budget office regularly preaudits every single expenditure

item. By moving to a postaudit of smaller expenditures and preauditing only the largest expenditures, significant amounts of time are made available for more important activity.

• In a purchasing process, a purchase order goes back and forth between the purchasing agent and the fiscal officer in two separate loops. The process is streamlined—the purchasing agent does all his work when he has the order, and the fiscal officer does all his work at one time, eliminating substantial back and forth activity as well as misplaced and lost orders.

Almost any clerical operation will benefit from systematic workflow analysis. Examples of unnecessary work exist in every organization.

Increasing Productive Time

On every job time is wasted; in other words, not all time is used productively. The focus of public attention is often on types of nonproductive time such as coffee breaks or washup time, won at the bargaining table by labor unions. Those losses of working time are often dwarfed by time which is wasted as a result of poor management. Substantial amounts of nonproductive time are generated in waiting time, for example, for a piece of equipment to be delivered; in travel time to different locations, or from field to headquarters often just to check in; or in downtime, when a piece of equipment breaks down, leaving the worker with little or nothing to work with. Allowing workers to be idle because their equipment is broken is particularly pernicious because it encourages workers to be careless.

Most jurisdictions do not have a measurement system for keeping track of productive time. Clearly, the solution to problems of nonproductive time begins with finding some way to measure the number of hours that a worker is actively working compared to the number of hours that he or she is not. Strategies for increasing productive time include better scheduling and routing so as to eliminate unnecessary trips.

• Inspectors would regularly check in in the morning to get their field assignments for the day. By arranging to have them pick up their field assignments for the following day when they check out at night, a trip from home to headquarters is eliminated and they are able to check in directly in the field.

- Street sweeper operators often come in in the middle of the day because their equipment is damaged. No alternate work is provided for them. When the procedure is changed so that men whose sweepers are damaged are handed a broom to sweep by hand, the number of such breakdowns decreases.

In some situations nonproductive time can be seasonal. Parks workers, for example, are notorious for "hibernating" during the winter season when there is no grass to mow or litter to collect. The winter season is a wonderful time for preventive maintenance, for rebuilding indoor equipment, and for carrying out an inventory of facilities and workload. In some jurisdictions park personnel work closely with street personnel in snow removal and street repair during the winter. There is no reason that the personnel who clean the parks during the summer cannot participate in cleaning the streets during the winter.

A broad approach to productive time focuses on the *elimination of roadblocks*. Most people want to work if given the chance. Performance failures are often the result of frustration with working conditions. If a vehicle runs out of gas in the middle of a tour because it was not gassed up the night before, a worker cannot complete his route. If equipment is faulty and breaks down frequently, it is not reasonable to expect people to be productive.

One way to increase productive time is to substitute lower-paid, less skilled staff for professionals. The whole development of paraprofessionals in health and education is an attempt to do this and to free professionals for higher-level responsibility. Civilianization in a police department is a classic example of this strategy. Having civilians do clerical work is supposed to reduce the cost of that work and at the same time free police for patrol and other police activity.

Another way to increase productive time is to change staffing patterns:

- One-man police cars make it possible to put many more vehicles on patrols and/or reduce the number of police required to cover a city.
- In rough neighborhoods the pattern was to send two inspectors

for safety reasons on every assignment. By substituting an inspector and an aide the security aspects continue to be covered, but trained inspectors are not wasted by having two cover the same route.

Work Measurement

Work measurement has evolved a great deal since Taylor first used his stopwatch to time the tasks of individual production workers. To a significant extent the challenges of work measurement in manufacturing industries was met by the 1930s. It is only recently that service industries have begun to make any serious progress in measuring service work. While a great deal remains to be done, some of the basic concepts have been established and are certainly applicable to government as well.[1]

The problem has to be subdivided into measuring the quality of work and measuring the quantity of work. Even in service activity, there are quantities associated with much of the work, and quantities *are* more easily measured than quality. Most people who have looked at the service measurement problem have correctly observed that in many instances the quantities produced are not nearly as important as the quality of what is produced. From this correct observation, people have tended to draw two erroneous conclusions: that it is pointless to measure the quantities because they are irrelevant, and that quality cannot be measured.

A tax auditor reviewing tax returns *can* easily do twice as many returns in one day by doing a much skimpier review on each individual return. The same is true of an auto mechanic, or a building or health inspector. By cutting short the inspection, many more inspections can be done in one day. This is even more true in "people" contact. Certainly a doctor or a social worker can easily increase output by 30 times by seeing each client for one minute instead of for 30 minutes. The solutions for these kinds of measurement problems are threefold.

First, one should be pragmatic—work measurement should not be used when it is not meaningful. Within government, work mea-

[1] For a general introduction to work measurement for state and local government, see *Improving Productivity Using Work Measurement*, (Washington, D.C.: Public Technology, 1977).

surement can be applied far more easily to some services than to others. Police and fire activities are extremely difficult to measure; sanitation, waste collection, and street paving are relatively easy to measure. Despite popular perceptions, most clerical activity, including vast portions of health and social services, are relatively easily measureable. Even in a police department, where the classic functions of patrol and detection do not lend themselves to work measurement, there is the possibility of measuring police performance in other ways.

Second, quantitative measurement needs to be done carefully and systematically. Most modern systems of work measurement in a service environment revolve around the concept of work units. A work unit is defined as a block of time required to perform some basic task. It is the building block of the work measurement system. Thus, for example, if it takes 20 minutes to repair a tire, then a seven-hour day is divided into 21 work units. Each more complex task is measured by the number of work units which corresponds to the amount of time necessary to do this more complex task. Thus, an engine tuneup might be worth three units. A worker's output is measured in terms of the number of work units completed each day. The time standard needs to be based on some analysis of how long it takes to do a task well, so to some extent a qualitative judgment is built into the specification of the quantitative standard.

Third, qualitative standards also need to be established and checked via a process of quality control. There is no systematic way to verify whether welfare caseworkers really care about the people that they are supposed to be trying to help, or how good an understanding they really have of the problems of the client and, therefore, how good their advice or counsel really is. But if there is a form to fill out, it is possible, through pulling a sample of such forms, to find out whether caseworkers are at least asking the right questions.

Another way to get at the qualitative issue is through "profiles" or "protocols." For example, a department of investigations was concerned that it did not seem to have a way to evaluate the work of its individual investigators. There was an intuitive feeling that some people did a good job while others did a poor job, but there did not seem to be any way to quantify or measure. It was suggested that they get their best investigators to write down the process that they went through in carrying out an investigation and to prepare a model brief. Using this model, it was possible to evaluate the work of each investigator. In addition to measuring how many cases an investigator completed during a month, it became possible to assign a qualitative score based on the level of deficiency compared with the model. Thus, investigator A might have completed eight cases of which two were rated excellent, three acceptable, and three poor. Investigator B might have completed only four cases, each of which was excellent.

Another problem in work measurement has to do with the heterogeneous nature of the work of professionals, such as engineers, who are reviewing plans. To say that engineer A reviewed only three plans while engineer B reviewed six plans is not to tell you very much unless you know something about the complexity of the operation being reviewed. Here, too, crude solutions are possible. If a supervisor classifies each building plan to be reviewed on the basis of the size and complexity of the project into complex, moderate, and simple, and assigns to each an average time value which is translated into work units, then it is easy to see that engineer A, who reviewed three simple projects, in fact did do quite a bit less work than engineer B, who reviewed six moderately complex projects during the same time period. Or in work unit language, engineer A completed only six work units, while engineer B completed eighteen. Here, too, some form of quality control is necessary to ensure that in fact engineer B did an acceptable job of review.

Work Standards

Closely related to the question of work measurement is the specification of work standards. The issue of work standards has been the subject of collective bargaining in the United States and abroad. Workers fear speedups because of what they perceive as the bottomless appetite of management for more and more output and profits, and they firmly resist the imposition of work standards wherever possible. Stories are legion of a new worker coming on a job and being told by the seasoned hands to slow down, lest the newcomer's zeal end up in imposed higher standards of work. A crucial problem for management is not only to convince workers to accept work standards but, what is even more basic, to find out what fair and equitable standards are, since for all but the simplest tasks, the amount of time it takes to do something can differ widely, depending on the individual, the work environment, and even variations in the quality of apparently similar tools. Implicit here is the question of how hard it is reasonable to work. Most work management efforts built around the idea of "forcing people to work harder" are doomed to failure. Motivation, morale, esprit de corps, and a sense of urgency are all extremely important intangibles—but they cannot be turned on and off like a spigot. Sometimes on-site measurements in the old-fashioned Taylor mode are feasible if they are done in an environment where negotiation is possible and there are not too many opportunities for either the worker or the observer to manipulate the experiment so as to bias the result.

The best approach for developing work standards is an incremental one, starting with data on the work actually being performed at the time the program begins. Except in the smallest governments, there is more than one group or individual performing the same function. There is likely to be significant variation in the amount of work performed by each of these groups. Thus, for example, if there are four paving crews, it is not surprising to find one crew putting down 100 tons, another crew putting down 200 tons, another crew putting down 300 tons, and a fourth putting down 180 tons for the same time period. The initial work standard in this environment can be established by the average output per crew, or 195 tons. The efforts to improve should focus initially on the crew putting down only 100 tons of asphalt and then on the crew putting down 180. If improvement efforts are successful with these crews, for example, if their production is brought up to the average of 195, then a new average of 225 tons would be the standard and the focus now becomes extended to the second crew, which is performing only 200. At some point the situation will stabilize. Even if the three crews manage to maintain their 225 standards and the third crew declines slightly, to say 275 tons, the total tonnage of 950 represents better than a 20 percent improvement over the initial 780. Such an exercise is far superior to bringing in an industrial engineer who through classic field measurement techniques decides that 300 tons is the appropriate level, only to have the workers deny the validity of the effort and express their disapproval by dumping the asphalt into a vacant lot.

Rigorous work measurement and systematic use of work standards is still the exception rather than the rule. Phoenix, Arizona, with 40 percent of the city's positions monitored by engineered time standards, is considered to be an outstanding example of the use of this approach. In the attempt to move forward from this situation it is important to keep in mind the need to keep work measurement systems relatively simple and to allow the standards to evolve out of the current levels of work performed rather than out of an abstract ideal as set down in some engineering manual.

In summary, although there remain certain areas of government in which work measurement and work standards are neither feasible nor useful, the majority of government work *is* measureable as long as there is the willingness to develop the measures and to take the results with a grain of salt. It is also important to reiterate that work measurement or "productivity" is just one, and by no means the most important one, of a series of ways of evaluating the performance of government. This point will be elaborated in Chapter 11.

Work Incentives and Sanctions

Introducing work measurement and standards into a previously unmeasured environment is likely to produce increases in the quantity and quality of work by itself. But there is a limit to what measurement itself can do, and a logical follow-up to introducing a measurement and standards program is the question of incentives and sanctions.

The need for greater use of incentives and sanctions in the public sector is one of the themes of this book; it is introduced in Chapter 1 and is discussed in Chapter 2 in the personnel area and in Chapter 11 on management systems. The discussion here focuses on *work* incentives and sanctions, that is, the promise of reward or threat of punishment to people directly involved in the work process—workers and/or first-line supervisors—as a way to motivate them to improve their work. To apply work incentives and sanctions it is useful to divide the problem into two parts: the nature of the promised rewards, and the criteria used to decide that the reward has been earned.

Four types of rewards are used in incentives programs. The most popular, of course, are monetary rewards, either in the form of one-time bonuses or regular pay increments. The second is in the form of time, the opportunity either to leave early when the job is done or to take extra days off. The other two types of reward are more subtle: flexibility, such as the freedom to set one's own hours as long as a certain number of hours are worked, and recognition, involving modest sums of money or awards.[2]

There are four types of criteria for deciding rewards, the most popular of which is the production of more or better products or services, measured either competitively—the best of a series of teams gets the reward—or against some standard or previously agreed-upon level. The other three types of criteria involve some other benefit to the organization: improving work conditions— having fewer accidents or a better attendance record, producing at lower cost, or suggesting a better way or better procedure to do something.

In principle, sanctions are the inverse of rewards. Sanctions may be monetary, like the loss of pay, or may involve having to work extra hours, losing privileges or flexibilities (having to adhere to a more rigid schedule than other workers), or being singled out for blame in a way that other workers are aware of. Almost none of these sanctions are systematically used. The sales clerk whose register shows a shortage might have that amount deducted from his or her pay. The other categories are even less likely to be used in any formal sense. Of course, the work situation is replete with examples of supervisors and managers applying informal sanctions, such as publicly chewing out the worker whose performance is below par or inventing various restrictions on the flexibility of workers who are "not trusted."

The criteria for sanctions should be the inverse of criteria for reward, such as producing less service at lower quality. The worker who really fouls up, who costs the organization money, or who rarely comes to work is much more likely to be fired or otherwise sanctioned in private industry than in government. The worker whose shoddy work produces a badly filled pothole that results in injury to a citizen who sues the city for substantial sums of money should be sanctioned in some way, although examples of such sanctions are likely to be few and far between because of political constraints.

[2] As was pointed out in Chapter 2, the possibility of promotion may be the most powerful work incentive of all.

The most comprehensive survey of incentives and sanctions in state and local government was published by the National Commission on Productivity in 1975.[3] The results, based on 1973 data, are suggestive even if out of date. California led all other states in the number and variety of incentive-related actions with 32 localities reporting some efforts in this area. Sanctions (called negative incentives in the study) were virtually nonexistent among the 509 local jurisdictions and 41 state governments responding. The most popular state programs were suggestion awards, output-oriented merit increases, and variations in working hours. The most popular local programs were output-oriented merit increases, task systems, suggestion awards, attendance incentives, and variations in hours.

Any well-run organization will use incentives and sanctions, recognizing the importance of the motivation of individual workers in achieving better overall performance. Thus, it is easy to argue for greater use of work incentives in the public sector. Yet there is an ambivalence about the use of incentives and a skepticism about the conditions under which they are used. The reason for some skepticism is the tendency in the public sector to use incentives as a substitute for ordinary good management procedure. The introduction of output-oriented bonuses in an environment where most workers are not working up to a reasonable level or in an environment where output is not measured and no standards for reasonable attainment have been set is a costly way to reach mediocre performance levels. Incentives make sense in an environment where a control system is in place and where average levels are reasonable for the type of organization or department. In such an environment incentives can legitimately help people do better than the average. The same is true of sanctions.

The issue of workplace safety illustrates this point. In an environment where safety standards have not been set, where regular safety inspections are not made, and where there is no effort to monitor and modify work conditions to make work safer, it is premature either to offer safety incentives or to punish workers who follow unsafe practices. The first job is to get a working safety program in place. Then it is reasonable to think about incentives for even better

[3]*Employee Incentives to Improve State and Local Government Productivity* (Washington, D.C.: National Commission on Productivity and Work Quality, 1975).

safety and sanctions for workers not meeting safety standards. In other words, where management systems and procedures are clearly established to manage the work process and where *ordinary* levels of work are regularly attained, the introduction of incentives and/or sanctions is a highly intelligent management strategy to get *extraordinary* levels of attainment.

Using New Technology to Improve Public Services

In some circles there is a great deal of fascination with the idea of using advanced technology to "solve urban problems."[4] The space program, in particular, excited the imagination of many and the question "If we can get a man to the moon, why can't we . . . ?" became part of the conventional wisdom of American urban thinking in the sixties. Given the American faith in gadgetry and the relative success of the space program, it is remarkable that even more attention has not gone into the attempt to solve local and state management problems with new technology.

The source for a good deal of the writing and thinking about public sector technology does come from the aerospace program. In a classic attempt to apply some of this thinking to the public sector, the state of California invested a tremendous amount of energy in the late 1960s in the effort to involve the aerospace industry of that state in solving public sector problems. A better course would be for government to look to service industries to see how they have used technology to help them manage more effectively. The typical service company—a bank, utility, or insurance company—like government, is people-oriented, process-oriented, and service-oriented. Typical aerospace ventures, on the other hand, are oriented to production, projects, and objects.

As much as possible, computerized information in service industries is being used to make the individual worker more effective in direct contact with a client. The customer service representative of the gas or electric company who can call up a customer's file in a

---

[4]For an analysis of experiences with and potential for technology application to public management, see James L. Merce and Ronald J. Philips, eds., *Public Technology: Key to Improved Government Productivity* (New York: AMACOM, 1981).

matter of seconds is clearly in a good deal better position to deal with that person's problems than the typical public servant confronted by an irate client.

There are three major ways in which technology can be used to improve government services and/or reduce costs: (1) computer-assisted service delivery, (2) automation of office functions, and (3) the development and use of new materials and equipment.

Computer-Assisted Service Delivery

In most technological innovations today a computer lies at the heart of the effort. This is true of all three of these categories of technology application. In the first area, however, computer-assisted service delivery, the computer itself is integrated into the field application. Computerized traffic controls in major cities have made a substantial difference in improving the flow of traffic on congested arteries. Computerization of Medicaid files in large metropolitan cities has begun to make it possible to get a handle on substantial problems of eligibility, fraud, reimbursement, and disallowance. Computers are being used in dispatch operations in police and fire service to match a responding unit with a call for service.

Computerization of assessment files and inspection violation files speeds access to data and eases problems of updating often mammoth files. Optical scanning devices offer substantial promise for such government functions as building inspections and water and sewer meter readings. The inspector or field worker marks a sense card which can be used to trigger both the billing system and the timing of future inspections or readings.

Office Mechanization

The second major area of technical application is in the area of office mechanization. An enormous amount of what goes on in any government happens in offices which are unlikely to have any major direct contact with citizens or users of city services. Budget, personnel, purchasing, timekeeping, billing, audits, and accounting—these are typical back-room office operations. Almost every function— police, housing, finance, environmental protection, consumer affairs, parks, buildings, health, human resources, and transportation—has substantial office (white collar) operations. The talk of a wholly automated office in the near future is probably just that, talk. While tremendous advances have been made in automating specific repetitive office functions, a good deal of what goes on in an office is highly judgmental and difficult to automate.

Developments in word processing, data system communication, information processing, and automated file and retrieval systems have begun to revolutionize office operations in private industry and are beginning to have some serious impact on advanced governments as well. There is no question that new and improved products are constantly being developed in the area of office automation. These products should have a major impact on improving accuracy and reducing errors ("they lost my health record again?") and should improve speed of government operations and allow for reductions in workforce.

At present word processing is the most promising of the new office technologies for government applications.[5] A word-processing machine is simply an automated typewriter that allows the typist to enter typed copy. Thereafter, the machine aligns the margins, a viewing screen allows editing, and virtually any number of copies can be produced, each with a slight variation (such as a different name and address). The applications in government are legion. At one extreme, the production of large, complex government reports typically involves a great many rounds of successive redrafting in response to different interests and concerns that must be reconciled in the final product of the report. Word-processing machinery makes it possible to make many changes incrementally without retyping the whole draft. In another area, "boiler plate" contracts and purchase orders can be loaded into the memory of the machine and produced with extremely low probability of errors which could be very costly, and with enormous savings in the time and energy of both clerical and supervisory personnel in the rigorous review, editing, and proofreading required when legally binding instruments are prepared. Introduction of word processing should reduce the need for typists and clerical personnel.

---

[5]For a discussion of the application of word processing in government, see James L. Mercer and Edwin H. Koester, *Public Management Systems* (New York: AMACOM, 1978), Chapter 12.

New Materials and Equipment

The third area of technology application in the public sector, the development and use of new materials and equipment, has received a good deal of attention, particularly in engineering-based departments. The development of slippery water in New York made it possible to deliver far greater volumes of water to a fire within a given time span. New road-patching materials can be put down in any weather and are supposed to last longer (although at substantially higher initial cost) than traditional materials such as asphalt. New forms of sanitation trucks make it possible for one- or two-man crews to collect more garbage than was formerly collected by a three-person crew and to work less hard at the same time. In Denver, Colorado, smaller crews collect greater tonnage through the use of a sanitation truck which automatically lifts and dumps a small container into the truck. High- and low-density sodium vapor lighting has been credited with enormous reductions in the cost of street-lighting programs in localities where these lights have been installed. In one particularly intelligent application of technology in fire service delivery, the Syracuse Fire Department uses Opticom (Optical Communication), an electronic device which, when activated from a moving fire truck, changes traffic signals to green. Smoke detectors in homes, stores, and factories provide a whole new decentralized fire-fighting strategy.

In a number of crucial areas the new technology has not yet been very effective, although the needs are tremendous. The most important of all is probably in the area of waste disposal. It is no secret that many American urban localities are running out of landfill sites. Resource recovery, energy recovery, and pollution-free waste disposal are all in their infancy. In other areas, too, new technology could be important. The street-cleaning and park litter problems could benefit from the introduction of some new and more effective equipment.

Developing a Customer Service Orientation

The third area for improving service and/or reducing costs in state and local public services has generally been overlooked in the productivity literature. In the private sector a great deal of effort has recently been invested in the effort to improve customer relations. The essential step is the development of a customer service orientation, that is, viewing services from the perspective of the consumer of the service rather than from the point of view of the provider. Developing such an orientation in service industries has not been easy. The airlines, banks, insurance companies, and utilities have invested a great deal of effort in this area. The rise and fall of large department stores is often a function of their ability to handle customer relations with rising labor costs and declining sales forces.

The problem in the public sector was identified many years ago by Herbert Gans, who pointed out that the standards and values used in such public service systems as parks and recreation typically reflected the values of the providers rather than of users.[6] This crucial insight has not really been understood or applied in a good deal of public service activity and has become lost in the larger issue of citizen involvement.

Community boards, citizen advisory committees, and federally mandated citizen participation processes have all focused on involving the citizen per se in the decision-making processes affecting government. This is not at all the same as developing systems and procedures to move the provider of the service to view it from the customer's or user's perspective. All citizens or residents of an area are not necessarily users of a particular service. Much citizen involvement takes place in a vacuum—unrelated to resources, responsibility, or firsthand experience as a user. Citizens are not necessarily good decision makers about operations any more than the stockholders of a typical company. Low rates of participation in community board meetings and elections provide evidence for the view that most people would prefer to delegate decisions about operations to professional managers and elected officials, holding them accountable for the results.

Basically, building a customer service orientation into government requires the providers of public city services to view the users of service not as *clients,* implying a kind of dependence, but rather as *customers* who determine the economic success of the enterprise and, ultimately, the well-being of the individual workers. Obviously,

[6] Herbert J. Gans, "Recreation Planning for Leisure Behavior: A Goal-Oriented Approach," unpublished Ph.D. dissertation, University of Pennsylvania, 1956.

in the case of government, this is a "pretend" exercise; nevertheless, it's useful.

Customer service orientation can take a variety of forms, but two major expressions of it are complaint response systems, and service delivery procedures to respond to the user.

Complaint Response Systems

The average citizen often reflects general confusion about who does what to whom in government. "How do we get information about buying and fixing up an abandoned house?" "I had to call five different offices before I could find out why I got two separate water bills for the same property." "After 20 rings, I finally gave up on trying to get some information about my bus schedule." This sense of either no response, a lackadaisical or uninterested response, wrong information, or a runaround is a widely shared perception of government.

The solution to this problem is the design and operation of an effective system for tracking and responding to complaints, inquiries, and calls for service. The purpose of such a system is threefold: (1) the improvement of service delivery through enhanced ability to respond with an emphasis on equity, speed, and quality; (2) the fine-tuning of service standards in response to priority of concern as reflected in citizens complaints; and (3) the use of complaint information by management as a proxy measure for evaluating service quality.

Why are complaints so rarely well handled in government? In part, it is because the problem has rarely been given systematic attention, but in part it is because the problem is rather a tricky one in communications. Many citizen complaints do not fit neatly into an obvious category. For example, a person whose basement is flooding may not know whether to call the highway people (who may have just repaved the street), the sewer people (is it a backed-up main?), the water supply people (perhaps a main is broken), or the building department (which may have approved the plan for a recently completed renovation next door). Or should one call the mayor's office, one's congressman, or the councilman? If one finally determines to call the highway department, does one call the borough superintendent or the commissioner? Most citizens may not even know that there is a borough superintendent. Is there a district superintendent? The issue may even involve different governments. Water and sewer responsibility might be regional. The county might operate the highways, and the city the buildings department. Here is an example of the complexity of government missions at work. People are not usually confused about whether to call the gas company or the telephone company when they are having problems with their telephones. But a government typically performs more different functions than a private company.

Some people have approached this problem by calling for the establishment of a single telephone number for complaints. In fact, newspapers sometimes set up a highly publicized action-line to deal with this problem. Those who have argued for an office of ombudsman have in mind identifying one person or office in the system whose job it is to be sympathetic to the individual and knowledgeable about responsibilities in the system. The dilemma inherent in the design of an effective complaint-handling system is whether to build it around the complaints or to build it around the capacity to respond. The closer the system is to the citizen (for example, a citywide ombudsman with a single telephone number), the more likely the citizen is to get a sympathetic hearing; but the closer the system is linked to line service delivery, the greater the chance of getting results and having the complaint resolved.

The key to resolving this dilemma is the recognition that a specific system needs to be designed around both the complaints and the capacity to respond. Specifically, a network with four linked elements is envisioned: a set of contact persons (linked to each other and also to a set of action persons), a switching system, a tracking system, and a reporting system. This concept is diagrammed in Figure 6.

The first element is a group of highly publicized contact people who have consistent and accurate information about who handles what type of problem, cross-indexed by department and / or bureau. Contact persons should be distributed in a number of different locations: some in departments, some centralized (as in a mayor's office), and some decentralized (as at community advisory boards). A program of training is needed for the contact persons who are in effect the customer service agents or representatives. Quick and efficient processing of complaints does not preclude handling calls with courtesy. Yet public callers can be extremely demanding, and without a reasonably high level of training, most people will have difficulty maintaining their calm in the face of abuse and frustration.

The second element in the system is a switching component, whose function is to put the complainant directly in contact with the actor, that is, whoever has the capacity to either resolve the complaint or determine that a resolution is not possible. This is a rather different concept from referral, which implies that the client does the chasing around. The referral process is dependent upon highly precise information which rapidly becomes outdated. The switching concept implies that various contacts and actors in the network talk to each other on a regular basis. Ideally, the citizen is connected to a potential actor within the same phone call or shortly thereafter.

A third element, a tracking or monitoring mechanism, is also needed to ensure that a complaint or inquiry is followed up, that is, that something really happens. The switching mechanism merely makes sure that the person with the problem is connected to the right source for getting it solved. The tracking or monitoring mechanism tries to find out whether or not the problem was solved. The

Figure 6. Concept for complaint response network.

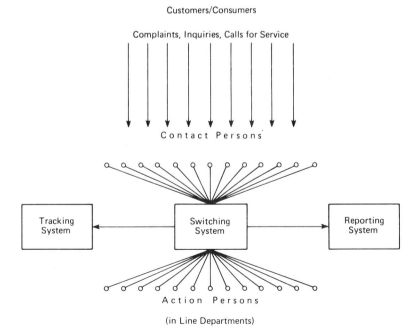

Customers/Consumers

Complaints, Inquiries, Calls for Service

Contact Persons

| Tracking System | | Switching System | | Reporting System |

Action Persons

(in Line Departments)

system should also have a provision for citizen callback. Both contacts and actors should be able to effectively communicate to individuals information on the status of their specific requests or complaints.

The final element is a reporting system which permits management to analyze the volume of complaints and inquiries to get a better handle on where operational problems exist and to help evaluate the quality of what service is being delivered.

One interesting issue in the design of a reporting system is the definition of a complaint. Some systems don't distinguish between complaints, inquiries, and calls for service. The distinction is often difficult in practice. "Who is responsible for flooded basements? My basement is flooding and I need help. I was told it would be taken care of two years ago." Is that an inquiry, service call, or complaint? For obvious reasons it would be simpler not to try to make the distinction. Yet these three types of calls—complaints, inquiries, calls for service—each have very different consequences for management reporting.

A *complaint* usually means that something is not working. Complaints should be counted, last year's should be compared to this year's, and similar divisions operating the same function should be compared. This provides a crude measure of the quality of service being performed. An *inquiry* is merely a question of fact. More inquiries do not necessarily mean a growing problem. If the number of inquiries measures anything, it measures the general level of public interest in a program. It obviously is not a criticism of that program. A *call for service* is a direct reflection of the need or demand for service. It is one measure of workload—a department may do both complaint-based work and cyclical work.

From a reporting point of view it is worth trying to separate these three. For the workers filling out a form who find it hard to make these distinctions, it is useful investing in some simple guidelines based on a definition of precedence. For example, if the call sounds like both a complaint and a call for service or inquiry, treat it as a complaint.

Installing a complaint tracking and response system by itself is no insurance that everything will improve. In a typical government management environment, many functions need to be redesigned from the point of view of the customer.

Improving the Capacity to Respond

Government relates to the individual citizen through four means of communication: direct contact (a policeman making an arrest); walk-in, that is, the citizen physically comes into a government department or office; telephone; or mail. In a few, increasingly rare situations the service comes to the citizen (as in postal delivery or home care). Each of these modes of communication offers some unique opportunities for improvement.

The establishment of a 911 emergency telephone system was based on the perception that in a crisis or emergency a person needs a relatively simple, easily remembered, universal way to make contact and that increasingly the telephone is the device. The development of dial-tone-first pay phones where one can dial 911 without a coin is a further extension of the recognition of emergency needs. Of course, police departments complain that the system gets cluttered with a great number of "junk calls," and fire departments complain that since they have relatively fewer calls within the total system, they tend to play second fiddle to police calls that cost valuable response time. The average citizen probably views the installation of 911 as a tremendous increase in government's ability to respond.

Walk-in systems in general offer the opportunity for extensive improvement or change. In response to complaints about the long waits and low level of courtesy associated with some services, a number of jurisdictions have switched to mail systems. Thus, in many states it is now possible to get a driver's license renewal by mail without ever having to go to the local motor vehicles bureau.

A major change in walk-in service is the establishment of one-stop service for permits and licenses. Citizens are often forced to travel to different locations, sometimes inconveniently situated, in order to receive the different licenses and permits needed for one project. Developers and residents require an understandable, predictable, and manageable system to obtain the necessary approvals, permits, and licenses from various agencies. A well-designed walk-in facility is responsive to such client needs. It is not hard to tell whether the consumer or the provider is dominating the conception. For example, in one government, window A indicates permits needed for rehabilitiation, and window B indicates permits needed for new construction. In another government, window A says "land permit," window B says "utility permit," and windows C, D, and E each reflect a different type of regulation or permit. The latter is clearly provider-oriented; the former is consumer-oriented.

Sometimes the emergence of a situation involving new government responsibility requires the development of a system which incorporates complaints, calls for service, and inquiries in a system requiring both walk-in and phone-in contact. Such a system was designed in the winter of 1980 to respond to the anticipated home heating fuel crisis in the city of Hartford. The case is illustrative of some of the issues in this general area.

Case Study: Using a Customer Service Orientation in Designing an Emergency Energy Program, Hartford, 1979

In the fall of 1979 concern grew in both business and government circles that the city of Hartford, with a substantial low-income population, faced a potential fuel oil crisis of staggering dimensions. The problem was twofold: Would supplies be adequate? And would people be able to pay the inflated prices? Because rental stock accounts for over 80 percent of the housing units in Hartford, there was substantial concern that increasing demands for fuel associated with a cold winter and high prices would cause increasing numbers of landlords to walk away from their buildings. In response to this concern, the city manager in Hartford appointed an energy coordinator with a reputation as a doer; and the state and federal governments together developed a funding program which was to be funneled through the local antipoverty agency, Community Renewal Team (CRT). The Hartford management study staff was asked to help CRT and the city "get their management act together," as there was some concern that the program might collapse at the level of operations.

Three problems surfaced very quickly: First, the city and CRT were going their separate ways. Second, confusion and uncertainty with regard to the level and type of state and federal funding were having a paralyzing affect on CRT's ability to organize itself. Third, months of policy research had been so advocacy-oriented to generate support and the sense of urgency that virtually no usable operational information had been collected with regard to the number of potential consumers, the level of their needs, and the like. A process was begun to try to understand and close the gap between the operations of the city and CRT. A set of questions were put before CRT to begin to focus attention on those details of operational planning that needed to be put in place regardless of the ultimate level of fundings and specific guidelines with regard to their use.

The initial impression of the CRT-city conflict was that it was based on mutual suspicion, which in turn was based on some unfortunate history in previous relationships. More detailed probing soon revealed that there was also an important programmatic difference relating directly to the unstated question: Who were the consumers of the service and how would they be expected to communicate with the provider? The city system was implicitly based on a cry for help: "Help, I'm cold"—a no-heat complaint. The CRT system was also based on a cry for help: "I'm poor, I can no longer pay for my heat." CRT, with its network of local centers, was concerned with how to get money to poor clients and with protecting itself from disallowances by the federal government. The city quite understandably was concerned with getting heat to the clients.

The Hartford management study team was able to show both sides that the "I'm cold" call was, in fact, closely related to the "I'm poor" call. The tenant who paid for heat in his or her own apartment might be calling because he or she was running out of money, or the landlord had disappeared, or the boiler had broken down—the call for help might include any one or all of those components. The solution was to combine the emergency-oriented, 24-hours-a-day, seven-days-a-week thinking of the city with the walk-in, weekdays-only concept of CRT—and to design the system from the point of view of the consumer.

A single phone number was established for all heat-related problems and complaints in the city of Hartford, and the number was widely publicized. Crude estimates were developed of the probable number of calls, standards of calls for operators, and the number of operators needed. The call-in function was linked to a "war room" established at CRT, but staffed by city as well as by CRT personnel. In addition, CRT staffed walk-in centers. People who called the number were referred to the center near them if they appeared to be eligible for financial assistance on the basis of poverty, but at least they came to the center knowing what information to bring.

Despite a late start and a host of difficult and complex operational problems, but helped substantially by a mild winter, the program worked relatively smoothly. The point of this illustration is that a set of responses to a public problem had initially been organized around the institutional structure for service delivery. The introduction of the consumer perspective radically changed the whole approach. Starting with the user brings the service out in another and hopefully better place.

9

Improving Basic Services and Development Programs

The direct service programs of government deal with public education, safety, and health and welfare. They also attempt to cope with major social and economic problems through development programs. Each basic service has its own traditions and characteristics, which may lend themselves to certain kinds of performance improvements. Some are particularly susceptible to technological improvement; others, for example, the public safety area, are constrained by extremely powerful and vocal labor unions. Moreover, each program area is dominated by a special mix of professional groups with their own interests, values, and styles of management. For example, the human services area is dominated by medical and social work professionals, with very strong biases with regard to not only the content but the style and method of service delivery. In addition, basic service is characterized by a specific constellation of constituency or interest groups. Parent groups, for example, play an integral part in the delivery of educational services in many communities.

The complex interplay of these various forces shapes a pattern of management improvement opportunities and constraints which is unique to each service system. Three of the most important service areas of state and local governments—education, human services (health and welfare), and public safety (police and fire)—are discussed in this chapter, with special references to their unique management improvement opportunities and constraints. The final section of the chapter is a discussion of managing development programs to improve the social, economic, and physical conditions in the jurisdiction. Each is a subject in and of itself, and a detailed examination of management systems of any of these major programs deserves its own volume. In this discussion it is only possible to skim the surface.

Schools Management

Elementary and secondary education in the United States is usually under the direction of independent or quasi-independent boards of education, typically elected, sometimes appointed. In most places teachers are strongly organized, and where there are elected boards, it is not unusual for the teachers' union to dominate the electoral process even more strongly than municipal unions dominate municipal elections. Boards of education tend to be local, with the state overseeing the setting of standards and providing funding.

Public program education is dominated in public discussion by strong emotional issues of policy and program: desegregation and busing, and community control are classic emotional issues dominating much discussion of education. Other fundamental issues have a significant emotional tinge: Should the schools be teaching basic skills only (reading, writing, and arithmetic), or should they be educating the whole person (after Dewey)? Should classrooms and schools be highly disciplined in structure, or should they be open and free flowing?

There is little agreement about what affects the quality and results of education. Some literature seems to indicate that the family may be more important than the schools in how well a child gets educated. Even more specifically, others have argued that the socio-economic class of the family is the key determinant. The teaching/learning process is not really clearly understood, and it is not unreasonable to talk about "the mystery" of teaching and learning. To what extent should schools view themselves as systems for preparing children for the world of work and to what extent should schools view themselves as the basic system for transmitting the values and knowledge of the culture?

Much argument revolves around the importance of classroom size and school size. A small classroom in a small school seems more manageable and is clearly valued by teachers, but there does not appear to be any definitive evidence that classroom size is closely related to the level of learning. Similarly, in urban school systems a great deal of investment has gone into new school buildings to replace the old plant. At capital budget hearings the groups pressing for a new school building usually are at the forefront. There is certainly no evidence, however, that a new school building encourages more learning than an old one.

Some have argued that the public school system itself, as historically structured, is obsolete and have urged movement toward a voucher system, where parents choose which school to send their children to and pay with a government voucher. There has also been substantial controversy over the use of teaching machines and programmed education—is it an appropriate use of new technology to help learning, or does it depersonalize the system, cutting down the contact with a human teacher that lies at the heart of the educational process? There have even been a few experiments in which public schools were turned over to a private firm to operate under a performance contracting agreement.

With so many controversies, it is not surprising that mundane operational management issues in the education business have received relatively little public attention. It *is* important to keep the management questions in perspective: the values and resources of the family and the quality and commitment of individual principals and teachers all have a greater impact on the quantity and quality of learning that takes place than the way a school system is managed. However, school systems are under as much pressure as any other unit of local government to do more with less. Federal mandates without corresponding federal resources have exacerbated a very tight cost-revenue squeeze for most school systems. Managing more effectively is virtually the only way that school boards can cope with this squeeze without doing irreparable damage to the educational process itself.

The overall goal in management improvement in the educational system is to remove the impediments to learning so that learning and teaching can take place. A popular image of the typical urban school system is that it is so burdened by administrative regulations (red tape) that very little learning actually takes place. Many employers and parents, particularly in older urban areas, believe the public schools are unable to produce a "product" that can read, write, and hold a job. The facts are hard to come by, but the impression is strong that the nation faces a decline in the quality of education, with potentially serious consequences. While management improvement may contribute only a small portion to the capacity to improve educational quality, even this small contribution could be very important.

There are several specific management areas where improvement opportunities occur frequently in education: the reduced need for space, the use of paraprofessionals, the role of the principal, performance measurement, and administrative and headquarters staff. In addition, school systems face a larger and more complex management issue; the need to create a manageable organization structure. These areas are discussed below.

The Reduced Need for Space

Many schools in the United States in the early 1980s face declining enrollments resulting from the generally declining birthrates. In some areas, the loss of students has been so great that there are large numbers of empty seats, a situation that generates support for school closings. In many areas, however, the declines are relatively gradual, and thus a struggle begins between those who wish to consolidate and close some schools to save money and those who wish to maintain the neighborhood school. In such an environment of gradually rather than dramatically decreasing enrollment, it is urgent that schools develop and use an ongoing space management function. This concept is discussed in detail in Chapter 10; here it is merely useful to point out that most large companies with complex space requirements have an ongoing process for planning, allocating, and monitoring the use of space. Most governments do not have such functions, and in fact, in relatively stable environments, without substantial changes in staffing patterns, very often the informal systems work fairly well (see Chapter 10).

The Use of Paraprofessionals

The schools were one of the first systems in the public arena to use paraprofessionals. The theory was threefold: to give jobs to low-skilled, unemployed people; to involve parents (often of troubled children) in the schools; and to free teachers for their primary responsibility, that is, promoting learning. Teachers' aides were supposed to reduce the burden of paperwork and disciplinary activities for the teachers, leaving them free for teaching responsibilities. In many systems, however, teachers' aides work alongside teachers and do not have any specific responsibility. The result is simply more teaching personnel at higher costs with no increase in professional teaching time or net reduction in the cost of the whole operation.

It seems that most school systems have not thought through clearly the role and use of paraprofessionals, having reached the first objective of giving jobs to unemployed people. From the point of view of the quality and cost of service, this appears to be counterproductive. School systems need a clear strategy for the use of their paraprofessionals, who should have specific jobs and responsibilities based on those specific tasks that are removed from a teacher's job description.

The Role of the Principal

One of the crucial dilemmas of the management of school systems is the role of the principal. In most reasonably large school systems, the school principal is caught in the middle between the perceived needs of the teachers and students of his or her school and the dictates of a sometimes remote headquarters operation. It is often unclear what exactly the role of the principal is. This is particularly ironic because there is some evidence that the quality of the principal's leadership is the single most important determinant affecting the overall quality of the school. On issues such as budget accountability, teacher assignment, responsibility for absence control, and the like there is substantial lack of clarity as to whether the principal or headquarters is responsible. Can a principal who feels that he or she needs another science teacher more than an art teacher trade the art position for a science position? In many systems this is not possible, because that judgment is made at headquarters.

The principal is the logical person in the school system to become a responsibility center manager. The principal should have greater control over recruitment and assignment of personnel and over budget planning and implementation, as well as greater performance accountability. The concept of the principal as the key responsible manager is difficult to implement in part because some principals prefer to be seen as educators, and they deprecate the role of administrator or manager.

Another point of pressure is more practical. Principals in many jurisdictions have formed associations or unions that bargain collectively. There is some fear on their part that the more they function as managers, the poorer their case will be for maintaining their collective bargaining status, which they believe is the only thing that assures them reasonable treatment in terms of salary and working conditions.

Performance Measurement

A major management issue that has received a good deal of public attention is the question of performance measurement,[1] involving the evaluation not only of students but of teachers and principals as well. These are highly controversial areas, and teachers' unions have resisted performance evaluation on the grounds that the qualities of a good teacher are too subtle to be measured. Similarly, with regard to students, many have argued that objective tests reduce the learning process to mechanical and rote test preparation. While there is merit to both of these points, it is difficult to conceive of seriously improving the school system or any other organization without at least some rudimentary notion of how to measure performance. How can a student, a teacher, or a system improve without a way to assess progress? A sense of perspective about the *use* of performance data is needed. As a rigid substitute for human judgment, it is bound to be useless. If one is reasonably alert to the deficiencies of the measurement system, then it can be tremendously useful.

The two forms of measurement are connected. The best way to evaluate a teacher is on the average performance of the students in his or her class. The best way to evaluate a principal is on the average performance of the school. The whole thing does rest on some capacity to evaluate, no matter how primitively, how well students are doing. The rank order of an individual, a class, or a

[1] Public performance measurement is the subject of Chapter 11. The discussion here is restricted to some specific schools measurement questions.

school based on the relative score on standardized reading and arithmetic tests has got to provide at least a rough clue about performance. The schools at the very bottom of the list and the schools at the very top certainly are deserving of some special scrutiny. The scrutiny may reveal that from a qualitative point of view, a school with high scores is doing a terrible job, and a school with low scores is doing an excellent job. The objective data provide a framework for asking sharp rather than vague questions.

The best way to use performance measurement is in conjunction with performance incentives. Such a system has been used in the Houston Independent School District. The incentives program, called the Second Mile Plan, awards a bonus stipend to teachers, using a point system where each point is worth $100. The first of the seven categories that qualify eligible teachers for incentive pay is contributing to outstanding educational progress by students. This is worth 8 points ($800) and is awarded when the school average for students' rate of academic improvement as measured by standardized tests is greater than the median for similar schools in Houston measured by socioeconomic variables. The other six categories are: extended educational service (extra hours), outstanding attendance, teaching in areas of critical staff shortages, teaching in a high-priority location, participating in professional growth activities, and recruiting other teachers.

Administrative and Headquarters Staff

The popular perception of the crucial management problem in school systems is the growth of headquarters bureaucracies. Partly in response to federal programs and mandates, partly in response to the need to control local decentralized school districts, and partly out of inertia, school headquarters have surged in growth, particularly in the large school systems. In some systems, the administrative and support staff (including both field and headquarters) is larger than the teaching staff.

It is difficult to disentangle the fact from the myth. In recent years, under the pressure of fiscal constraint, school systems do seem to be reducing some of their relatively exotic headquarters operations. One of the problems is that like all staff operations, it is extremely difficult to evaluate. For example, do curriculum development specialists contribute enough to the improvement of curriculum to justify their salaries? This is particularly difficult to answer when there is no general agreement as to the importance of the curriculum itself. The only way to separate fact and myth is for each element of the operation to be justified on the basis of an explicit contribution to the organization. When in doubt, the function should be eliminated and the results carefully monitored. This may reveal that a terrible error has been made, but it is much more likely to indicate that probably the position was not crucial in the first place. The advocates of decentralization have argued that the simplest thing to do with large headquarters staffs is to decentralize and spread them around the system. This can be a very costly trap. For example, if headquarters has an art coordinator for the entire system, decentralizing this function might very well mean appointing an art coordinator for each school or at least each group of schools. So one art coordinator might be replaced by six or seven.

A Manageable Organization Structure

The last important issue pervasive in school systems is perhaps the most basic of all. It is usually not difficult to find a management structure in a typical city or state government. That is, there is usually an executive at the head of the organization, division or department heads with specific functional responsibilities, and middle managers and supervisors who are responsible for specific task areas. There is a comfortable similarity to the typical business organization. When one attempts to use this model to analyze the typical school system, however, one is at a loss to find some of these classical managerial roles. For example, who is the first-line supervisor in a typical elementary school? There is a series of teachers, perhaps 30 or 40, all of whom "report" to a principal. Looking for the next level in the classic hierarchy one searches in vain for positions parallel to that of department or division head. An assistant superintendent responsible for elementary schools might have 20 or 30 schools "reporting" to that individual. With this weak a line structure, perhaps it is no surprise that enormous staff organizations have grown up to try to help the hapless superintendent or chancellor get control.

The absence of a first-line supervisor or a department head is not a semantic problem; it makes it difficult to devise solutions to specific management problems. For example, all of the assembled wisdom on the subject of lost-time control indicates that the first-line supervisor is the crucial individual because of his or her close contact with the working personnel on a day-to-day basis. The department head is the individual accountable for the overall management of lost time. For the school board, however, the lost-time problem is difficult to solve because there usually is neither a first-level manager who has reasonably frequent contact with the teachers nor a department head who is in a position to evaluate, monitor, and hopefully improve the overall lost-time situation. Some school systems do have a supervising teacher who combines a light teaching load with some accountability for the work of the teachers in his or her "group." Similarly, some school boards have experimented with a district concept in which there is a director or local superintendent in charge of a manageable number of schools.

Human Services (Health and Welfare)

A second large area of state and local expenditure is for human services (health and welfare). Two large programs in this area are income maintenance and medical assistance. These programs tend to be open-ended, that is, any eligible client is served, and the greater the demand, the greater the expenditure. Local government, in particular, caught in a mass of federal regulation and with rising demand, has felt trapped. These programs are administered differently all over the country. Some are state funded and run, some are state funded and county administered, others are state and locally funded and administered by cities.

Income maintenance is a highly paper-oriented operation, very similar to typical insurance company operations. There are essentially three processes. A process of eligibility determination and review (in the case of medical payments including both clients and providers); a claims review and verification process; and a payments process. The system is characterized by large intergovernmental flows of funds with substantial implications for cash management, a process of federal audit and review resulting in fairly frequent disallowances, and an extremely complex structure of guidelines susceptible to court challenges of all kinds. The opportunities for fraud are numerous, and the levels of audit are as numerous as agencies involved in these systems.

Traditionally, the social welfare issue has given rise to two warring camps: the advocates of the poor, who have focused on lobbying to increase payment levels and liberalize eligibility standards on the one hand, and, on the other, those who insist on making sure that ineligibles are off the rolls and that there is some form of fraud control in the system. The former are often social workers, the latter typically fiscal or business managers brought in to try to get aspects of the system under control. This is a silly argument. There is an obvious operational philosophy that should guide the operation of human services programs. Those who are not eligible should not be in a program. Those who are eligible and are capable of work should be helped to get off the welfare rolls into gainful employment. And those who are eligible and cannot work should be treated with dignity and respect and subjected to a minimum of hassle.

Given the volume of transactions characteristic of even medium-size governments, and the enormous flow of paper, the area is exceptionally ripe for the kinds of automation characteristic of modern insurance or banking companies. Hospitals are beginning to computerize claims and payments; welfare departments in some states (such as California and New York) have made significant investments in automation of aspects of eligibility review.

An important characteristic of the clients of human services programs in the United States is that a relatively small number of people need many different kinds of service. The users of health services are likely to be the users of homemaker services, to be on welfare, to need psychiatric help, and so on. Given the fragmentation of services in this area despite years of effort to promote human service integration, the typical user bounces around from desk to desk, from office to office, in an attempt to deal with what are often interrelated problems.

Improvement Opportunities in Income Maintenance

There are two groups of management improvement opportunities in the delivery of human services. The first involves methods of working: reducing error rates, particularly ineligibility rates; speeding up processes, especially verification processes; and automating the paperflow to speed payment processes and reduce error and loss. These call for computer matches, forms redesign, workload simplification and reduction, and accounting and auditing standards.

A second group of opportunities for management improvement arises from the needs of clients: speeding up referrals; installing a case management approach; balancing intake and service locations to minimize travel time; and reeducating social service workers to minimize the mismatch between their expectation of helping people and the reality of substantial paper-pushing.

The Hartford Management Study review of the social services operations found this typical pattern of management improvement opportunity. The study focused on the General Assistance Program in the city of Hartford, which had been plagued by staff shortages and very high and increasing welfare caseloads. Hartford had three times as many welfare recipients on general assistance as Bridgeport and two and a half times as many as New Haven with roughly the same population. The pattern dated from the 1940s, when Hartford already had substantially more welfare recipients than the comparable cities of Bridgeport and New Haven. The relatively poorer population and the relatively higher skill requirements of the mostly white collar jobs available partly explained why Hartford's General Assistance caseload was so high. The other explanation was that Hartford had not had a formal program of quality control. In this context five major improvement programs were recommended: quality control, automated paperflow, case management, service delivery areas, and a customer service program.

The first recommendation, which was implemented by the city, was the establishment of a quality control program. It was estimated that an initial sampling of case files could show a 20 to 25 percent error rate. Since many of these errors lead to inflated costs, it was estimated that an effective quality control program could reduce caseload costs by as much as 15 to 20 percent. An important element in quality control was the issuing of a photo ID card to each welfare recipient, in order to reduce requests for duplicate checks and to make it easier for eligible recipients to cash checks. To implement such a system, it is helpful to overcome client resistance by having each member of the department also receive photo ID.

The second major recommendation was to automate the

paperflow in the department, creating a master case file that includes both welfare and health payments, and setting up an automated billing system.

The third major recommendation was to install a case management approach. Hartford's typical caseworker is responsible for 130 to 140 cases, which means that he or she has less than 20 minutes a week for each client—hardly sufficient time to provide adequate social service. The case management approach would emphasize referral to appropriate existing social service and employment-related agencies, with a follow-up program to monitor progress. The first step was to group clients with similar needs and to train a group of caseworkers to specialize in each of these areas. For example, newcomers to Hartford may require special services to become self-sufficient more quickly. Those people on general assistance with the greatest potential for employment should work with counselors specifically prepared to help them. Despite the rhetoric of getting welfare clients to work, it was found that only 2.1 percent of the general assistance clients were actually enrolled in an employment training program.

The fourth recommendation was to establish a rationalized set of service areas. The department of social services in Hartford, following a national trend, had established centralized intake for the entire city in order to control the consistency of eligibility standards. But the department had decentralized service delivery, as opposed to intake, to seven field-office sites in order to promote neighborhood programs and to coordinate the department with other service providers. Although this approach seemed logical, it actually required the prospective client to visit an office (sometimes several times) that might be quite far from home before preliminary paperwork was completed, and then he or she was required to repeat the process once the caseworker was assigned in a field office. Operating in multiple locations in a city of 140,000 means that services and staff are often spread too thinly to provide adequately for clients. It was recommended that, to provide both intake and services in one location, the department operate from four field offices, each of which would include a basic service unit of one supervisor, seven to nine caseworkers, clerical support staff, and an intake manager.

The last recommendation was in the area of customer service. The department of social services did not have a formal process for collecting and following up on complaints, and such a program was recommended. Government agencies in general need to be more alert to the opportunity to treat people who use their services more like customers than petitioners. This is as true in social services, with a difficult and troubled clientele, as it is in any other part of government.

The implementation of these five improvement programs in Hartford was expected to cost about $350,000 over three years in increased staff and training time, but was expected to yield $1.3 million in savings to the city alone. Considering that the state pays 90 percent of the costs of general assistance grants, the savings to the state are likely to be many times as high as the estimated city savings. At the end of three years this program should yield a 25 percent reduction in caseload costs, improved client access to jobs and services, improved staff morale and reduced staff turnover, reduced travel and waiting time for clients, better supervision, and overall better client service.

While the whole package sounds slightly utopian and while it is difficult to point to any one jurisdiction that has implemented a total program of this kind and realized these benefits, various jurisdictions have implemented bits and pieces of this kind of program and have realized substantial improvements. New York City did substantially reduce its ineligibility rate, from 17.5 percent to under 10 percent in four years. Photo ID in Bridgeport and New York City was very successful both from the client's perspective and in achieving savings. Case management is increasingly the approach being utilized in the social service world. Computerization is proceeding, particularly in large, complex systems.

Public Safety (Police and Fire Service)

Fire and police service are *the* classic local functions, at least since New York City and New York State police forces fought a pitched battle in the streets of the city in the 1870s. Fire and police unions are among the most powerful on the municipal scene. Because they are uniformed paramilitary organizations, the classical management style has been authoritarian. Pride and esprit de corps have gone along with the uniform in most departments. These are among the best-paid municipal workers. While the two services have these commonalities, their basic work is very different. Fire fighting is the classic emergency service. They literally sit and wait for something to go wrong. On the other hand, at least in theory, more police work is oriented toward prevention. The police are active, on patrol constantly. Both of these services have been rather resistant to innovation and change. They are each very costly to operate: high salaries and high pensions, relatively high levels of disability with attendant higher costs. In most municipalities the fire and police departments are among the largest, if not the largest, in the city.

Like education, police work is slightly mysterious. To the extent that the function of police is to reduce or contain crime, surprisingly little is known about what effect police actually can have on crime. For example, there is very little evidence that adding policemen per se has any major impact on crime level. Citizens seem to prefer visible foot patrol, but there is some evidence that it is the undercover and anticrime decoy squads that have real impact in terms of arrest rates. It is extremely difficult to tell when a policeman is "doing a good job." When the number of crimes go up there is virtually no way to tell whether this is because of some lack in what the police did or because of other conditions.

Probably because of this confusion about role and impact, the field itself is characterized by important cleavages in philosophy and approach—the "old-time cop" versus the "new-time cop." The "old-time cop" has little higher education, is oriented to traditional police methods, and is partial to visible police presence, in the form of more police on the beat and more patrol cars. Those who favor this concept think that suspected offenders should be treated firmly, and that the policeman on the beat should know his particular turf. The "new-time" cop is probably college-educated, is oriented to working closely with the community, uses computers and analysis of data to develop flexible response and deployment, and prefers specialized anticrime and decoy squads to traditional patrol. Police are deployed in response to closely monitored crime information by time of day and location.

Because of the high expenditure levels, great citizen concern, and general importance to the quality of urban life, police and fire services lend themselves to management improvement, even though the deeply rooted traditions and the power of the unions are important constraints on the ability to implement change.

Management Improvement Opportunities in Police Service

Three areas of opportunity are described in relation to police service: civilianization, rank structure, and span of control.

Civilianization. In most police departments there are substantial opportunities to substitute civilians for uniformed personnel in clerical and support activity. In such functions as administrative and clerical operations, data processing, and dispatch, civilians with training can replace uniformed officers, freeing the uniformed officers for professional work and performing the clerical or administrative functions at lower costs. Clerical personnel do not usually earn the same salaries as policemen and certainly do not have the same level of pensions.

Rank structure. Police rank structure is firmly embedded in tradition: officer, detective, sergeant, lieutenant, and captain. Higher ranks such as inspector are also often official civil service ranks. Leading departments around the country are questioning the relevance of this traditional rank structure to modern management of police work. First, the duties and responsibilities of sergeant and lieutenant need to be more clearly differentiated, or the two ranks should be consolidated.

Second, there is significant question about the relevance of the rank of detective. Police officers are often very effective in investigatory work, particularly in following up on a case that they themselves initiated. Promotion to the rank of detective has often served as a reward for good performance. To the extent that detectives are people who have performed well, it is not obvious that they should focus explicitly and completely on investigatory work. There is some advantage to having seasoned and expert officers available for a variety of difficult and sensitive assignments.

Third, many departments have been plagued by a civil service system which is so rigid that all appointments up to the top are based on the ability to pass tests. In the New York City police department the highest civil service rank is captain. All positions above that rank are filled by appointment. This gives the police director or commissioner substantial flexibility in assigning personnel for specific positions but does not violate the traditional rank structure (where lieutenants command captains). Salary and responsibilities are then a function of the job in the organization and not of the civil service title per se.

Fourth, most police departments do not have an entry-level position. A police officer in a typical department costs the taxpayer $25,000 to $35,000 a year (including pension costs and other fringe benefits). In most organizations that is a middle-level job. Yet there is a great deal of police work that is relatively routine but that cannot be safely performed by a civilian. The solution is to establish the position of assistant police officer to take over such functions as traffic control, crowd control, and parking enforcement. Such a program could provide recruitment, training, and career development for minority applicants. Activities such as parking enforcement raise revenue, and this new rank could be at least partially self-supporting.

Span of control. Closely related to the question of rank structure is that of span of control. In many departments, faced with attrition in the ranks, the ratio of superior officers to police officers and detectives has declined. The pressure for promotion as a legitimate reward for good work is often hard to resist. Superior officers are reluctant to retire early or to move to other jobs because of their substantial stakes in the pension system and the opportunity to retire at a relatively young age. The police department, more than any other, needs to maintain and establish average ratios based on reasonable span of control standards. For example, if a reasonable span of control is one captain to three to five lieutenants, one lieutenant to four to six sergeants, and one sergeant to seven to ten police officers, then in a city with one to four, one to two, and one to seven, respectively, there is probably a reasonable number of sergeants and captains but too many lieutenants. Once standards are established and surpluses if any identified, then departments need to use classic management responses, all of which take a relatively long time: retirement incentives, loan of experienced police managers to other departments with important vacancies, and the creation of special task forces which otherwise would be difficult to staff, such as arson control.

Management Improvement Opportunities in Fire Service

In this discussion, five examples of management improvement opportunities are described: the location of fire stations and manning levels, reduction of false alarms, arson control, use of smoke detectors, and deployment.

Location of fire stations and manning levels
In the northeast, in particular, fire stations are located roughly the way they were when originally built. One hundred years ago, stations had to be more numerous than today, because horse-drawn apparatus was slower and thus had to be closer to the sources of potential fire. Under the impact of fiscal pressure, cities sometimes get in a bind: there is not sufficient personnel to man their engine and truck companies without overtime, yet there is at least a political commitment to cover all stations for all shifts. For example, by early 1979, the city of Hartford had accrued almost $600,000 in unscheduled overtime costs. This is the least cost-effective solution: maintaining a given manning level using overtime at roughly one and a half times the cost of filling regular positions.

The cost-effective approach is to take a fresh look at the number of companies the city needs to deliver effective fire service and to maintain those companies at full strength. Of course, the number of companies a city really needs involves managerial, psychological, and social judgments. In Hartford, for example, with 20 companies and 13 stations there is one station per 1.4 square miles. In the oldest parts of the city, where fire stations were established years ago, they are even closer together. Careful analysis indicated that Hartford could effectively protect residents with three or four fewer companies. Through the use of a computer model developed by the Rand Corporation, it was calculated that the probable increase in the average time that it would take an engine to get to a fire is less than ten seconds. Of course, people are comfortable if they have a fire station nearby, even if that fire company is not the one that responds to an alarm from their house. The removal of a fire station is as difficult an action as government can take, because it involves people's basic sense of security for themselves and their families. Local governments willing to bite the bullet and make the difficult choices involved in closing unneeded existing fire stations can generate tremendous resources to improve fire service in ways more consistent with today's technology and needs: newer and better equipment, a comprehensive false alarm control program, comprehensive arson control, and publicly subsidized smoke detectors.

Reduction in the number of false alarms

Many areas face a serious and growing false alarm problem. In Hartford, for example, between fiscal year 1971 and fiscal year 1979, false alarms went up 251 percent from about 2,300 in 1971 to about 8,000 in 1979. In fiscal year 1971, one-third of all alarms were false alarms. By 1979, 55 percent of all the alarms were false alarms.

Reducing false alarms is not easy. Fire departments all over the country have tried a variety of educational programs aimed at reaching young people, who are responsible for most of the false alarms. Cities need to experiment with two basic approaches: (1) to test voice-response technology, and (2) to develop working partnerships with their neighborhoods.

The old-fashioned pull alarm box on every street corner belongs to another era. Today more real calls come in by telephone. Some cities have completely removed the street boxes, relying on telephones. This program was implemented in Dayton, Ohio, with substantial reduction in false alarms and relatively little impact in delaying fire responses. Other areas are experimenting with new types of street alarm boxes. The voice response box has proved very effective in places such as New Haven and Bridgeport; it has been less successful in New York City.

The second approach to reducing false alarms involves a step-by-step neighborhood strategy. First, the local government identifies high-incident areas. Some boxes, sometimes adjacent to schools, have hundreds of false alarms while others have very few. Second, neighborhoods with high false-alarm rates need to be made aware of the cost to the neighborhood when real fires could be in progress. Third, neighborhood groups should be asked to make suggestions and volunteer to help in neighborhood-based education. Fourth, if neighborhood-based education does not work, a variable response should be instituted. During the time of day when there are the most false alarms (typically 3:00 to 4:00 P.M.), the department would send only a car instead of a fire truck to high-incident boxes. Fifth, and only as a last resort, alarm boxes could be removed. Even the reaction to the removal of a box can be softened if a public telephone with no-coin emergency capacity replaces the alarm box which is removed. In working with neighborhood groups it is important that they be asked to make suggestions and volunteer to help with the understanding that if their suggestions do not work within a specified number of months the government will have to move forward on its own.

Arson control
Many cities and areas have experienced substantial increases in arson, including arson for profit as well as for mischief. In Hartford, for example, while building fires went up 24 percent between 1971 and 1979, incendiary-type fires (where there is reason to suspect that the fire was deliberately set) went up 232 percent during this period. Insured losses in fires in Hartford went up three times as fast between 1971 and 1979 as the number of building fires. Many jurisdictions are experimenting with data-processing improvements, an early warning system, training, laboratory facilities, and the early involvement of the state's attorney. The key to successful arson control is the development of coordinated police, fire, and prosecution task forces. Seattle and New Haven have developed models based on this approach with reasonably good results.

New prevention strategies: smoke detectors
Traditionally, 80–90 percent of a fire department's resources have been devoted to fire fighting and suppression, and only 10 to 15 percent to prevention. The rhetoric of prevention is easy; yet there is no substantial evidence that traditional fire inspections have much impact on preventing fires. On the other hand, effective prevention activity could substantially reduce the cost of a fire-fighting operation as well as dramatically reduce the probability of injury and property loss. The key to a successful prevention program appears to be the wider use of smoke detectors. A study of the use of smoke detectors sponsored by the National Fire Academy shows significant reductions in the chance of injury or loss of property with the use of detectors. Governments have three options in helping to encourage the use of smoke detectors. Allentown, Pennsylvania, for example, used community development resources to actually purchase smoke detectors, and West Hartford, Connecticut, passed an

ordinance requiring home owners to have smoke detectors. The third option would use property-tax incentives to encourage the use of smoke detectors.

Deployment and dispatch
Other significant management improvements are being made in advanced fire departments in the areas of deployment and dispatch. The concept of variable response, depending on the area and time of day, rather than the standardized full complement of equipment to every call, is being used in progressive departments. Scottsdale, Arizona, has become justly famous for its advanced approach to fire fighting. For example, a complete information base on a property can be filed with the department. When a call comes in, the apparatus on the way to the fire receives a full report (printout) on the nature of the structure, occupancy, and hazards. Firemen will know, before they reach the fire, that there is a two-year-old sleeping in the northwest upstairs bedroom and there is a back staircase with direct access to that bedroom.

These relatively brief comments on three of the most important program areas—police and fire, human services, and education—illustrate the kinds of management improvement opportunities and constraints that are typical of large-scale state and local service systems. These programs are rich in management improvement opportunities; of course, the constraints are real, too.

Managing the Development Programs

Aside from delivering basic services, state and local governments are deeply involved in a wide variety of development programs to improve the social, economic, and physical conditions of their areas. In the context of the effort to change social and economic conditions, the essential management concern—better services at lower cost—is radically different from the relatively straightfoward job of delivering a service.

If little is known about how government can achieve effective education or police service, even less is known about how government can improve the economy, maintain housing and neighborhoods, or develop human resources (manpower and poverty programs). Assessing the performance of basic services is difficult; assessing the performance of development programs is *extremely* difficult. There is often no agreement about the role of government in relation to development, or indeed, whether government should be involved at all; there is little agreement as to what constitutes improvement; there is very little understanding of cause and effect; and resources are rarely adequate for the task. These four points are worth some elaboration.

There are those who still argue that such matters as neighborhoods, the economy, and the environment are not appropriate areas for government, but should remain in the province of private industry. And even those who agree government should be involved do not necessarily agree as to when success is achieved or what constitutes effectiveness.

Whereas most people would agree that cleaner streets and operational playground equipment are better than dirty streets and broken swings, not everyone is in agreement on defining better neighborhoods or better economic development. For example, urban renewal was a successful program in that it replaced substandard units; it was a failure in that it brought about an increase in rents and displacement of former residents. Those who favor environmental improvement clash with those who favor less regulation. Those who favor use of government incentives to upgrade industry clash with those who point to a public giveaway and the erosion of the tax base.

It is difficult to evaluate and improve programs when there is a lack of understanding of what works. For example, we really do not know how to reduce juvenile delinquency. As a consequence, there is often very little relationship between even substantial effort and results.

There is often a significant gap between the goals and expectations of developmental efforts and the ability to deliver with the resources, program tools, and knowledge available. The classic example of this mismatch between expectation and capacity was the national effort in the early 1960s to eliminate poverty: "Promise a lot; deliver a little. Lead people to believe they will be much better off, but let there be no dramatic improvement. Try a variety of small programs, each interesting but marginal in impact and severely underfinanced. Avoid any solution remotely comparable in size to the problem you are trying to solve."[2] These programs are also characterized by political confrontations that make them difficult to operate: between neighborhood groups and city hall, between conflicting ethnic groups in the same or adjoining neighborhoods, and between citizen groups and business interests.

In short, in service delivery there is a reasonable amount of evidence in the public and private sector that better management does lead to better services at lower costs. In the development arena, on the other hand, there is much less reason to be confident that better management will mean more effective programs. Perhaps we can borrow from the philosophers to say that in the case of development programs, better management is *necessary but not sufficient* to ensure success. Adequate funding, methods for involving citizens in decision making without causing the process to take forever, policies which encourage private investment while at the same time protecting the public interests, and competent and strong political and professional leadership—each is probably more important than effective management in good development programs.

Nevertheless, better management in the development area can make a difference. Some CETA programs were better run than others. Cities such as Baltimore have made significant progress in their housing programs not only because of good programs and an appropriate housing stock and adequate resources, but also because a sensible organization and effective management system made a tightly run program possible. If developers or neighborhood group sponsors become frustrated because of delays they do not understand, or are confused as to which department is responsible for which aspect of a proposed project, or are getting contradictory information from two or more departments, then proposals will bog down or even close down altogether.

In other words, the overall management opportunity in government's development function is to improve the quality of coordination. Increasingly, the best development projects have a number of highly interdependent components. A typical project might include a mixture of public and private financing, involve the rehabilitation of

[2] Aaron Wildavsky, "The Empty-Head Blues: Black Rebellion and White Reaction," *The Public Interest,* Spring 1968, p. 3.

housing for moderate-income families, and call for a program of job training to train people in the skills needed in housing rehabilitation. The traditional divisions between economic development and housing, between job development and job training, and between residential and industrial or commercial land development are no longer meaningful.

Various cities and states have tried to meet this coordination need in different ways: creating a single superagency (putting all development activity in one large department); keeping departments separate but appointing one person with centralized decision-making powers; or creating a neighborhood and development task force that includes all key departments heads and has a strong chairman. To illustrate the management opportunities typical of government development programs at a more specific level, it is useful to look at two sets of programs that have been among the most important in this area: economic development, and housing and neighborhoods.

Economic Development

As a relatively new function of state and local government, active involvement in economic development has been an incremental and piecemeal activity. Typically, there is no clear division of responsibility between the state and its constituent cities and counties. Much public economic development activity has been competitive, with different jurisdictions attempting to lure industry with high taxpaying potential. States in the South have been highly successful in encouraging industry to move from the Northeast to their states through a combination of tax incentives, land writedown, and just plain hustling. Cities and states have two kinds of economic development tools: the manipulation of existing programs to better support economic development objectives, for example, by offering tax incentives; and specific economic tools and programs such as land writedown and land assembly, which tend to be new, somewhat controversial, and difficult to get started. Against this background of incremental growth and multiple programs often with competing objectives, it is not surprising that two themes dominate the attempt to improve the management of economic development programs: eliminating or reducing red tape, and reorganization.

Dealing with red tape

The typical businessman who needs to expand or begin a new economic enterprise views government with trepidation and alarm. The image is one of a mass of regulations, often contradictory, administered by people whose sole job in life is to make things difficult for the businessman. This perception of endless red tape strangling individual initiative is firmly part of the conventional wisdom. The facts are that most business expansion does require a series of permits and licenses. Even a relatively simple project requires approval of the plans and designs, a building permit, a certificate of occupancy, an environmental impact statement, and approval from the parking regulation authorities. It might also require a zoning change involving several departments and a street closing. In addition to the multiplicity of permits to get and regulations to conform with, the businessman is often troubled by a genuinely negative attitude on the part of those administering regulations and licensing activities. The reasons for this perception are not complicated but the solution is. To the governor or county administrator faced with an eroding job base and threatened tax resources, it is extremely frustrating to find that one's own people are not helping.

Government's historical role has been as a watchdog in this area: to ensure that economic activity does not threaten public health and safety. The notion that economic activity is good for the public welfare—the key supposition of economic development public programs—is the newer thrust and is often in real conflict with the older responsibility to protect health and safety. Eliminating red tape may mean eliminating the regulations and permits which *do* protect public health and safety. It makes good rhetoric but is not a feasible management strategy.

It *is* feasible, however, to attempt to get the process under control. To make the regulatory process accountable in the carrying out of economic development objectives, a number of jurisdictions have experimented with forms of one-stop service. This is a central permit application center where permits and licenses for various departments can be efficiently processed and where prospective developers can get information about all aspects of government's interest in their development proposals. In the state of Georgia all economic development proposals can use a one-stop service for information and permits related to the building and development process.

The apparent logic of such centers is defeated in many places by the traditional reluctance of departments to yield any of their responsibility for the issuance of their permits. Since the health department, for example, is charged with protecting the health of a city's residents, that department is likely to be reluctant to yield control over the issuance of health-related permits because in the end it is responsible for any damage to the public health that results from the inappropriate granting of such a license or permit. This legitimate concern is often closely intertwined with the more basic bureaucratic concern of losing turf.

With vigor and care this concern can be accommodated. For example, the one-stop service could be staffed by experts from each of a series of departments to ensure that no errors are made. In such a situation, representatives of a number of different departments would all sit together, dealing with inquiries and processing applications in the same place. Ideally, in such an environment conflicts between different departments can be ironed out face to face, obviating the need for the businessman to trek back and forth from health to transportation to consumer affairs to reconcile three different perspectives on the same proposal. Or the permit application center could be restricted just to getting the application and the relevant information. The contact involving approval or rejection would still be with the relevant department.

Reorganization

The Lindsay experiment with the creation of superagencies in New York City made it abundantly clear that simply making the organization chart neater by combining apparently related departments does not solve anything. Combining three smaller troubled units merely creates one big troubled organization. Yet the reorganization of economic development activities, usually by combining a series of small operations into one larger one with higher-level status, does have substantial appeal, because economic development projects, particularly if large-scale, place tremendous burdens on the need for coordination. In a political bureaucratic environment, at least as much as in industry, lateral coordination is extremely difficult to achieve. In other words, four department heads of equal status are not likely to want to spend great amounts of time dealing with each other's problems; quite naturally, they prefer to deal with their own problems. Let the other guy take care of himself. Effective coordination usually requires someone at the top pressuring, forcing, or cajoling peer managers to work together for some common objective. Since development projects tend to have many interdependent components, it is urgent that there be someone with sufficient authority to make the different elements work together.

Another reason for looking toward high-level consolidation as an appropriate management strategy in economic development is based on the nature of much of government's involvement. The bane of most economic development efforts is that, particularly in a large government, there are likely to be half a dozen different people all of whom either do, or think they do, speak in the name of the municipality or the state. It is perfectly feasible to find three people in the same organization each negotiating with a different developer for the same piece of land. It is equally likely that none of the three actually has the authority to shake hands and make a deal, an absolutely fatal flaw in the deal-making world of development. With consolidation, there is a single person in a government who is the negotiator: who can shake hands on a deal involving a series of different participants, some public, some private.

Housing and Neighborhoods

The depth and extent of government's involvement in economic development is exceeded by its efforts to improve housing in residential neighborhoods. Public housing, urban renewal, the model cities program, and most recently the Community Development Act were major national initiatives in this area going back to the days of the depression. The environment is one of great organizational complexity, with often cumbersome citizen participation, multiple competing constituencies, and needs greatly exceeding available resources. Housing programs, practices, and policies tend to be contradictory and implicit—clear and explicit policies would be construed as government favoring one constituency or interest group over another to the detriment of elected officials. One of the baffling and frustrating consequences of this situation is that even with resources substantially less than demonstrated need, many jurisdictions have tended to spend their community development money very slowly, and the ability to spend the money—regardless of purpose—has become a measure of the effectiveness of community development. Like economic development, housing and residential development programs are characterized by poor coordination and cumbersome organization. They need to speed up the development process, clarify who is in charge and can make decisions (organization), and provide devices to improve coordination.

At the peak of urban renewal in the late 1950s and early 1960s many cities established the position of development coordinator. These redevelopment czars—Robert Moses in New York, William Rafsky in Philadelphia, Edward Logue in New Haven and Boston—had wide-ranging powers to move development along and cut red tape. In their zeal to get renewal projects built and on the ground, they were often accused of careless or thoughtless relocation, disregarding the interests and wishes of local residents, and playing havoc with existing governmental processes. Because of these criticisms and the shift from large-scale redevelopment projects to more mixed housing rehabilitation, new construction, and maintenance programs, development czars have gone out of fashion, although in the main, they did get their job done. And yet the need for organizational mechanisms to achieve coordination is still real.

Sometimes an informal structure works better than a formal one. In New York City in the late Wagner administration, the housing policy committee was composed of the commissioners of half a dozen departments involved in housing and residential development. The committee was reasonably effective because of its close relationship to power in city hall, the availability of a systematic research and analytic base in the community renewal program, and the experience and strengths of the participants, who could protect their own turf without being involved in endless squabbles and who had a high level of mutual respect. The housing policy committee was probably a more effective coordinative mechanism than the highly publicized Lindsay reorganization in which many of the same departments became part of the Housing and Development Administration or superagency. The link to city hall was severed, the downgrading of departments to be part of an administration made it difficult to attract the same caliber of individuals, and the link to the community renewal program was not maintained. While the housing program looked more coordinated on paper, it was probably less so.

At a minimum, cities and states should have a development working group or committee involving the existing housing, planning, and development departments. This working group should have specific responsibility for preparing a formal two-year development program scheduling the projects which it is committed to complete within a two-year period. The schedule should be public, and delays which will certainly occur should be explainable. The emphasis in much of the formal public scheduling of expenditure in the development area has been on the planning end. Thus many jurisdictions have multi-year plans. These plans tend to stress the *start* of projects rather than attempt to anticipate their *completion*. This approach creates expectations which cannot be met. The public quite justifiably is more concerned with results and completions than with starts and plans.

Some governments use formal processes for keeping track of projects. In facing the problem of implementing complex multifunctional projects, private industry, especially in technology-based companies, has developed and refined a variety of techniques which can be loosely grouped under the general heading of project or program management. This approach is particularly useful where projects are relatively large, are composed of a large number of separate elements or steps, and require contributions from many different departments. The heart of project management is the appointment of a specific individual to be responsible for all aspects of a given project. A second major aspect involves the development of a specific schedule composed of all the separate actions needed to complete the project. Progress and costs against the planned schedule and budget are carefully recorded and monitored. If such an approach is followed faithfully, problems can be identified early. Where delays or cost overruns are unavoidable, participants are aware of the delay and the reason for it. The critical path method (CPM) and program evaluation and review technique (PERT) are two examples of specific scheduling techniques. The technique is not as important as the concept.

Specific opportunities to improve coordination in the development area vary in different areas. In some jurisdictions the consolidation and integration of separate inspectional forces (health, housing, fire, and buildings) into a single coordinated inspectional system provides a crucial assist to the development process. In older areas typical of the Northeast and Midwest, cities are often faced with a growing stockpile of city-owned buildings as a result of tax foreclosures and abandonment. Such cities often find themselves without any real-property management capacity. In Hartford, for example, it was found that there were 22 separate steps in the city's property management involving 12 different departments, and yet important functions were not being performed by anyone. For example, there was no systematic way for getting city-owned property back into private hands. There was no early warning system that would alert public agencies to potential abandonment. Many cities are working hard to increase the number of housing units through new construction and rehabilitation while at the same time they are losing more units through abandonment because of inadequate coordination of the available tools to encourage maintenance of the existing housing stock.

Conclusions

Whether as a stimulator of private enterprise or as an actor on its own, government at all levels is now deeply involved in social, economic, and physical development. As the approaches grow more sophisticated, and with more highly interdependent components involving private industry, government, and neighborhood and other nonprofit groups, the pressures and requirements for improved management similarly increase. I did not even go into the more obvious problems of auditing and fiscal controls; here the requirements are not essentially any different from the means and solutions discussed in Chapter 6. But it is true that many of the development programs under tremendous pressure to get going and solve major societal problems quickly have been less than careful in auditing and fiscal controls. Congressional discomfort with many of the programs created at the national level often has as much to do with the failure of local groups to maintain adequate books as it does with the supposed shift away from a philosophical commitment to using government to solve problems such as unemployment.

10

Managing Support Services

Support services, or overhead services, are those activities in government whose client or user is another government department or function rather than the public. The quality of public services often depends on the efficiency, quality, and effectiveness of invisible (to the public) support or overhead services. These services typically include vehicle maintenance, building operations and maintenance, purchasing, data processing, as well as telephones, energy, and legal, architectural, and engineering services. In any organization the contribution of overhead functions is difficult to evaluate, and in the public sector it is even more difficult.

This chapter considers the role of operations support in public management; reviews several of the largest and most important support systems; and suggests ways to adapt the best practice in the private sector to improve the management of these functions in the public sphere.

The Role of Support Services

It is early autumn. The days are still fine, but the leaves have begun to fall. The parks department is inundated with calls from irate golfers because the greens are so covered with leaves that they are in unplayable condition. At first glance, it appears that the solution lies with a management improvement in the parks department. But in fact, the solution lies elsewhere. Some years before, because of the large number and extent of golf courses, the city had purchased a special leaf-raking machine. It now turns out that this machine has been down for three months, because a crucial part was broken. The part was not replaced because of a problem in the purchase order for getting the part in. The purchase order was not correct because of some failure in the legal department to negotiate and approve the appropriate contract with the vendor. Whose fault is it? Difficult to tell, but three-quarters of the problem lies not in the department responsible for the delivery of the service—maintenance of golf courses as part of the parks program—but in one or more of the support services—vehicle maintenance, purchasing, and legal services.

Because of their public invisibility, support services are often allowed to deteriorate during periods of fiscal crisis. It is tempting to cut data-processing personnel and other "back-room" operations rather than the more visible policemen or teachers. But tempting as it is, this strategy is risky. Because of the difficulty of evaluating support or overhead functions in any organization, it is likely that closely mixed in with crucial support activity are some inefficient, overstaffed, and unnecessary activities. In New York City during its recent fiscal crisis, there was so much concern about the tendency to cut key support services that a major recommendation of the data-processing task force of the Mayor's Management Advisory Board was the protection of critical applications. "Continued staff reductions could ultimately result in nonperformance of functions vital to the city's continued operation. Late or incorrect payrolls or income maintenance disbursements could create havoc and delays, or errors in revenue applications could aggravate the already difficult cash flow program."[1]

A support activity in the public sector is very similar to the same activity in private industry. Data processing, vehicle maintenance, building facilities maintenance and operation are virtually identical in government and in industry. And it is in the support areas that the clear superiority of industry over government management appears most obvious. In principle, functions such as vehicle maintenance are identical in business and in government.

In practice, however, the differences between support services in the public and private sectors are striking to the managers who move between the two worlds. In the private sector, the purchasing man-

[1]*Data Processing* (New York: Mayor's Management Advisory Board, 1976), p. 18.

ager is supposed to understand that his or her business is helping the line manager. In the public sphere, the support functions are viewed as a series of checks and balances against the line manager, rather than as aids. To the city department head struggling in vain to get something accomplished in face of the heavy constraints as set down by the purchasing or legal department, the very term "support services" to describe those activities is likely to be met by a laugh of derision.

Support services are important for management improvement for these three reasons: improving support services is often the key to more effective service delivery; money saved from eliminating unnecessary or inefficient support activity can legitimately be used to pay for services which would otherwise be threatened by fiscal stress; and support services are foremost among those government activities that can benefit from the transfer of experience from the private sector.

Centralization versus Decentralization

The management issue which dominates thinking and discussion about support services in every organization is the question of decentralization versus centralization. The General Services Administration of the federal government is one model of an attempt to centralize support services. That little sign on the side of federal cars—"the interagency motor pool"—is the result of the federal government's strenuous effort to gain control over a serious problem—the proliferation of vehicles. The conventional wisdom has supported centralization.

Miles has pointed out that centralization of support services has a major hidden cost in the loss of flexibility. The issue is typified by everyone's war over photocopy machines. As these devices have become indispensable in the office of today, many organizations have opted for bigger and more powerful machines. Small ones seem to appear anyway all over the organization. Miles says that that proliferation may not be all bad. "*Dissatisfaction with services tends to rise rapidly when the provider of the services becomes bureaucratically bigger, more remote, and less flexible, even if costs are somewhat lower* [italics in original]. This maxim says to managers, especially to top executives: Don't accept, without extremely careful consideration, the recommendation of a feasibility study that tells you that you can save X dollars by centralizing any particular service."[2] In other words, there is likely to be a tradeoff between centralized control and somewhat lower costs on the one hand and increased flexibility and usefulness on the other.

The implication of this dichotomy is that there is no grand solution. To centralize or decentralize a support service is a judgment that must be made in terms of the specific situation. In this discussion, I have a slight bias toward centralization. I have a strong bias toward a common planning and reporting system, so that there is someone at a high level who has a picture of the total effort in the area of, for example, space management. The decision to decentralize as a deliberate strategic choice in order to maximize flexibility is very different from the pattern of gradual growth by accretion so common in the public sector. For example, the decision to give each department a minicomputer to deal with its own processing requirements is very different from the more common situation in government where there are several competing centralized computers of varying size, power, and modernity, each probably underutilized. Owning a larger powerful computer becomes such an important status symbol that all the important department heads have to have one.

One of the reasons that centralized support services tend not to be responsive to the users is that they have no incentive to be so. Where there is a chargeback system for centralized services, and the line department has a degree of choice between buying service centrally, going outside, or doing it itself, one is likely to see a substantial improvement in the quality and quantity of centralized service, particularly if the central service is held accountable for its own "billing" results. Most governments do not have a formalized chargeback system for most of their services, but the more advanced governments are beginning to.

By far the most important support area, and its importance is increasing all the time, is that of information processing. The second

---

[2]Rufus E. Miles, Jr., "Miles's Six Other Maxims of Management," *Organizational Dynamics*, Summer 1979, p. 38.

most important area, and in terms of dollar expenditure often the most important, is the maintenance and operation of public buildings. A third important area is vehicles management. These three examples of operations support are discussed in this chapter.

Information Services

The development and transmission of information is the most rapidly growing support area in both dollars and personnel, and the definition of the area is constantly expanding. According to one estimate, 50 percent of the workforce is now involved in gathering, processing, and distributing information.

Information-processing as a field is growing so rapidly that even the best-managed operations are hard-pressed to stay abreast of new technology and to devise intelligent managerial and organizational strategies. The hardware is expensive and becomes obsolete quickly. Government is not typically well situated or staffed to make these extremely sophisticated and difficult choices between alternative systems and approaches.

Clearly, the computer lies at the heart of the information explosion. For the nation as a whole, it has been estimated that computer-produced information is growing at a rate of 12 percent per year. The available total processing capacity that exists in the world has increased 20,000 times in 20 years.

For government, the crucial unifying principle of this activity covers all services designed to provide information useful for decision making and action. It is the rare government that has an organized information service. More typically, a number of units produce data largely to support a position, to impress public constituencies, or to overwhelm. Much information is produced for its own sake, sometimes as a government responsibility, as in the development of census-type information. Relatively little government activity is oriented to provide its own management with information needed to better provide services. In the typical government organization, for example, research capacity is diffuse, unfocused, and often undirected. Improving the quality of governmental management information depends on an adequate system for formal decision making.

Developing a management information system in the absence of a planning and control system is a good example of placing the cart before the horse.[3]

Managing Data Processing

Tales of the wasteful use of the data-processing resource, even in industry, are very common. When the first big increases in computing power came with the introduction of the IBM 360 and 370, the stories revolved around capacity: "Almost all of the machines in the country are underutilized." By the 1970s excess capacity tended to get soaked up by increasing demands for information, and it is now obvious that inelegant programming and improper operating procedures can rapidly fill a computer to capacity. Today's tales relate to unneeded reports: "A management audit of Division X in Company Y shows that a major monthly report had been generated for three years for someone who had left the company one year after ordering the report and it was never used again." Beyond the question of meaningful reports is the relationship between the size and nature of the job to be done and the power of the system designed or purchased to do the job. You don't use a jet plane to get across the street. "Company Z bought a $12 million system and all it gets used for is purchase orders."

Despite these stories and the general belief among professionals in the field that industry wastes a tremendous amount of its computing resource, overall, industry is still ahead of government in both level of investment in and sophistication in the use of computers. It is only the most advanced governments that are making effective use of the computer resource. Private industry appears to be spending two to three times as much as the average government on computers. Two recent surveys showed that cities typically spent only about 1 percent of their resources on data processing. It is fair to say that the computer has become a central tool of private sector management whereas it is still somewhat on the periphery in most aspects of governments. The search for new and better computer applications is the driving force in the explosion in the use of computers.

---

[3] A performance-oriented planning and control system for government is the subject of Part IV (Chapters 11, 12, and 13).

The major innovations of the 1970s were remote/on-line systems to supplement and sometimes supplant the large batch processing operations characteristic of the 1960s and the introduction of minicomputers and microcomputers. Both of these forces made possible the decentralization of computing power and increasingly available interactive programming systems, from war games to consumer banking. Today, computer people speak of integrated networks of computing machines: central batch processing, minicomputers, and remote terminals all hooked together and all capable of "talking to each other." This decentralization and the increase in interactive capacity offer the average line managers the challenge of using the computer to improve their own operations; in industry the computer is no longer "over there belonging to those computer people."

Most cities and states, however, are still at the stage of development of private industry in the sixties and early seventies. If government can benefit from the lessons learned by industry in the seventies, it will save a great deal of time, energy, and grief.

Improvement Opportunities in Data Processing

Studies of the management of data processing in New York City, Hartford, Connecticut, and Allegheny County, Pennsylvania, all find a common core of issues and improvement opportunities:[4] (1) Government is characterized by "unplanned decentralization" in dealing with the proliferation and fragmentation of responsibility for computers, software, and personnel. (2) As in other areas discussed so far, data processing in government is characterized by the virtual absence of formal systems for planning and control. (3) There is need for clear leadership in developing and improving applications and in a rapid transition to the users rather than the providers as the leaders in application development. (4) Government struggles with substantial problems in recruiting and holding on to skilled data-processing personnel.

The findings and conclusions of the computer services task force of ComPAC (Allegheny County) are typical:

[4]*Data Processing* (New York: Mayor's Management Advisory Board [MMAB], 1976); *Report of the Computer Services Task Force* (Pittsburgh: Committee on Progress for Allegheny County [ComPAC], 1977); *Data Processing* (Hartford: Citizens' Committee for Effective Government, Hartford Management Study, 1980).

The task force found the computer services function in Allegheny County to be operating in an unstructured and informal manner, a natural response to the decentralized management environment in county government. As a consequence, the data processing capability is fragmented into pockets of activity. . . . For the county as a whole, . . . the task force found that the function received little direction and oversight from higher management. It found few management planning and control tools for establishing priorities, measuring progress, and determining what things cost. It found no formal process for requesting, evaluating and approving the need for additional computer services. Data processing people appear to promise all things to all users, in spite of an inability to deliver on the promise. They appeared more anxious to start new projects than to maintain good support on the old ones. Employee turnover, particularly in the critical skills, is excessive.[5]

These four issues are discussed below.

From Unplanned Decentralization to Coordinated System

In a typical government one finds computers in many different places with no apparent relationship to each other, incompatible software in different installations, lack of standards for purchasing computers, and many different people involved in ordering and/or operating systems. Size, complexity, computing capacity, and costs can become important status symbols in any organization. Independently elected officials and the three branches of government almost always want their own computers because of some mixture of legitimate confidentiality concerns and generalized pride and turf considerations. An independently elected board of education, for example, usually does not want to share computing facilities with the municipal government that operates in the same community.

It is easy to respond to this issue by saying that everything should be centralized. However, massive consolidation of all data-processing facilities and personnel into a single installation is not necessarily the best or most feasible approach for most reasonably large governments. For example, systems that are tightly linked to delivery such as traffic control or dispatching emergency service should not be centralized, but should be integrated with the service system that they support. On the other hand, citywide, countywide,

[5]*Report of the Computer Services Task Force,* p. 8.

or statewide systems such as personnel, financial management, and management planning and reporting should be under central control and integrated with each other. The availability of distributed networks of terminals, microcomputers, minicomputers, and large central batch-processing machines all linked together makes a new alternative possible: planned decentralization. There is no doubt that planned decentralization is a better computer strategy than unplanned decentralization (the current situation), and in most states, counties, and medium-size or large cities, it is also a better strategy than maximum consolidation. In the planned decentralization system, some departments have their own installation, others do not; smaller departments use a "service bureau" that provides not only machine time but programming and systems support as well. This approach increases the probability of innovation and responsiveness to diverse needs. The new technology also minimizes the dependence on layers of technical staff; the user and the machine can be in direct communication.

Even in a decentralized environment, there is a great deal that needs to be coordinated. For example, there should be regular meetings at the technical and professional level, through, for example, an intergovernmental data-processing committee. To the maximum extent possible, software and operating systems should be compatible. This facilitates the development of a shared or pooled reserve capacity and some ability to handle the largest processing jobs on a cooperative basis. Even more important, it provides a fail-safe backup arrangement so that one system or center can cover for another in case of system failure.

Planning and Control for Data Processing

The second major opportunity to improve public data processing, the development of systematic planning and control, flows from the first—eliminating unplanned decentralization. If many people may order computers and there is little compatibility between the hardware and software of different installations, then there can rarely be a formal or even an informal basis for setting priorities among competing development or utilization needs. There are few formal controls or even measures of how the available data-processing time and personnel are being allocated. New systems are developed by the initiative of some individual. There are few if any controls on running time and how it is distributed. Utilization may be high in one installation and low in another; one may run on two shifts, another on three, a third may have barely enough work to keep one shift busy. The criteria for adding hardware or developing new software tend to be informal or out of date. Ask the typical government manager to see his or her data-processing plan and one gets a blank stare.

As in industry, governments need to recognize that their data-processing people and machines need to be carefully and intelligently allocated and the use of those resources carefully monitored. A formal data-processing plan for at least one year and ideally two or three should be part of every jurisdiction.

> The lack of a long-range planning program or for that matter, a viable short-range (operating) plan process has placed the Bureau of Systems and Computer Services (BS/CS) in an environment where it is constantly being surprised by new project requests, and is unable to accurately project its resource requirements, both people and machine with any degree of accuracy. This constant fire-fighting and direction changing will continue to plague the county until such time as a formal planning program can be initiated and appropriate procedures, schedules and methods can be put into action.[6]

A number of jurisdictions have made a significant start in developing systematic and logical computer planning processes. Significant progress in this area has been made in Fairfax County, Virginia, and Alameda County and Santa Clara County, California. Over the past decade, private industry has come to recognize that productive utilization of computer capability requires: planning and control based on a three-to-five year period; a process for setting priorities among competing potential applications, systems, and hardware; and explicit criteria for setting priorities on a cost/benefit basis.

As difficult as it is to establish plans in government, it is important to make the effort in the data-processing area. Computerization mistakes are very expensive, especially mistakes in overall direction;

---

[6]*Report of the Computer Services Task Force*, recommendation 2, p. 3.

undoing is always more expensive than doing. Large-scale system development projects take more than one year, thus a multiyear perspective is very helpful. But most jurisdictions do not even have a one-year operational plan, and this is a useful place to start.

Increasingly, it is important to have a clear handle on the "make vs. buy" decision: when an installation should do its own programming (make) and when it should adapt an existing package (buy). It is often difficult to get the funds allocated to buy existing software, and so data-processing and systems staffs in government often tend to get involved in reinventing the wheel.

A useful way to start a planning process is to estimate the probable costs in staff time and consultant resources for each proposed new application. This relatively modest first step gives data-processing leadership the capacity to project for the decision makers what might be the applications of data processing at any proposed budget level; and it begins to put the lid on the endless expectations for information of competing interests. But the next step is crucial: developing some capacity to project probable benefits.

Cities and states need to resist the temptation to use the computer to generate information for its own sake. Priorities must be set to ensure that the computer is used in the way most likely to improve service and/or reduce costs and/or increase revenues. The computer *is* an intriguing toy and there are many "interesting" potential types of information that it could generate. It requires strong will and good analysis to focus attention on the potential benefit of each proposed data-processing application. Even without the relatively rigorous return-on-investment criterion typical of advanced business computer decision making, cities and states can make reasonable judgments about the relative potential benefits of proposed uses of computers.

A simple planning and control system starts with a year-round process in which systems and applications people work with departments in identifying potentially high-priority applications of data processing to improve their operations. At some point each department submits its proposals for the following year with some estimate of potential costs and benefits. These are collected and analyzed by some central person, and recommendations are prepared for a central decision maker. In advanced environments there is an opportunity for major department heads to express their perspective in a data-processing advisory committee. Explicit criteria are developed to help rank order potential applications, future resources are projected, and a cutoff point is established. The decision maker starts with the project ranked highest, deducting its costs from the available resources, and keeps going until resources are used up. This set of priority projects is the basis for the annual data-processing plan. Since each proposed project includes by definition an estimate of needed resources (people as well as software and hardware), adding up the requirements of priority projects in effect generates an estimate of total resource needs. The plan is then used to track progress of all priority projects through the year and to measure the actual benefits as compared to those projected or expected. Of course, plans have to be negotiated, and they can be amended. Neither the process nor the product is cast in stone in this planning and control process.

Toward User Leadership in Developing and Improving Applications

Even though computer technology and the range of potential applications is expanding at an incredible rate, many government managers are only dimly aware of the potential for their own operations. In advanced private sector systems, the enthusiastic driving forces behind the development of new applications are the users—the division and department managers who recognize that the computer is a tool which can help them do a better job and look good. Line managers recognize that they themselves have to become reasonably sophisticated—not in computer technology per se, but in knowing what the computer can and cannot do, and why their own involvement is key. In the actual development of applications there is a close working partnership between the data-processing department and the line manager.

Most managers in cities and states, however, are not so sophisticated in the uses of computers. It is the exceptional rather than the average department head who is both enthusiastic and knowledgeable about the potential application of computer technology to his or her area. If there is a driver in the data-processing seat, it is perceived to be the data-processing department, not the user. In any city there *are* likely to be a few enthusiasts, but there is not likely to be much correlation between the distribution of enthusiasm and the distribution of computer potential. For example, in Hartford the police chief was an enthusiast; the police department was, by far, the greatest user of the development time and running time of the data-processing center. The fire chief, on the other hand, presiding over a department where the opportunities were at least equal to those of police, had no programs on line and little new work projected.

Data-processing managers, like any other support service managers, need alliances in order to maintain their positions. They are naturally attracted to working with and investing in the program areas where there are enthusiasts, that is, potential allies. This places a tremendous distortion on data-processing priorities. Priorities are often set not on the basis of the largest potential benefit, but on the basis of the largest actual enthusiasm. In some jurisdictions the enthusiasts are planners or research personnel who have an insatiable appetite for computer-generated information and who make virtually no contribution to the delivery of services or the operation of development programs.

Putting the user department into the leadership position is not an easy or a quick task. User departments need to know how to recognize a potential cost-effective use of the computer, how to enlist the aid of the data-processing department in solving their problems, and how to develop specifications for the computer. Simultaneously, the data-processing department should be trained in that high level of analysis which elicits the user's needs on a basis which both parties understand. The development of a common language can result in improved specifications and removes much of the frustration that stems from unrealistic user expectations.

As part of the planning and control system, a system performance contract should be developed. System performance contracts, which are becoming common in private industry, are intended to ensure clear understanding of expectations with regard to responsibilities and results on both sides: data processing and user. The system performance document defines and establishes standards, for example, batch turnaround and scheduling, acceptable error rate and date entry, standards for user documents, and teleprocessing availability. Development of such a contract between the user and the data-processing departments can eliminate confusion as to expectations and have a major impact on workload. For example, in many cases, 90 to 95 percent reliability is found to be a reasonable expectation; 100 percent reliability is a major expense and source of delay (exceptions include such areas as payroll). Such contracts also commit the data-processing professional to meet production standards and schedules agreed upon. Data-processing professionals are notorious for being optimistic and confident souls, often breezily overcommitting both in results and time. A performance contract helps them keep their feet on the ground.

Under the impact of major fiscal crises and personnel shortages, one of the first things to go is the development of new applications. Typically, when the alternatives of maintaining current operations or developing future enhancements are considered, development activities are the first to go. Clearly, this is a counterproductive strategy. It is better to drop low-priority current operations and to ensure that at least some time and effort go into continuing development of those new applications which are the highest priority from the point of view of saving money or improving service.

Recruitment and Retention of Computer Personnel

It is no secret that good data-processing managers, systems analysts, and programmers are in heavy demand. It is difficult for government to compete effectively for good data-processing personnel. The only carrot that government has is the nature, challenge, and excitement of the work itself, which *is* important to data-processing people.

Position classification systems, job descriptions, and job titles in the typical civil service system tend to fall behind the private sector in attractiveness, specifics, and potential career paths. Job titles that accurately connote status, coupled with job descriptions that specify attractive responsibility and with a clear career path for the superior performer, are important tools used by private sector firms in their competition for top-quality data-processing professionals. Frequent review of formal position descriptions and statements of duties and frequent updates of the title structure are important. The traditional tendency in government to downplay the importance of titles and job descriptions is particularly harmful in data processing. It is difficult to organize a data entry center if the civil service system has no slot for data entry clerks; similarly, heavy investment in database management will be undone if the personnel system never heard of database managers. The typical civil service title structure does not allow for high-salaried, highly technically skilled programmers and systems analysts who do not take on supervisory responsibility. Perpetuating that structure is a good way to lose good programmers.

Cities and states are often unable to respond quickly to the changing employment environment typical of the data-processing market. The combination of ordinances, personnel rules, union constraints, and other administrative regulations affecting position classes, duties, and responsibilities impedes quick responses to changing markets. By and large, position classes are reviewed only occasionally and then usually in response to a challenge. In the volatile world of data processing this is not adequate. Slow movement in this area contributes to the competitive disadvantage against private sector companies which are able to quickly modify job requirements as dictated by internal corporate needs for systems talent or adjust compensation scales as dictated by market conditions. Capacity to review and update salaries frequently is urgently needed.

High turnover is characteristic of the field: the national average was 28 percent in 1979. In this environment, cities need to: (1) invest heavily in a full-time data-processing recruiting effort; (2) review and update position descriptions and titles at least annually, if not semiannually; and (3) develop individual plans which chart a course of career growth and development for each individual professional employee. Performance should be monitored so that in fact the very best people are fast tracked. This is the only way to hold on to them. Cities and states should sample the professional data-processing labor market at least semiannually and develop a procedure to respond virtually automatically to the market changes observed. Cities and states need to work to ensure that they are at or slightly ahead of the market at all times. This can be done if salary levels for critical technical positions are established at approximately 110 percent of the survey market salary, recognizing that survey data are two to six months old when published.

Public Buildings

If information service is the newest support function, management of public buildings is probably the oldest. The management and operation of public buildings is often a major part of the responsibility of a public works department. If the department is also concerned with basic functions such as waste collection and disposal, the operation of buildings often gets little attention. Functions such as building security or space management are often not specifically assigned to any one bureau or department. Private industry has made a major effort to get this area of support under control. The escalating cost of energy has brought dramatic attention to the heat, light, and air conditioning of public buildings. These costs have long been viewed as uncontrollable. It is now recognized that these costs are controllable, but that government systems and procedures are simply not up to the job.

Dollar expenditures for public buildings are typically quite substantial. In Hartford, for example, costs associated with operating public buildings exceeded $6 million out of a general fund of about $160 million in 1979—virtually all of it in city funds. The management of facilities is important not only because of the dollars spent, particularly on energy, but also because of the impact on safety and morale. In many cities and states the contrast between a public and a private building is appalling. The public building is dimly lit; offices are piled high with files and a clutter of paper; either workers are sitting on top of each other or there are vast drafty rooms with very little activity; the floors are likely to be dirty. The private office building is probably newer, is well lit and well maintained, and has a balanced allocation of space. Of course, some public offices do resemble their private sector counterparts.

In the following section, three topics are discussed: space planning and control, building operations and maintenance (including custodial service), and energy conservation.

Space Planning and Control

Major companies give significant attention to controlling their space utilization. This function is usually not highly developed in cities and states. In New York City, for example, at the onset of the fiscal crisis in 1975, the management of the city government's own space was tucked away inside a real estate department whose primary function was the acquisition and disposal of real property that came to the city because of tax default. At that time, there was no inventory of city-owned space that was accurate, complete, and up to date. Cities and states, particularly under fiscal pressure, need the same type of formal space planning and control that exist in private industry and that are likely to lead to specific improvement opportunities.

One area that tends to receive insufficient attention is lease management. Many cities are involved in substantial leasing programs. For example, the development of new human resource programs with federal funds in the 1960s (such as day care) created pressure for opening large numbers of sites in less time than it takes to raise capital funds and construct buildings. But since public leases are sometimes handed out as a political reward, the cost of leases and the amount of space leased is sometimes unrelated to real needs or market conditions.

If the workforce contracts, the government is often stuck with too much space. A cursory look at the leases that a city holds usually indicates that the commitments are relatively long range. People shrug their shoulders and simply accept the cost of paying for space that is really no longer needed. A systematic analysis of the costs of getting out of leases compared to the costs of continuing to operate unneeded space may lead to substantial savings. In the absence of a professional lease management capacity governments often lack the expertise to effectively negotiate leases, particularly in areas experiencing upgrading.

Other activities which could have substantial impact on reducing costs and improving morale and workflow include: setting standards (square foot per worker by type), estimating space needs, evaluating expansion proposals, and planning and implementing contraction of space use where the number of personnel is declining. The managers of such activities are responsible for maintaining an inventory of existing space. Wherever possible, they reallocate space to new functions rather than add new space. Periodically, they develop a formal plan for space utilization and have ongoing responsibility for monitoring the vacancy rate. Even where substantial reductions in workforce take place, as in New York City, where the workforce declined by 20 percent within just a few years, the space used does not tend to decline proportionately. The remaining workers tend to spread out. And a systematic program is needed to make sure that the amount of space is in balance with the size of the workforce.

A great deal of space is also wasted because of the tendency to hold on to records that are not needed or are out of date. Since many states have rather strict archival requirements, it is often difficult to throw anything out. But even in areas of government where public records do not have to be kept for hundreds of years, records retention programs are a rarity. Standards for what kinds of records should be kept and what should be thrown out and more systematic plans for storage would open up space in the typical city office and add substantially to the usability as well as to the appearance of that space. It has been estimated that as much as 25 percent of the usable space in government offices is wasted by dead storage.

Another area of concern is the quality of public space. There are often tremendous disparities: the quality of space in city halls or state capitols—the highly visible symbols of government—is usually fine, but more remote field locations often are allowed to deteriorate seriously. Conditions in sanitation garages and welfare centers are often appalling. The development of qualitative standards is as much a part of the space management function as the quantitative standards. In the absence of space planning and control there is often a wide disparity within the same organization as to the amount and quality of space occupied by different managers. Giving managers at a different level in the organization comparable amounts and quality of space, regardless of department, is a useful reinforcement to the establishment of a managerial service.

A word of caution, however. An analysis of space use in a city or state may reveal that although a formal space planning and control program with clearly defined staff responsibility is not in place, space management appears to be handled reasonably well on an informal basis. In Hartford, for example, it was found that the existing informal space management effort had resulted in average amounts of space use comparable to private industry. The city averaged 113 square feet per person, and a sample of private companies was only slightly higher. An analysis of the lease program found that the city leased only 2 percent of its working space, the cost of leased space was relatively low, and standardized leasing procedures had been put in place. Even in Hartford it was felt that the city would benefit over the long run by centralizing the responsibility for the space management function within a single department. At the time of the study, the purchasing division, the city architect's office, and the planning and community development departments had all played some partial role.

Building Operations and Maintenance

The operation and maintenance of public buildings often calls to mind the old saying "out of sight, out of mind." In other words, unless a building blows up, neither the public nor elected officials nor important appointed officials even notice this management area. In New York City's Human Resources Administration, for example, 600 people in custodial operations were responsible to a relatively low-paid manager. He had neither training nor technical assistance in such basic matters as the selection of the best type of cleaning equipment and supplies, and he received neither praise nor blame from his superiors unless there was a catastrophe. Contrast this with private sector experience. Mr. K. is the manager of a small building owned by a major insurance company. He is young and ambitious. His job is to make sure that that building runs smoothly. He has resources to draw upon and is carefully watched by his superiors. His future career depends on how good a job he does at running this one small building. He must be sure that he stays within budget and that the "tenants" of the building are satisfied with the quality of cleaning and maintenance. If he succeeds, he will move up the ladder and have a group of buildings to manage.

The proper maintenance of public buildings, including necessary repairs, painting, and maintenance of heating systems, can be done a good deal more efficiently and effectively. In Hartford, for example, it was found that the span of control of different supervisors performing parallel work ranged from 1:2 to 1:20. There was no inventory of tasks to be done and therefore no workload measurement. Thus, there was no way to tell whether three painting crews were too many or too few. Because the work is concrete, it lends itself to productivity work measurement and standards, but manuals of procedure and operating standards were either absent or out of date.

Custodial service can be substantially improved through the installation of a relatively simple performance rating system, like the one used by the Bell System: an independent inspector is trained on visual standards of cleanliness and rates various areas of a building to derive an aggregate score ranging from 0 to 100 percent. Three Hartford city buildings, rated on cleanliness by an independent inspector using this system, were graded 34, 59, and 94. A passing grade would have been 80 to 85. The municipal government, like most private companies in Hartford, contracts with private firms for most of its cleaning services. The building with the high score (94) was the only one of the three that had a regular system for passing along complaints to the contractor through a single responsible person. With a regular inspection program, independent quality rating, a log book, and a person in charge to follow up on complaints, dramatic improvements in cleanliness are possible without spending more money.

School systems with large physical plants in many decentralized locations are particularly susceptible to potential improvements in facilities operations and maintenance. Custodial and operations budgets are often very large both because of the amount of square feet and the heavy use that buildings get. The problem of management improvement in school systems is complicated by the decentralized nature of the system and by some counterproductive traditions. For example, it is traditional to have a head custodian in every school regardless of the size of that school. That means that very large schools have a maintenance staff of 20 or 30 reporting to a head custodian while smaller schools might have only one or two. Pooling the maintenance and operations responsibilities of two, three, or four smaller adjacent schools under a single head custodian would be a better allocation of work in many instances.

Energy Conservation

With energy costs sky-high, the biggest challenge in public buildings is to reduce energy use. While the rising cost of energy is probably the best-known fact in American life, the impact on public budgets is worth restating. In one public service—the Hartford school system—rising fuel prices caused the cost of energy to double over a four-year period. Some state and local governments tend to focus more on energy policy and crisis planning as it affects all citizens and to attend less to their own buildings. Among those who do focus on building energy conservation, there is a further tendency to equate energy savings with complex computerized systems and/or expensive rehabilitation. With the prodding of eager vendors, the focus is on payback periods for initial scarce capital funds and on the relative benefits of different expensive computerized control systems.

Examining the best practices in the private sector suggests that attention to energy conservation can yield substantial results, and that there are modest as well as elaborate approaches that can be quite beneficial. Most specific proposals to save energy fall into one of three categories: (1) retrofitting buildings, (2) automating controls, and (3) managing building energy use.

Retrofitting buildings
The most complex and expensive approach to energy conservation is the long-run strategy of modifying buildings themselves to make them more energy-efficient. Replacing heating and/or cooling systems, installing devices to capture and reuse waste heat, modifying roof structure and materials, replacing normal windows with thermal panes—these are all examples of major modifications requiring very careful analysis of capital costs and future operating gains. Especially in periods of high interest rates, a payback period of more than three to four years (that is, recouping the original investment through annual savings) should probably be avoided.

Automating controls
The intermediate strategy for energy conservation involves the installation of computerized controls which carefully regulate the supply of heat, cool air, and light to various time and area zones depending on need. Public buildings receive highly variable use depending on time of year and day (for example, the IRS office at tax time); similarly "front-office" areas are heavily used, back-office areas less so. As with retrofitting, these systems are not inexpensive and require careful payback analysis. The costs do tend to be somewhat lower than all but the most modest retrofitting; the changes also tend to be somewhat less permanent than those associated with retrofitting. If the controls do not produce the promised savings and the contract with the vendor is intelligently written, the controls can be removed. It's a lot harder to remove a new roof.

Managing building energy use
The short-term strategy, and the one more frequently overlooked, is the development and implementation of a program to manage energy use. Without requiring any fancy technology or major capital investment, it should be possible to reduce consumption levels in the face of continuing price increases. With a careful and ambitious program, savings from conservation can balance at least some of the cost increases resulting from increasing prices. Experience in the private

sector indicates reductions of energy use in the 15 to 25 percent range with such a program. Common to these efforts is a strong and clear policy commitment from top management to specific reduction objectives along with the assignment of responsibility to specific individuals to achieve these targets. Experience in the private sector underlines the importance of assigning responsibility for energy management to persons with mechanical engineering experience and practical hands-on knowhow. They need to understand how heating, lighting, and cooling equipment is designed to operate at maximum efficiency and to know when it is not being efficiently used. The job of energy coordinator is not an especially good one for the generalist whom no one seems to know what to do with.

An additional ingredient in a successful program is the development of efficient building operating procedures and standards by the energy coordinator. Successful programs normally require monthly reporting to top management of variances from established targets for all facilities. Reports of such variances are based on an ongoing monitoring of consumption levels. A measurement system is needed to express various forms of energy use via a common unit, such as BTU/sq. ft./degree day.

With relatively modest initial investments in training and equipment to carry out initial energy audits and begin monitoring use, a program can be undertaken that builds on common-sense approaches such as:

Reduced lighting
  Turning off unnecessary lights
  Reducing lighting levels
Temperature regulations
  Reducing thermostat settings according to occupancy patterns
  Night and weekend setbacks of temperature
  Monitoring and control of demand
Fine-tuning of equipment
  Reducing ventilating air volume
  Reducing air intake volume
Operating equipment on a schedule that parallels work schedules
of occupant employees
  Continual monitoring of building consumption levels
  Monitoring and control of demand[7]

---

[7]*Management of Municipal Facilities* (Hartford: Citizens' Committee for Effective Government, Hartford Management Study, 1979), p. 10.

In four buildings in Hartford, where such an effort was made, consumption actually went down 21 percent in a single year. Once a short-term program is accomplished, then more basic and long-term approaches such as retrofitting can be examined. These three dimensions of better public building management—space planning, building operations and maintenance, and energy conservation—illustrate the issues in this area. Other issues, such as security, may be important in specific situations. Obviously, these different areas interrelate. An illustration of a comprehensive program for improving the management of public buildings is in Figure 7.

Vehicles Fleet Management

Fleet operations in the public sector are the perfect example of the intensive interaction between politics and operations in public management. In the private sector, fleet administration can be based on a fairly straightforward set of calculations—who needs a car and how frequently, or when it is more economical to buy a new car than to run an old one.

But this relatively straightforward calculation is twisted and gnarled under the winds of the political process. In the political arena the auto is even more a status symbol than it is to the average American. A large amount of newspaper space in the early days of the Koch administration in New York City focused on that important policy question: what kind of car should the mayor drive? Should a Chrysler which was defective be repaired or should the mayor drive an old ceremonial Cadillac left over from the 1960s? The key vehicle issue in the public sector is not the economics of vehicle operation, the size of the fleet, the number of mechanics needed, or the most rational time to replace a vehicle, but the administrative procedures governing the use of cars. The issue is frequently joined when an irate citizen calls to say, "I saw a city car at the supermarket." In this environment, it is not surprising that public fleets tend to be too large and too old, with excessive downtime and too many mechanics. Why do public fleets tend to get too old? Why are they not replaced on a rational schedule?

Spending now to save later is never popular with political leaders. No city councilman wants to be identified as the one who added a

Figure 7. Comprehensive program for improving management of buildings, Hartford.

Issue Area	Improvement Opportunities	Anticipated Benefits	Performance Standards
Energy Conservation	Energy Management Program	Reduction in BTU consumption per location by 10–30%	Review of energy consumption in 9 City buildings (McCook, Street yard, 3 City garages, City Hall, Library, 525 Main, new Police Station)
Building Operations and Maintenance	Building Operations and Maintenance Program	Square feet maintained per worker increased to 24,000 square feet	Complete inventory of 9 City facilities (Burgdorf, McCook, City Hall, 525 Main, new Police Station, 3 City garages)
			Complete 90% of all scheduled routine maintenance activities
Custodial Services	Contractor Inspection and Control System	Improve quality of custodial services to standard per building score of 80–85	Building inspected every other week
			Contractor contacted whenever score 79 or lower
			Whenever contractor interface necessary, follow-up inspection within 1 week
Building Security	Coordinated Building Security Program	Improve protection of persons and property in municipal facilities	Analysis of incidents occurring on City property including: • trends in occurrences • security recommendations • security measures taken
Space Management	Space Planning and Control Program	Improve quality of office space by reducing amount of spaced devoted to storage	Program released to all Department Heads Follow-up conducted to ensure compliance by each department head

Source: *Municipal Facilities* (Hartford: Citizens' Committee for Effective Government, **Hartford Management Study**, 1979). p. 5

mil to the tax rate to "buy the civil servants a lot of shiny new cars." In the case of heavy trucks, with the slow implementation of public purchasing practices, it is unlikely that the trucks could even be delivered and on the street within a year of being purchased. Since citizens believe that public servants use cars for their own purposes, they see the investment in new vehicles as a waste of tax dollars. In one community, trucks were on a rational, regular three-year re-placement cycle; passenger cars, which were obviously more sinful, were at the whim and mercy of the city council.

Why are public fleets too big? No one ever throws a truck out. The new director of operations in New York City spent six months trying to get the sanitation department to retire the worst trucks from its fleet. By definition, this would reduce downtime and avoid the endless waste of repair time and energy on the most hopeless vehicles. Why did the department resist? Because all the old-timers in the department knew from sad experience how hard it was to get new trucks, and an old truck may be better than none. Moreover, old trucks can be cannibalized for parts—everyone remembers the time the budget bureau "lost" the requisition order for parts, and some of the equipment is so old and specialized that the parts are not made anymore. A bigger fleet, particularly of cars, means more perks. In a system with relatively few managerial perks—there are no stock options within government service—an assigned vehicle is one of the few rewards that the top management has to hand out to managers.

A big, old fleet does need more mechanics than a modern one appropriately sized, and cities do tend to have too many mechanics, sometimes not enough clerks, and almost invariably too few ana-lysts. In this environment, with no work measurements, no work standards, and little or no ongoing management information, the costs of operating fleets can be incredibly high. In New York City in 1976, 30 to 40 percent of the sanitation trucks were out of service at any one time. The Hartford Management Study found that most of Hartford's municipal vehicles are in poor condition. These vehicles are expensive to maintain, dangerous to drive, and do not do an effective job in getting the streets swept or paved or in allowing inspectors to cover their routes. It appears that as a result of several years of fiscal pressure, the city has been pennywise and dollar foolish; not enough money was spent each year to replace a significant portion of the fleet. This policy can only result, as it has already, in *increasing* rather than decreasing costs."[8]

For the Hartford city fleet, replacement accounts for only 15 percent of the annual vehicles budget, which is low compared with well-managed private and public fleets. The size and deployment of the workforce are not correlated with actual workload. Hartford had one mechanic for every 14 vehicles, whereas two private sector companies surveyed had one mechanic for 27 and 43 vehicles, respectively.

The average time required to return vehicles to the using department is unpredictable and appears excessive. Because of extensive downtime, a larger number of vehicles are in the fleet simply to take the place of vehicles waiting for repair. It was recommended that Hartford modernize its fleet over a period of two to three years in order to be able to deliver services to its taxpayers in the most cost-effective manner. With relatively newer cars and trucks, the city will be able to operate with a smaller fleet; as mechanics retire, the workforce can be reduced. The costs of regularly replacing old trucks and cars will be more than made up by dollar savings.

As for vehicle maintenance, the task force in Hartford found a modern garage being operated in an old-fashioned and chaotic manner. Because of the fiscal crunch, clerical positions had not been filled, and virtually no records were being kept. There was no central control over work coming into the garage. The city operated three shifts, with virtually no supervision on the night shift, and it was widely believed that no municipal work was being done. Most of the mechanics were on the first shift, where they were constantly being interrupted by requests for service from city employees. The task force recommended that the third shift be eliminated and that the bulk of the force be concentrated in the second or evening shift, when there would be fewer interruptions but when supervision could be adequate. They also suggested that a control center be established to screen requests for work, and that the preventive maintenance program be reestablished. Figure 8 shows the workflow diagram developed by the Hartford management study. Scheduled work becomes the major focus as opposed to trouble

[8] *Vehicles Management* (Hartford: Citizens' Committee for Effective Government, Hartford Management Study, 1979), p. ii.

Figure 8. Recommended garage workflow, Hartford.

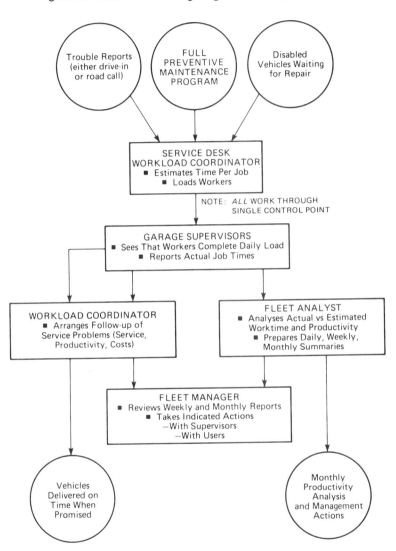

Source: *Hartford Management Report, Working Draft* (Hartford: Citizens' Committee for Effective Government, Hartford Management Study, 1980), p. 10.

reports. A workload coordinator estimates time per job, and the supervisor(s) see that the work is actually done. The fleet analyst develops the standards and reports on actual work accomplished, and the fleet manager runs the entire operation. With this program it was estimated that at the end of a five-year period, the city would be operating with at least $130,000 less per year as compared with current budget, using very conservative estimates of dollar savings. The improvement to service and morale should be enormous.

Other governments have also solved their problems in this area. Phoenix developed a work measurement system (using work units) to generate standards of how many mechanics are needed to maintain a fleet of given size and characteristics. They instituted a chargeback/rental system whereby departments "rented" vehicles from the central pool. This discourages the normal inclination to want excessive numbers of cars. The money for "rentals" went into a central equipment fund out of which new equipment was bought on a regular cycle. The Phoenix plan has been widely studied, and elements of it are being replicated elsewhere in the United States. San Jose, California, and Denver, Colorado, have also made substantial strides in modernizing fleet management.

Conclusions

These three support services—information, public buildings, and vehicles—typify the management improvement opportunities and constraints in this sector of governmental activity. Public vehicle management is the classic example of the intimate interaction between political imperatives and operational needs and the conflict between the two. Public buildings management is the classic instance of operations support management covered with cobwebs, but stirring into life as energy costs change from nuisance to monster. And information services and data processing—the newest and most important support services—incorporate all the important issues: the struggle between decentralization and centralization, the lag in planning and control, the conflict between established areas of turf and procedures, and the need to recruit fast and adapt flexibly to rapidly changing technology. Complex as these issues are, and as invisible as support services are to the general public, improvements are both possible and necessary if public services and development programs are to operate effectively.

Part IV

Putting It All Together:
Public Performance Management

Formal performance-oriented management, commonly known as management by objectives (MBO) or management by results (MBR), may be the most important management idea of the last third of the twentieth century. Most companies have adopted some form or other of this approach. It has been widely supported and widely criticized. Some have found it to be a success and have become advocates; others believe that it has failed for them and have become its critics. MBO was explicitly adopted and then dropped in the federal government during the Nixon administration.

It is useful to reconstruct the logic that underlies the interest in MBO. Odiorne in his seminal work of 1965 argued that the dominance of the large-scale, anonymous, hierarchical corporation had lost the entrepreneurial spirit that was the key driving force which in earlier years had improved the performance of American industry.[1] When companies were smaller it was the entrepreneur's drive that spurred the growth, inventiveness, and success of American business. In a large corporation, except perhaps at the top, there was no systematic incentive for working harder in order to succeed. If the owners of a grocery store did a poor job, they were likely to be out of business and lose their livelihood. If a middle manager in a large company did a poor job, how would anyone ever know? It was very difficult to assess the impact on the overall corporate situation of an individual or even a subunit doing well or poorly.

MBO is based on a motivational theory linked to the nature of corporate enterprise in America and the perception that something

---

[1]George S. Odiorne, *Management by Objectives: A System of Managerial Leadership* (New York: Pitman, 1965).

was needed to get this enterprise "juiced up." The need to find a way
to get organizations to perform is as relevant to government in the
1980s as it was to business in the 1950s and 1960s and perhaps more
so; but the *specific* approaches that are likely to work in government
are radically different, because the environment is radically different. Since MBO has become associated with a set of procedures and
techniques some of which may not be relevant to the public sector, it
is better to use the more generic term "performance management."

Performance management involves three elements: (1) A plan establishes a desired level of future performance in relation to a level
of resources. Ideally, the plan should be negotiated between a
superior and a subordinate. (2) Progress in reaching the plan is
tracked on some periodic basis and reviewed. (3) Good performance
(exceeding desired results) is rewarded in some way; poor performance (not attaining desired results) is sanctioned in some way. While
various systems differ in the nuances and subtleties, virtually all
who have used performance management would agree that these are
the three key elements. The next three chapters outline a comprehensive management system based on performance and accountability tailored to the special circumstances of the public
sector.

Many cities, counties, and states have tried to develop performance measurement in one form or another—a productivity program
with some process for measuring how well government programs
and services are performing.[2] Chapter 11 presents an approach to
public performance measurement which blends some new perspectives with the experience to date.

The necessity to connect the performance measurement system to
the ongoing (informal) system for making decisions is sometimes
overlooked. All the forms and procedures in the world will have no
impact on the quality and cost of public services unless there is an
explicit strategy for using the information generated in real-world
decision making. An approach to using performance information to

[2]These systems go under various names; some have been supported by the U.S.
Department of Housing and Urban Development (HUD): Dallas, Texas, *Performance Report;* Dayton, Ohio, *Program Strategies;* Fairfax County, Virginia, *Monthly
Report to the County Executive;* Jacksonville, Florida, *Resources Management System;* Portland, Oregon, *Goals, Objectives and Performance Measures;* Washington,
D.C., *Performance Monitoring System;* Wilmington, Delaware, *Productivity Management Project.*

improve public decision making and thereby improve public services is explored in Chapter 12.

In Chapter 13 both of these approaches are illustrated in a case study describing the New York City management plan and report system—a sophisticated effort in the late Beame administration (1975-1977) to institute performance management.

11

Measuring Public Performance: How Do We Know How Well We're Doing?

Contrary to most of the literature in the field, it *is* possible to measure performance without reference to explicit goals and objectives. On the basis of this somewhat novel approach, this chapter (1) constructs a workable definition of public performance management, and (2) outlines four practical principles of public performance measurement.

Management by Objectives Without Objectives

Almost every manual, handbook, training course, or book on the general subject of management by objectives, performance management, or planning in general starts out with step 1: Set your objectives. For years I had been intensely uncomfortable with this dictum in relation to government management. Somehow it didn't fit. After watching people try to make it fit, including an abortive effort to install planning-programming-budgeting in New York City in the 1960s, I ended up feeling vindicated in my discomfort, but as everyone else in the business seemed to agree that objective setting was the heart of the exercise to improve management in government, I was out of step. In preparing for NYC's management plan and report system, I resolved to try to avoid long philosophical arguments with people who believed objective setting to be as basic as breathing: we just never asked for objectives.[1] I am now prepared to argue

[1]The development of the New York City management plan and report system (NYC MPRS) is discussed in detail in Chapter 13.

that that is a distinguishing hallmark of successful performance management in government: Management by objectives without objectives. But how is that possible? Isn't it a contradiction in terms? Can one have a performance-oriented system without objectives?

The heart of most performance management systems is a set of objectives or goals, that is, desired end-states. Many systems are based on a hierarchy. Goals are the broadest desired end-states and objectives are more specific ones. Broad goals are translated into specific objectives; performance standards are set up to measure progress toward achieving objectives. This process, which sounds so logical and straightforward, is devilishly difficult to implement in the typical public environment. And the results of this exercise often are less than outstanding.

The difficulties begin with the effort to define broad goals. A tug of war is virtually endemic: The professional managers try to make the goals relatively specific so as to help in the later selection of specific objectives and measures of performance. Political managers like to make the goals as general as possible so as to minimize the political costs of alienating important constituencies. Tremendous amounts of time and energy are consumed in hammering out the precise wording of goal statements. In the end, the goals tend to have little operational content. The tendency toward promising all things to all people is classic.

With such a general statement in hand, the central analytic staff and department managers are likely to use up another huge batch of time and energy trying to justify the derivation of specific objectives from the broad goals. Achieving this linkage between goals and objectives usually involves so many tortuous assumptions that the results lack credibility.

Another set of difficulties exists at the level of objectives. The literature tells us that good objectives are specific as to time and amount: that is, my objective is to make 175 widgets per week by December 30, 1983. The knowledge, experience, and specific data necessary to project *meaningful* objectives are typically nonexistent in most corners of most governments. Because information as to what things cost is usually so imprecise, a department head often doesn't know what he or she can achieve with a given budget. Sometimes objectives are set in a vacuum of information about available resources.

Since objectives are set before performance measures are specified, there is sometimes no regard to their measurability. For example, a parks department faced with a ten percent budget cut set as its objective performing 90 percent of the previous year's maintenance. But with no definition of "maintenance level," and no measurement system in place, there are no data on last year's maintenance levels and therefore no way to know at the end of the year whether more, less, or the same maintenance was achieved.

At the end of a long and difficult process of setting goals, deriving objectives from goals, and specifying objectives—with all the attendant negotiation—the selection of performance measures (the last step) is likely to be hurried. At this point, it is discovered that knowing whether an objective is being achieved or not requires performance measures that have never been defined. Since there is inevitably more than one possible performance measure relative to any objective, another level of debate and discussion ensues. Even where agreement on the appropriate performance measures can be reached fairly quickly, it often turns out that the systems for collecting and aggregating data to conduct actual measurements are not in place. By now so much time has elapsed that there is no time to do more. So the cry on performance measures goes up: "Wait till next year." With all participants surrounded by mounds of data that no one knows how to apply or use, and that everyone has invested heavily in generating, there may not be a next year.

The purpose of this long, negative, somewhat exaggerated description of a typical performance measurement process is not to deride a great many serious, hard-working, and intelligent people who are committed to it. Rather, the purpose is to demonstrate that, as in many other complex environments, the best approach to performance management in government is not necessarily the most logical one. In my experience a good system does not proceed in the logical sequence of goals, objectives, and then performance measures. Rather, it starts with performance measures. Objectives are specified later, and goals, last of all, if at all. In the governmental environment the specification of objectives—that is, defining precisely where one would like to come out by a specified date in some measurable term—is certainly not appropriate for a first- or second-year cycle of a performance management system. Perhaps the third or fourth year of a working system is the appropriate time to think about setting some specific objectives.

In this apparently backward process, the first step is to define missions, functions, or programs—reasonably coherent "hunks" of governmental activity built around a common purpose. For each mission or program, a set of measures is specified. If there is some history, a target is set which refers to last year's results: up, down, or the same, depending on resource levels and other factors. This target is negotiated. There is no attempt to justify the selection of the measure or the specification of the target in terms of a hierarchy of goals and objectives.

Why is this approach likely to be more effective than the classic goal-oriented approach to performance measurement? There are two reasons: one political, one practical. The political reason is that it is easier to reach agreement about a performance measure than an operational goal. Two people who disagree violently on the goals of the social welfare program are likely to agree, for their own reasons, that it is important to track the welfare caseload as an important performance measure. They may even agree on a realistic target— one with a sense of glee, the other with a sense of despair. The practical reason is that eliminating the steps of setting goals and objectives simply reduces the number of steps in the process. In an environment not accustomed to analysis and information, this is all to the good. The available time is shifted from the relatively abstract to the relatively concrete.

Following from this approach—performance management without goals or objectives—the remainder of this chapter focuses on performance measurement in the public sector: some useful ways to think about performance measures and to actually implement measurement systems.

A Definition of Public Performance Measurement

Public performance measurement has been bedeviled in part by conceptual struggles: effectiveness versus efficiency, input versus output measures. There are those who argue that only effectiveness measures are real and efficiency measures are not important. Others have argued that only productivity measures are real because they relate resources to results, whereas output measures simply measure volumes and therefore are not meaningful. The theoretical distinctions between these different kinds of measures are probably interesting, but they have very little operational significance in a world in which good data and meaningful measures are scarce.[2]

Efficiency versus Effectiveness

Those who focus on the impact of services have tended to favor effectiveness measures. Those who focus on internal management control have tended to favor efficiency measures. In evaluating an air pollution control program it is perfectly feasible for an active and well-run regulatory operation to have no effect on air quality, which is worsening because of wind and climatic conditions (like the tendency of New Jersey's pollution to drift over New York City). If we evaluate the pollution control program on the basis of its *effectiveness*, that is, the quality of air in the city of New York, it is obviously an unfair and irrelevant measure of the actual work of the people in the department and gives us no handle on whether they are doing their best or not.

On the other hand, efficiency measures alone are not likely to be very revealing on the question of how worthwhile the whole enterprise is. In the air pollution example, inspectors may be making a very large number of incinerator stack inspections each week but if the whole program can have no measurable impact whatever on the quality of air, then one has to seriously question the value of the whole enterprise. So it is foolish to debate whether effectiveness or efficiency measures are "better": both are important and address rather different dimensions of the performance question.

On a more basic level, those who debate the relative merits of effectiveness versus efficiency measures miss an important point. There is no clearcut demarcation between what is an effectiveness measure and what is an efficiency measure. Measuring the number of inspections performed per day is primarily a measure of

[2]For a discussion of various types of performance measures and the distinction between efficiency and effectiveness measures, see Harry P. Hatry and Donald M. Fisk, *Improving Productivity and Productivity Measurement in Local Government* (Washington, D.C.: National Commission on Productivity, 1971).

efficiency; measuring the quality of the air before and after the inspection program is an effectiveness measure. But what of measures like: the number of violations recorded; the percentage of the recorded violations removed after an inspection period; the level of stack emissions before and after a period of inspection? Each of these performance measures lies on a continuum between the extremes of a pure efficiency and a pure effectiveness measure.

Controlled Variables and Performance

A more useful way to think about measurement for performance management is to consider the extent to which the organizational unit being measured controls the variables affecting the results. Performance is always the result of some mixture of controlled and uncontrolled variables.[3] The greater the control exercised by the unit being measured, the more useful the measure is as a tool of accountability. Different services vary. For example, evaluating the cleanliness of the streets as a way to measure the performance of a street-cleaning operation is not nearly as useful as measuring the frequency of garbage pickup as a way to measure the effectiveness of garbage collection services. In the case of street cleaning, it is perfectly feasible for a crew to do an excellent job of cleaning a street only to have it dirty an hour later because of heavy density and extensive littering. In the case of garbage collection, either the crew does make the pickup or it does not. If it does, then the service is effective; if it does not, then the service is not.

Often the extent to which the organization being measured and evaluated actually controls the variables affecting its performance is unclear, and evaluations may be highly judgmental, particularly evaluations of the impact of programs. If the crime rate goes down, is that because of effective crime prevention, and is the police department to be congratulated, or should the decline be attributed to socioeconomic conditions outside the control of the police department and simply be viewed as a reduction in the volume of work that they have to do? Or should one conclude that a smaller proportion of actual crimes are being reported to the police? (Nationally, reported crimes tend to be only a fraction of actual crimes.)

[3]Russell Ackoff, *Scientific Method* (New York: John Wiley & Sons, 1962).

With this discussion as background, it is possible to construct an operational definition of public performance measurement: For our purposes, *a performance measure or indicator is any piece of information that provides evidence as to how well a given function is being performed and that can be tracked over time to gauge whether a service or program is getting better or worse in some specific sense.* The best performance measures are those that measure results and at the same time reflect variables that are essentially controllable by those being held accountable. In the public sector, *measuring performance* is the activity of collecting clues, that is, bits and pieces of evidence as to how well a program is being carried out or a function is being performed. A performance measurement *system* includes selection, collection, analysis, and presentation of performance-relevant information.

Principles of Public Performance Measurement

Several principles distinguish a useful from a fruitless system: (1) Think incrementally; (2) build interpretability into the selection of measures; (3) represent performance measurement as a framework for discussion, not as a certainty; and (4) focus analysis of results on the variance between what occurred (actual) and what was expected (planned). These principles are elaborated below.

Think Incrementally

Many people who try to design performance measurement systems, particularly if they start with broad goals and objectives, are frustrated to find that they are inventing a system for which no data have been collected. It is much more useful to start collecting in a systematic format the performance-relevant information that is available, including but not limited to what is being used to manage with already. This avoids a great deal of thrashing about on the question of what is or isn't measurable.

Given the generally primitive state of public data systems, it is not hard to question what is available. Here, too, the objective should be to gradually improve measurement, not throw everything out at once. For example, one of the silliest measures in New York was the count of the number of potholes. The number could be manipulated almost at will; it included both minute cracks in the surface as well as gaping craters—all counted as potholes. But the data were being collected and measured, and that was a starting point.

Starting with already available information has two purposes: First, it establishes a baseline as quickly as possible for those measures which later turn out to be meaningful and ensures historical continuity for at least some measures. Second, it buys some time—people can learn to adjust to performance management while new and better measures are being developed. Thinking incrementally means tracking what is available and what has been used historically, and in an ongoing process, gradually dropping measures that are not meaningful and adding new measures as they are developed. It *is* important to collect hard numbers and to gradually increase the rigor of the definitions involved. Particularly for multidepartmental measures, such as vehicle downtime, the measures do need to be explicitly and uniformly defined. But here, too, the starting point is to find out how departments are measuring vehicle downtime, if at all, and to assemble what data are available before moving on to the question of improving definition.

A useful tool for improving the quality of data and measurement is an audit program. Periodically, a central staff person should actually penetrate the workings of the organization in order to generate the information to review how the numbers are being put together—not so much to catch "cheaters" but to ensure that there are documented trails for data collection and aggregation and to ultimately achieve some uniformity of definition and measurement. In New York City, such apparently straightforward measures as the number of men on patrol in the police department turned out, after such an exercise, to be fairly complex and required a number of improvements in the way the data were collected.

There are really very few directly useful measures of performance in the public sector. In New York City we had several hundred measures of the performance of the police department and I would cheerfully have traded all of them for one measure as useful as a profit and loss statement in industry. In other words, there are relatively few public sector parallels to the widget-making factory's simple, direct, quantitative measure which can be used to hold people accountable and as a basis for reward or sanction. But remember, the same is true of most private sector service organizations. Government, too, can overcome.

Build Interpretability into the Selection of Measures

Once this system is going and data are flowing on a regular basis, and one has made some initial attempts to interpret, analyze, and use the information, suggestions begin to come in for new and better ways to measure performance. At this point one needs criteria to evaluate proposals because some of the suggestions may involve fancy computer models and elaborate systems of information that can actually impede rather than help the delivery of services. Before sending 300 parks maintenance personnel out to measure the width of the slats in playground benches, one wants to be sure that it is a fruitful exercise.

Conceptually, the approach is simple. The criterion for selecting an indicator or performance measure to track is whether a decision maker should react to the results. *If a decision maker is neither pleased nor disappointed if the number increases or decreases, there is significant doubt that the measure is worth collecting or tracking.* So evaluation and interpretation on the one hand and selecting or establishing measures on the other hand are interdependent, and interpretability should be built into the selection process. Interpretation is often difficult, and sometimes one continues to collect information while being slightly puzzled about what it means. For example, the incidence of venereal disease in a community is usually considered to be an important public health measure. Now apply the criterion. If the V.D. rate goes up, is that good or bad? From the point of view of the ability to *detect* venereal disease, an increase in the rate is good because it suggests that the jurisdiction's systems for detecting and reporting V.D. are improving. From the point of view of the level of the disease in the community, clearly an increasing V.D. rate is bad.

One would hardly conclude from this confusion that we should stop collecting the information. Rather, it means we should struggle harder with interpretation and be prepared to collect more measures before one can begin to discriminate. In a probation department it is reasonable to count the number of cases that each probation worker handles. In many environments one would conclude that when a caseworker handles more cases that is an improvement, and in fact, in New York City's old productivity program, improvement was counted that way. Actually, however, the state of New York had established rather strict standards of a *maximum* number of cases per worker on the simple theory that beyond a certain caseload the individual probation workers cannot be doing an effective job for their juvenile charges. Thus an increase beyond a certain point in the number of probation cases per probation worker in fact was negative, not positive, because it violated state guidelines and risked the loss to the city of state reimbursement.

In principle, the aim is to collect the fewest measures necessary to give a reasonable picture of how well a function is being performed. In practice, since performance measures in the public sector are merely bits and pieces of evidence, a great many of them may be needed before any conclusions can be drawn about how well a mission or program is being performed. This means that at almost any point in the process, more information is being collected than it is comfortable to digest, and the information is of poorer quality and offers less clarity of interpretation or meaning than one would like. Which leads to the next point: Be prepared to recognize performance measurement as a framework for discussion rather than as a certainty, and build this recognition into the design of the system.

Present Performance Data as a Framework for Discussion

Treating performance data as evidence (clues) rather than as conclusions suggests a specific format for organizing and presenting performance data. First, a structure of missions, programs, or functions is a prerequisite for intelligent and orderly performance measurement. Remember, the query is how well we are doing at performing X or Y. The X's and Y's are programs, missions, or functions, and they need to be explicated. Then for each program or mission it is possible to identify the performance measures that are most likely to give useful insight on how well the program or function is being performed. Since the indicators are only clues, they may not move in the same direction. The total number of catch basins cleaned may be increasing, but the number cleaned per work crew may be decreasing. The evidence may not add up to a clear picture. Some indicators suggest performance is better, others may suggest performance is worse.

Since the answers don't pop out of the numbers, it is necessary to

Figure 9. Format for quarterly summary of department performance.

AGENCY: DEPT. OF ENVIRONMENTAL PROTECTION   FIRST QUARTER FY77
                                                          (Quarter, Fiscal Year)

MISSION: "B" COLLECTION & CONVEYANCE OF STORM WATER & SEWAGE

Level of Performance Achieved:

☐ Exceeded Expectations   ☐ Reached Expectations   ☒ Below Expectations— Uncontrollable Factors   ☐ Below Expectations— Controllable Factors

EVIDENCE		Explanation
From Management Plan & Reports	From Other Sources	
Sewer Maintenance Catch Basins Cleaned and in Service Crew Shift 1 Day 13.3 vs. 12.5 Planned Total Catch Basins Cleaned 8248 vs. 8933 Planned Catch Basin Backlog 3105 vs. 1500 Planned		Catch Basin Productivity has exceeded targets due to the implementation of the "Catch Basin Cleaning Task Force," while the total Catch Basin cleaned was below the plan because of ongoing attrition (while 6 BMO's were hired to implement task force, 3 other BMO's retired). The task force was implemented 6 weeks later than planned due to hiring delays. There seems to be a problem developing in the vehicle maintenance section in the Agency. An in-depth analysis is being undertaken to develop a solution. The Catch Basin Backlog remains high, although reduced from nearly 4000 due to the above mentioned problems and also the heavy flooding caused by hurricane "Belle."

Source: New York City Management Plan and Report System, 1977.

be prepared to present information in a way that allows judgments to be made about relative emphasis and importance. Two approaches to this problem are shown in Figures 9 and 10. Figure 9 was used as a quarterly summary report form in New York City. For each mission a conclusion as to overall performance is reached and the evidence to support the conclusion either from within the performance measurement system or from other sources is presented. Figure 10, prepared as a report for the confidential use of the mayor, shows another approach to the same problem in the form of a set of achievements and problems in the overall performance of a department.

Good performance measurement systems do not concentrate only on numbers and output; they also measure timing (speed), frequency, and progress from established milestones as well as toward quantitative targets. Good performance measurement answers the question, how well are we doing, on several levels of generality. At the most detailed level it provides an answer for the line manager; at the intermediate level, for the department head; at a fairly broad level, for the chief executive; and at the broadest level, for elected officials and the public.

Focus on the Variance Between the Actual and the Planned

To measure performance, an explicit standard of comparison is necessary. The two logical bases of comparison are, first, last year's comparable performance, and second, planned performance for this year. The previous year's level of results is a logical starting point in the incremental world of government. The next step is a plan, that is, some level of expectation with regard to anticipated results in the current year. This is the essential element of performance measurement. In some instances, however, coming back to the principle of an incremental approach, no historical data may be available and there may be no basis for setting a target. In such a situation, it is better to start measuring without a target than to wait a year for the data to accumulate, to construct a meaningless target, or to spend thousands of hours to reconstruct historical data that are not readily available.

Other bases of comparison, however, should not be overlooked. For some functions there are national averages. Looking at compa-

Figure 10.   Format for six-months summary of department performance.

Department of Correction

Performance Achievements	Performance Problems
Percentage of Inmates Delivered to Court by Judge's First Call for November is above target. A planned level of 75% of inmates delivered to Court by Judge's First Call has been surpassed, with 94% of inmates delivered on time.	*Overtime Hours Were 30% Over Target for October*—approximately 45,000, a planned 35,000. Overtime expenditure above target amounted to $568,000 in first 5 months of FY '77. DOC claims that a large number of officers on terminal leave and inability to control sick leave contribute to the problem. DOC/OMB are addressing the problem by implementing a sick leave control unit.
Disturbances and Incidents Have Been at a Low Level. In view of increasing "difficulty" of inmate population, program cutbacks, and legal-judicial climate—DOC has done well in keeping incident level down.	*Development of Computer Capability Continues to Lag.* DOC's plan to develop computerized systems to inform and assist management has fallen behind schedule.

Critical Management Issues

Manpower Requirements for Court-Ordered Directives:

- Compliance with single-cell and contact visit rulings will be maintained—Department must take actions to minimize the considerable expense involved.
- DOC & OMB are about to undertake an analysis of post coverage and possible civilianization of some uniformed positions. Goal is to reduce costs.
- Funding can probably be generated internally if overtime and post coverage costs can be reduced. Qualified personnel (see below) are essential to do this.
- Strategy of requesting double-celling for new admissions and inmates who damage cells at ARDC should continue to be pursued in the courts.

Appointment of First Deputy Commissioner and Other Qualified Professional Managers:

- Recent departure of First Deputy Commissioner has left this position unfilled. Appointment of a qualified professional should be made as soon as possible.
- Shortage of high-quality management and professional personnel has delayed analysis and implementation of needed improvements. Authorization and appointments need to be expedited.

City/State Interface

- City should explore contracting with state to house state convicts. Added revenues of $22 million in FY '78 are possible. City will have excess space with completion of "C-95" in Spring.

Source: New York City Management Plan and Report System, 1977.

rable cities—same size, same region, same general type of government—can be instructive. A very important and typically overlooked basis of comparison is to measure similar units against each other. In New York City the system for measuring the quality of street cleanliness, which was called Project ScoreCard, consisted of a planned cleanliness level for each district. The data compared each district against its own target and all districts against each other in terms of the extent to which they attained their targets.

As an extension of this principle it is important to always include some measures which allow for interdepartmental comparison. While it is impossible to make a direct comparison between the primary performance of a fire department and a sanitation department, because their work is so dissimilar, it is possible to compare their performance in the common support and staff areas. Some of these measures provide a fascinating proxy as to overall management of the departments being compared. Absence rates, tardiness rates, productive hours, affirmative action, energy consumption, spending in relation to budget, and vehicle maintenance (where decentralized) all can be quite suggestive. The capacity to rank and rate roughly equivalent units with regard to their performance on similar variables is a key to the use of performance measurement to get better service.

Of all these measures, the most important is the relationship between what was planned or expected and what actually occurred. This gap is the variance. Positive variance on an indicator means that as measured by this particular piece of evidence, the mission or program exceeded expectations, and negative variance means that as measured by this particular piece of evidence the program fell short of expectations. If the variance is judged by either the department or the central staff to be significant, then the focus shifts to explaining why the variance occurred. Then the focus shifts to how to reduce the negative variance and prevent it from recurring, and how to replicate the positive variance.

Conclusions

The cornerstone of public performance management is a systematic approach to measuring planned versus actual performance for key indicators. The selection of useful performance indicators requires a simple, pragmatic approach: picking measures that provide meaningful clues as to how well a mission or function is being carried out. Increasing the quality of evidence of good or poor performance requires constant effort to improve both the measures and the measurement systems. This effort is more worthwhile than the effort sometimes invested in classifying measures or in trying to derive specific measures from broad goals.

12

Using Performance Information: Systematic Ways to Do Better

It is one thing to have useful performance information; it is another thing to use it effectively. A good measurement system generates information which is highly structured in a way that is likely to help the organization. But unless the information actually feeds into the system for making decisions, the information will have no impact on the actions which are taken, and nothing will change.

Five elements are crucial for an effective system of public performance management:

1. Budget and personnel constraints need to be replaced with budget/personnel performance-based policies. In the private sector, some control over resources by the line manager usually exists, whether or not a formal plan of management by objectives (MBO) is in place. In government, this element needs to be explicity designed into the performance management system.

2. A structure for departmental incentives is needed. The link between reward and performance is the key to the original motivational theory underlying classical MBO. Trying to install a performance management system in government in an environment where rewards based on performance are absent is like trying to make an omelette without eggs. In addition to the individual incentives discussed in Chapters 2 and 8, there are important departmental incentives that are discussed in this chapter.

3. The question "How can we do better?" needs a formal answer within the system. The most useful concept is that of an improvement project, which is an action plan for those high-priority improvement areas that require special resources, procedures, or task groups. Doing better often requires a special effort, not simply

"trying harder." On the other hand, those formal MBO systems that require an action plan in every single performance area are doomed to collapse.

4. A systematic way is needed to overcome crisis management. The best way is a process of issue analysis and resolution. Time and time again, it has become apparent that government management is dominated by crisis, particularly at the highest level. A peculiar catch-22 is endemic. Senior government managers cannot spare time and energy to improve management because they are overwhelmed by crisis. But because they are overwhelmed by crisis, they cannot manage effectively. In good public performance management, systematic efforts to predict and defuse potential crises before they peak can move public decision making part way along the huge distance from crisis management to planned management.

5. New mechanisms are needed to inject performance information into public decision making. A management review and an operations cabinet are two useful devices. Most performance management systems are designed to fit into an orderly world. The system competes for the time and energy of senior officials with the normal, politically driven, issue-by-issue response style which exists in a democratic society. Periodic face-to-face contact between important decision makers with useful performance data on the table is crucial.

These five elements are discussed below.

Reduction of Constraints

Managers who are to be held accountable for results need to have some flexibility and control over the key variables which determine performance. In other words, they cannot do better next time unless they have some control over the things which could improve results. Even in the private sector, critics of MBO have cited the manager's inability to control constraints as one of the key weaknesses in the whole system. But at least in most private business, the line manager has some control over key input variables: budget and personnel.

In a typical government the line managers below the department head may not even know what their budgets are, and they certainly have no involvement in the selection of personnel. Budget decisions are made by a central budget bureau; in the case of personnel, the civil service system controls key decisions, with the personnel department acting to interpret and protect civil service (a pattern thoroughly documented in Chapters 2 and 3). For the line manager in government, then, the two major constraints are personnel and budget. The minor constraints are purchasing, the legal department, and, for some governments, a central real estate operation.

The most important personnel flexibility for a manager is the ability to hire, fire, and promote subordinates. This generally requires basic civil service reform. Minimal civil service change, such as some effort to consolidate civil service titles, can somewhat reduce constraint on movement or promotion. More modest personnel flexibilities can also be important: for example, decentralization of position classification, that is, allowing the line manager to classify a position in the civil service system. Deciding whether a given position is a secretary I or secretary II is an important power because it may be the only way to give a salary increase. The ability to process the hiring decision—distinct from the decision of whom to hire—can often save the department many weeks or even months in getting an essential new person on board.

The key change required in reducing constraints in the context of performance management is to shift central departments such as budget or personnel from a preaudit and review role to a postaudit and review role. If a department is free to move ahead on its own to make an important personnel or budget decision with the full knowledge that the action will be reviewed later for consistency with citywide policies, and that its flexibility can be removed if its actions are inappropriate, it is likely to be careful. In industry, auditors have a great deal of power, and department heads do have to justify expenditure, but they do so on a postaudit basis so that the auditing process itself cannot interfere with operations. Removing auditing from operations (that is, moving from preaudit to postaudit) eliminates one whole area of "excuses" for poor performance which is so often made available to the line manager in city government—"I couldn't perform because I couldn't get that crucial piece of equipment because budget wouldn't let me."

In the budget arena, where line item approval is the norm in many places, budget bureaus have enormous power, as was pointed out in Chapter 6. In a line budget environment, there are thousands of line modifications required all the time. The key flexibility response is to allow the line department to make all but the most important budget modifications on its own without previous budget approval. Shifting from a preaudit to a postaudit mode can mean having a budget modification go through in 48 hours instead of three months.

At an even more fundamental level, the automatic reaction to fiscal constraint is to impose a hiring freeze, in other words, position by position control. Removing the constraint of position control to allow the departments to fill a certain proportion of their vacancies within an overall dollar amount and salary range by category can make an enormous difference in department efficiency.

Budget control over individuals hired is often informal. It is often hard for people from private industry working in government to recognize that even though the money is in the budget, and no change in the budget is required, an approved position cannot be filled without the permission of the budget examiner. Removing this constraint from department heads is often the most important flexibility that they can be given: permission to fill already approved positions.

In addition to the extremely important personnel and budget constraints, the typical line manager in government also must contend with the constraints of centralized purchasing, legal, and real estate services. The historical tendency in public purchasing is to require central purchasing approval for every small item. The more widely understood reason for this revolves around the concern about corruption and the waste or stealing of public dollars. But the more subtle reason, which in the long run may be the more important, has to do with politics. Even relatively small numbers of dollars can be embarrassing politically for a mayor or governor. The department with a $20 million budget can cause major political embarrassment by purchasing a $2,000 rug or by spending $500 to travel to an island paradise at government expense for a "conference."

There *are* economies of scale and consistency of standards which can occur via centralized purchasing, but there is a tendency to forget or overlook the performance impact. The delays characteristic of many purchasing operations can be absolutely maddening to a line department head. The parks manager who gets a lawn mower in November instead of May and the streets manager whose snow blower arrives in May instead of October are going to have trouble reaching performance expectations for the season that they missed. The same is true of legal services. If the contract for street reconstruction is delayed six months, it can mean no new roads for a year. If the real estate unit fails to negotiate a lease promptly, gets a storefront when office space is needed, or gets space in the wrong location, the consequences are felt in the area of line departments' ability to perform.

A key tool for dealing with the problem of resources and constraints is to introduce a short-term planning component. If every department outlines its purchasing requirements over the next three months and its purchasing plan is approved, then it can process the actual papers itself without central preaudit. The central budget and purchasing department merely has to postaudit the actual purchase orders to make sure they conformed with the plan. Again, nonconformance with the plan means that the department loses its flexibility. A good planning and control system makes it possible to have your cake and eat it: to allow the departments to operate, and to control resources within a citywide policy framework.

In order to institute a performance management system one needs to sort out legitimate responsibility of staff agencies for overall policy from the responsibility of line managers for their own day-to-day operations including the management of their own resources. The department head who says "Just give me the resources and let me run with it" does not understand the real world situation. The central overhead staff or support agency, such as personnel, budget, or purchasing, represents the needs of executive management for consistency in application as well as some flexibility in response to changing circumstances. When the budget bureau does not allow agency Y to spend its budgeted amount to hire an approved group of workers it is probably because agency X is overspending. And the mayor, manager, governor, or county executive is seeking a balanced budget. This is the other side of the constraint coin. Thus, along with more control over the variables which determine the ability of line managers to perform there is some protection for legitimate preservation of the citywide or statewide policy framework.

Policy criteria do need to be explicit so that judgments will not be arbitrary, as when, for example, agency Y does not receive its budgeted amount because of an arbitrary judgment by a budgeting examiner (ranging from "I don't trust him" to "I can't find the paperwork"). This need for an explicit policy framework is as crucial to improving public performance as the need to free line managers from constraint.

Incentive Systems

The ability of department heads or bureau chiefs to give out merit increases is probably at least as important as their ability to earn merit increases on their own—for the former enhances their own ability to manage and to succeed. This ability presupposes (1) a performance evaluation system so that increases can be given on an objective rather than a subjective basis, and (2) a policy framework which defines the number and size of increases that can be given out in a specific group.

Rewards can be even more indirect and still work just fine. At one point in New York City "the reward" for "doing well" was getting into the MBO program and getting budget and personnel flexibility. Being allowed these flexibilities meant that the department head had demonstrated some capacity to manage effectively and could be trusted. A commissioner stopped me in the hall to ask, "Jack, when is my department getting into MBO?" Being "in MBO" meant that department heads could use part of their savings for special projects. It meant there was a merit pool—during the fiscal crisis of 1975–77 only MBO departments could give merit adjustments, whereas others could not.

There are other kinds of subtle and very important rewards which may be used to drive a performance management system and motivate its participants. For example, the climate during budget requests is crucial to a department in negotiations with the mayor or manager and council. In the typical environment, the department head with good personal relations and a good presentation style will do better in these negotiations and emerge with a better budget package than those who are less articulate on their feet and who have not cultivated the relationships to the same extent. In a working system of performance management, however, the department with a good performance record has credibility in budget hearings; with a poor record, poor credibility.

The ability to "keep" savings and to use at least part of the savings for special projects is an important public sector performance incentive. Usually there is no incentive for department heads to save money because at the end of the year that money just goes back into the general pot. Within the year, money is taken away from a department that has underspent and is given to departments that were overspending. The worst mischief occurs when agency Y's funding is reduced because agency X is overspending through poor management. The fire department in New York City always argued during the fiscal crisis (and with some merit) that it was being penalized for its careful management over the previous several years.

It is virtually impossible in most public budgeting systems to use savings made in one year for spending in the next. This is a particularly difficult problem because many management improvements depend on reinvesting short-term savings to get long-term gains. It can be done indirectly, however. If savings in one year are used as a criterion for size of budget in the next year, then, in effect, savings *can* be carried forward. This is the reverse of the typical public sector budget-making psychology: departments that underspend in one year have it taken away in the next year on the theory that "they really didn't need it after all." This, of course, generates pressure for the year-end spending which is famous in federal government circles. This can be reversed if an explicit criterion for more resources can be the amount of previous savings, but it does require a shift in budget-making attitudes.

Another approach is to take a sounding at midyear. The department that can attain its midyear performance targets with lower resources than projected should be able to use those saved resources in the second half of the year to do innovative programs.

Improvement Projects

Most of the literature and practice of public performance management places too much stress on systems for *measuring* performance and not enough stress on systems for *improving* performance. In most instances the typical reaction to the discovery of a performance variance, such as an above-target police department response time to crimes in progress, is "let's try harder." A more systematic approach is the development of an *improvement project.* Starting with the recognition of a significant negative variance between planned and actual performance, the process then calls for an operational review to get a better understanding of what is causing the problem. This review should result in a plan of action for improving performance. This plan may require additional resources or new ways of doing things.

A formal improvement project uses the techniques of project management. First, identify the steps required to generate improvement. Second, specify responsibility for each step and a project manager responsible for the whole effort. Put the task in a time frame and identify the probable anticipated results in terms of the amount of improvement expected and by when.

Asking departments to list a set of improvement projects as part of their annual plan turns up two types of projects. The best projects have as their anticipated result a service improvement, revenue enhancement, or cost reduction. That is, a good project is a systematic effort to improve program or mission performance as measured by the performance indicators in the system. But there are often many second-order projects: improvements in systems, methods, or procedures which "ultimately" will lead to better service. A classic example is an improvement project to develop a new performance measure and to install the data system required to produce it. Such efforts consume unusual time and energy resources, and one needs to make sure that they really will result in improvement. Departments need to be explicit about how some improvement to the data system specifically can be expected to result in better service or reduced costs even if the effect is a second-order one. Most important, one must be careful to have a reasonable balance between first-order and second-order improvement efforts.

In any event, there should be a significant number of improvement projects—every organization, no matter how well managed, can be improved. The number of first-order improvement projects is in itself a very useful measure of the seriousness and quality of the overall management of a department. A department head who cannot define a significant number of ways to make the operation better either does not understand the operation, is not devoting attention to it, or has given up. In any event, that person is probably the wrong one for the job.

Issue Analysis and Resolution

A critical issue is one that requires a higher-level decision than can be made by the manager of the operation whose performance is being evaluated. Systematic identification and resolution of critical issues is the bridge between crisis management and performance management and is crucial in the effort to gradually shift the emphasis in government away from crisis management. Without such a bridge, the whole structure of performance management cannot possibly penetrate public decision making. By definition, an annual plan and a system for controlling against that plan is initiatory planned management; in the world of reaction to crisis there is literally no opportunity to initiate.

Because senior managers are consumed with the crisis of today, they cannot deal effectively with the problems that are not in the crisis mode. Sensitive and difficult decisions that a department head cannot make alone must get delayed until they become crises in order to get the attention of executive managers in city hall. This delay in top-level decision making is the bane of existence of most senior line managers in government. Often such issues involve politically sensitive management choices. Since elected officials are reluctant to make decisions where strong political stakes exist on both sides, or where there is conflict between a managerial imperative and a political one, there is a preference for delay in the hope that the issue will go away before it becomes a crisis. But delay often makes it difficult for the line manager to perform. In one classic case New York City had to close a landfill that was technically full, and then had the unpleasant choice of whether to reopen the landfill or to truck garbage to another borough at greatly increased costs. The choice between offending neighborhood groups or placing the sanitation department budget in jeopardy was a paralyzing one, and for months there was no attention to the issue. Line managers in the sanitation department were in an intolerable position from the point of view of scheduling and deploying equipment and men.

Including critical issues in a management planning and control system surfaces issues in a way that forces analysis of the options. The options are systematically thought through ahead of time, the information relative to a decision collected, and the process of choice facilitated. In New York City this was a popular part of the process, because it gave the department heads something to hold city hall accountable for. The hall could delay a viable option, but if so, it did so explicitly and the department head knew about it. Most important, the potential impact on the department's ability to perform was preidentified. When a negative variance in a department surfaced, very often it was possible to pinpoint whether in fact it reflected a failure in the department's performance or whether it was due to factors under the control of a higher level of government or higher officials in the same government. Of course, some issues are so sensitive that they cannot be put on paper. But a substantial number are susceptible to prediction and analysis. Figure 11 is a sample issue analysis form. It includes the options for resolving the issue and the critical date(s) by which a decision is needed if performance is not to be impeded.

Some people define a critical issue as a potential policy roadblock. Failure to resolve a critical issue is a failure to make it possible for a senior line manager to work. Part of the analysis of the critical issue is identifying the consequences of a nondecision. A nondecision as an explicit management response is quite different from a nondecision because someone neglected to file an appropriate report with the federal government by a certain date.

New Mechanisms for Using Performance Information

Using performance management to enhance decision making may involve creating new mechanisms for making executive decisions. Several presuppositions are important: The chief executive has to want to improve services and reduce costs, to recognize the connection between better management and better services, to be willing to work hard to overcome the deficiencies of traditional public management, to be open to the development of a performance management approach, and to accept in principle the usefulness of a formal planning and control system as a way to implement performance management. This may be a tall order. The typical elected chief executive, city council, or county supervisor has little experience with formal management and a great deal of experience with political processes and probably believes that the way government is managed is inevitable. The frequent reaction of elected officials is to

Figure 11. Format for analysis of critical issues.

AGENCY: Department of Sanitation

MISSION(S): Waste Disposal/Land Resources Task Force/Engineering

TITLE: Close Pelham Bay Landfill on Schedule	CRITICAL DATE(S) Early: 12/31/77 Latest: 3/1/78

Description of Issue (& Impact):

Determine alternate disposal site and/or sites for the 15,330 average tons per week of refuse material disposed at this Bronx facility until the Baretto Point Marine Transfer Station is completed and on line (permanent replacement facility).

	Action Level(s)
Mayor/F.D.M	☒
Council/B.O.E.	☒
N.Y.S. _____	☐
Fed. _____	☐

Alternatives for Resolution (& Implications):

Reopen 100 acres of the Ferry Point Park Landfill site, North Bronx—additional cost over five-year period $632,000.

Barge Bronx refuse to Fresh Kills Landfill—3000-acre site. Staten Island—first-year cost $5,524,000, five-year cost $24 million.

Truck all Bronx refuse to Fountain Avenue Landfill, Rooklyn—first-year cost $15,341,000, five-year cost $76,705,000.

Citywide Interborough diversion (reallocate remaining disposal resources city-wide)—first-year cost $25,976,000, five year cost $104,500,000.

Critical Action(s): Action	Decision Maker	Critical Date
Determine Plan I (Ferry Point reopen)	Mayor	11/8/77
Allocate funds for Pelham closing final cover contract	OMB/Mayor	8/1/77
Present four alternatives including contract with Borough Improvement Board re: five-year limit and task force to plan and execute final use plan for Ferry Point to Community Board/Elected Officials and Borough Improvement Board	Comm/1st Depty Mayor and Corp Counsel	11/15/77
Amend Cap Budget to be able to fast track Barretto Point M.T.S. from June '81 completion to December '80 completion	OMB/Mayor/Counsel/BOE	12/1/77
Prepare Ferry Point for reopening, site preparation	OMP/Dept/Depty Mayor	1/1/78
Secure PRCA permission to reactivate operations	Mayor/Comm/PRCA	12/31/77
Reenter Ferry Point Park		3/1/78

Source: New York City Management Plan and Report System, 1977.

solve performance problems through some combination of speech making and public relations. But even if the will is there, it still takes some ingenuity to design mechanisms that can work in the political/bureaucratic environment. Two types of mechanisms have the potential for connecting the real decision-making process with the information generated by a formal performance management/planning and control system: the management review meeting, and the operations cabinet.

Management Review Meetings

The heart of any public performance·management system is a set of regular face-to-face meetings between a superior and a subordinate manager around the question of the relationship between planned and actual performance during a specific time period. Reducing the variance between planned and actual performance is the force that needs to drive government on a day-to-day basis, and the management review meeting is the key to making this happen. (In industry, this type of session is called the variance meeting.) The meeting takes place between a superior manager (for example, the city manager) and one department head. Each may bring supporting staff or not, but the essential quality of the meeting is a face-to-face discussion on the question of how well the subordinate manager's department is performing. The meetings should be held reasonably frequently, but not so frequently that no one has time to do his or her job, because in that case the meetings will stop. Monthly or bimonthly meetings seem to work well, depending on the size and complexity of the government, the number of subordinate managers at each level, and the size and importance of the specific department. The agenda should be based on exceptions—the key targets that were missed over the previous time periods, the missed milestones in improvement projects, and the current critical issues.

The reader is yawning. Surely, such meetings go on regularly in all governments. Not at all. Oddly enough regularly scheduled face-to-face, one-on-one encounters at the higher levels of government are the exception rather than the rule. Most governors, county executives, and mayors do *not* meet regularly with each of their department heads. If they do, there is rarely an agenda, and if there is an agenda it is rarely based on objective information regarding the department's performance. When such a system is working well the agenda is carefully defined and reviewed ahead of time by each of the major participants. It focuses on decisions and actions that are needed rather than a "show and tell" which is designed to advocate or convince. Follow-up assignments are carefully tracked following the meeting to ensure action. The agenda for the next meeting includes incomplete action on items from the previous meeting. To the extent possible, decisions should be made on the spot.

An Operations Cabinet

In addition to the management reviews, there needs to be some mechanism for fitting all the pieces of government together. Many governments try to do this through a cabinet with the chief executive and department heads. More often than not, however, these are ceremonial and the large numbers of people present make it impossible or difficult to conduct confidential business. The need to interrelate the different pieces of the government is widely understood in industry, where the job of executive management is precisely that: to see that the different units of the company work in harmony, not in opposition.

In government, individual departments are often viewed as separate fiefdoms. The independence of key department heads, such as police and fire, is sometimes zealously protected by civic and neighborhood groups. There is relatively little formal recognition of the interdependence of the various government functions. Working coordinative bodies are extremely difficult to sustain in government because of the constant struggles for power and turf. The policy planning council in New York, which was such a mechanism, set up in the early Lindsay administration, collapsed under the pressure of competition among its members. Cities and states need mechanisms that systematically balance political concerns with operational ones and that allow various central operational concerns to be balanced in harmony: budget versus personnel, labor relations versus management services.

A potential powerful contribution of a performance management system is the ability not only to inform decision making about individual departments but also to inform the more difficult and crucial decisions involving either multidepartment cooperation or difficult tradeoffs among different departments. In New York City such a mechanism was set up at the end of the Beame administration and was called the operations committee. This committee is discussed in greater detail in the context of the case study which is the next chapter.

Conclusions

Government as well as industry needs a comprehensive management planning and control system which is based on the concept of performance management. Unlike private industry, governments need to give special attention to reworking the structure of budget and personnel constraints on the line manager as a prerequisite to performance management; creating a new structure for departmental and individual rewards; including specific improvement projects; and overcoming crisis management by predicting important critical issues and making those decisions before they become crises.

13

Performance Management in New York City, 1975–1977: A Case Study

It is not widely known or understood that in the midst of the turmoil caused by virtually weekly brushes with bankruptcy and governmental collapse, New York City embarked on one of the most ambitious management improvement programs ever mounted by a government in the United States. Among the many significant components of this program, two had top priority: the development of a modern financial management and accounting system and the reduction of the workforce from over 300,000 to approximately 240,000. Altogether, there were ten major improvement efforts under way by early 1976.

The culmination of the program was the effort to install a comprehensive performance management system. In the end the effort was defeated by political transition. Carrying the Beame label into the Koch administration doomed most of the genuine reforms to misinterpretation and ultimately to atrophy. The tide of political transition has left only a few visible signs of the earlier work. But the lessons learned in this large-scale effort to reform a public management system under terrible pressure are instructive. If the basic principles for developing and applying performance information in public decision making could be made to work in those circumstances, they can work anywhere.

The case study is in three parts: (1) the MBO pilot program launched in October 1975, (2) the management plan and report system developed in May 1976, and (3) the operations committee launched in February 1977.

By August 1975, New York City's financial crisis had erupted in earnest. The city's inability to find any takers for a short-term bond issue had generated a genuine cash flow crisis in which there was real danger that the city could not meet its next payroll. This situation brought to the surface the basic budget problem: the city's operating revenues and operating expenses had not been in balance for years. The governor, with the support of the legislature and the federal government and with the grudging acquiescence of local officials, set in motion a process which on an emergency basis reshaped the entire pattern of state-local relationships during the crisis.

When the dust settled, there were four new entities on the scene, each playing an important role in helping to save New York City's government. One, the Emergency Financial Control Board, was chaired by the governor. With the mayor, the state comptroller, the city comptroller, and three business leaders as members, it had the power to make life and death decisions about the city's budget and financial plans. The second was the Municipal Assistance Corporation (MAC), set up to borrow money and empowered to use the city's tax resources to guarantee the money which was borrowed. The focus of MAC was debt, and its mandate was to develop a temporary rescue for the city and to develop a longer-term bailout program. These two were the organizations charged with immediate financial rescue.

At the same time, the mayor set up two parallel organizations: a Temporary Commission on City Finance to develop long-term solutions to the city's basic financial problems, and a Mayor's Management Advisory Board (MMAB), chaired by Richard Shinn, chairman of the Metropolitan Life Insurance Company, to advise the mayor on how to improve the operational management of the city.[1]

---

[1]Other members of the MMAB were E. Virgil Conway, chairman and president of the Seamen's Bank for Savings; William Ellinghaus, president of New York Telephone; Shelton Fisher, retired chairman of the board of McGraw-Hill; James L. Hayes, president and chief executive officer of American Management Associations; Lawrence Lachman, chairman and chief executive officer of Bloomingdale's; Alton G. Marshall, president, Rockefeller Center, Inc.; John F. McGillicuddy, president, Manufacturers Hanover Trust Company; Robert Rivel, president, Union Dime Savings Bank; and Harry Van Arsdale, Jr., president of the New York City Central Labor Council. Serving as codirectors along with Shinn were Herbert Elish, executive director of the Municipal Assistance Corporation, and John Zuccotti, chairman of the New York City Planning Commission. I served as the executive director.

The MBO Pilot Program—October 1975

The Mayor's Management Advisory Board (MMAB) convened in September 1975 and began its work in earnest in October. There were a number of high-priority management issues that needed systematic attention and study by the board, and a series of task forces were organized to study pensions, civil service reform, and computers. It was also recognized that the board needed to move quickly—even before the task forces reported—to make some relatively dramatic recommendations if it was to have an impact.

Shinn had had some recent positive experience with the installation of management by objectives (MBO) in Metropolitan Life, and he was prepared to recommend that the city install a similar program. The MMAB's recommendation to the mayor, made in late October of 1975, suggested that the city develop a pilot program of MBO in two test agencies. The mayor accepted the recommendation, and the fire and highways departments were selected as the departments to start with. Coincidentally, it developed that the fire department had already been experimenting with the attempt to put in MBO over the past year, working with the American Management Associations. John O'Hagan, the fire commissioner, had taken the presidents' course at the AMA and had returned full of enthusiasm for modern management methods. Although trained in an authoritarian mode, O'Hagan picked up the participatory MBO system and tried to install it in the fire department.

There was no one in the arena with any preconceived notion or commitment to any particular theoretical model of MBO. Everyone involved viewed it as an umbrella for getting the city ultimately, and the fire and highways departments in the short run, to manage more effectively. So MBO would be that management system which appeared to respond to the specific problems of managing in New York City. As the early discussions proceeded, three themes emerged clearly as the backbone of MBO: the need for more flexibility for line department heads in order to manage, the need for some way to monitor and evaluate performance, and some structure of reward for good performance. The concern about giving line managers more freedom from the constraints of the budget bureau and the personnel system was one of the driving themes of the proposed charter revision which had emerged from the Charter Revision Commission.

The reward idea was intriguing to everyone and was considered the key new thing.

The implementation of the flexibility concept involved the active involvement and approval of the personnel department and the budget bureau as well as the fire and highways departments. Bob Bott, the deputy budget director for management, became a key participant. He could easily have wrecked the whole enterprise; instead he was strongly supportive and was probably the first senior official in the history of the budget bureau who voluntarily gave up some of budget's review powers in exchange for something that he thought made sense for the city government as a whole. Weeks of discussions and negotiations went on throughout the fall and led finally to a three-part package that seemed to incorporate the basic elements of what was expected.

The results of the sometimes tortuous negotiations and discussions were three explicit, written documents which were signed by all parties in what was jokingly referred to as Magna Carta ceremonies. The agreements wrapped together the three aspects of performance management in the public sector: first, a performance agreement—a written commitment to meet certain performance expectations; second, a resources agreement—a commitment by the departments to stay within their budget with an understanding that they had relative spending flexibility within that limit and some capacity to keep savings (never fully operationalized); and third, the personnel and budget administrative agreement, which spelled out the flexibilities that department heads would have in exchange for a commitment to operate within overall city policy guidelines.

The crucial elements of this initial experiment were twofold: a shift from preaudit to postaudit of individual personnel and budget actions (the understanding that flexibilities could always be taken away if misused and that budget maintained preaudit responsibility on the largest dollar amounts), and a commitment to an overall framework of planning and control. The key things the departments were getting were the capacity to give merit increases in an environment where there was a salary increase freeze and the possibility to hire to fill needed positions under a "blanket certificate" in an environment in which there was a virtually total hiring freeze; even for critical hires the "normal" delay could be months.

Built into the flexibility agreement were a number of specific responses to the historical relationships between budget and line departments. For example, in signing the agreement the Budget Bureau agreed to explicate the criteria used to review those large budget modifications where they did have a preaudit review and to cite the sources for policy judgments. This attempted to address the criticism of budget examiners as arbitrary and to head off the misuse of power via the creation of instant policy. Postaudit of budget modifications below a certain amount were only for technical, not policy reasons and were essentially not reversible (although errors could be corrected). The personnel department allowed the line department to do position classification, but only after the people assigned from the department satisfactorily completed training carried out by personnel; and again, this was susceptible to postaudit to ensure that classification decisions were not being abused. Salary increases were possible but with an approved performance evaluation system and a formal salary adjustment plan in place. The goal was to remove much of the arbitrariness on both sides: operational procedures were in the hands of the departments, policy was in the hands of budget and personnel.

The Management Plan and Report System—May 1976

While the MBO program was being designed, events were moving, and by December 1975 Zuccotti was named first deputy mayor by Mayor Beame, with some prodding from the business community. As a codirector of the MMAB, he had been a key sponsor of the MBO experiment and, even while chairman of the Planning Commission, a key architect of the city's plan for getting out of the fiscal crisis.

Zuccotti arrived in city hall with an urgent need to get control of the government apparatus in order to implement the painful cuts required by the fiscal crisis without bringing city services into chaos. As a former planner, he was chagrined to find no regular flow of information from the departments to the center. He needed to move rapidly to learn about what the departments were doing and to get them under control. His first move was to set up a system of management review meetings with each department head. As he began to take over the day-to-day reins of government, he showed a renewed interest in the productivity program set up at the end of the Lindsay administration and still being kept alive by Bob Bott, the deputy budget director.

The city had so many separate management improvement efforts going that there was a danger that they would begin to trip over each other. To ensure coordination and cooperation Zuccotti convened an informal group consisting of the key staff involved in management improvement efforts. An early focus of those meetings was some attempt not only to get a handle on the management improvement efforts but also to develop a more systematic capacity to manage the city. The discussion centered on what kind of system should be installed; who should be involved; how it would be designed and implemented; and what the role of various existing pieces would be—the management review meetings, the MBO pilot, and the old productivity program. The discussions continued over several meetings, with Zuccotti getting increasingly impatient with the lack of action.

Some people in the group cited experts from the private sector who said that it would take two to five years to design, build, and implement a broad management system. Zuccotti's position was clear: "I don't have that much time." Others concluded that we could have a system designed and installed within just a few months if we were willing to make some sacrifice in quality. This was the view that prevailed. With only one and a half years to go in the administration, we did not have the luxury of designing the ultimate system. We needed something quick and dirty that we could start working with right away.

Bott and I were put in charge of the new effort. The mayor was briefed and agreed with the plan. The system as developed had three tiers: at the broadest level there would be a twice-yearly public management report, which would meet the charter requirement, on how well the city was performing and providing services. A second tier would be an executive report: the performance reports of the departments to the mayor. The third tier would be a management report for each department to use for internal management. Each tier had two dimensions: a plan which looked forward over the year and projected anticipated performance, and a report of results against plan.

The key tier in the system, that first year, was clearly the executive report. The mayor's management report was viewed as a by-product and was used to sell the necessity for the rest of the program internally within the administration.

The management plan and report system built on existing performance-oriented management activity. First, it incorporated and superseded the productivity program which was primarily built around specific indicators. This element folded neatly into the performance indicator component of the new system. Second, the MBO program was incorporated as a higher level of performance management: those departments that worked hard at management planning and reporting and demonstrated managerial capacity would "get into" MBO. Only MBO departments had administrative flexibility and the capacity to reward good performance. The management review meetings became the arena where management plan results were discussed. With a small staff assembled and a manual prepared to guide departments, the stage was set to launch the system.

With relatively little fanfare, the mayor announced the installation of the management plan and report system at a cabinet meeting with all department heads on May 6, 1976. The reception by the department heads was cautious. There were few questions asked, primarily by people from smaller departments. Most of the department heads seemed willing to give the new system a chance, but there was an air of skepticism in the room.

We recognized that the effort would not succeed if the department heads were not fully committed. We could not operate with "verbal cooperation"—superficial acceptance with the intent to ignore or even sabotage the effort. So we quickly followed up the cabinet meetings with four half-day briefings with groups of department heads. With the explicit support of the mayor and the first deputy mayor a week before, almost all invited department heads came personally and brought their chief aides. In general, the environment of fiscal stress increased the willingness of department heads to participate in management initiatives generated by city hall. At each of the four meetings the commissioners were asked in turn to react to the presentation made at the mayor's cabinet meeting and to the material which we had sent out to them before the meeting. Even though only two or three commissioners at each meeting were outspoken enough to publicly voice their skepticism about the operation and their belief that it was a waste of time, it was enough to provide a base to diffuse some of their real concerns.

The initial objective was to get a first set of approved management plans completed within six weeks. There were times when I didn't know whether to laugh or to cry at the notion of getting 30 departments of as many as 30,000 employees each, many of whom had relatively little experience or tradition of systematic management, to prepare an annual plan covering their operations. In retrospect, it seems like a hopeless agenda. In fact, almost every department was able to submit a plan before the first of July, the start of the new fiscal year.

Draft plans were carefully reviewed, and more than half had to be modified by the department before approval. Each plan included a statement of the department's missions ranked in priority order, and an attempt to relate the department's priorities to citywide priorities derived from the financial plan of the city. Each plan also included a set of indicators (broken down into operating statistics to measure workload and performance measures), resource measures (the number of personnel assigned to each mission), a description of planned improvement projects, and an analysis of anticipated critical issues.

Beginning in July, the departments began to submit monthly reports on planned versus actual results on the operating statistics, personnel levels, and performance measures. In addition, they reported on any missed milestones in improvement projects and on critical issues which had still not been resolved. Each department head met with the first deputy mayor in a management review meeting to discuss performance—the variance between what had been expected and what had been achieved. The agenda also included critical issues which were unresolved and which were deserving of the deputy mayor's attention. Key variances were red-circled so that in addition to the agenda, the first deputy mayor could scan some of the numbers themselves.

The pace and pressure of New York's city hall defy description to anyone who has not been intimately involved. To speak of constantly ringing phones and of potential crises brewing almost continuously does not really adequately describe the hectic atmosphere of pressure which permeated the operation. It is equally difficult to describe the amount of power and stress which flowed into the office of the first deputy mayor. Not only was he the mayor's personal advisor, the city's labor negotiator, and a key representative to the state government, federal government, and business community, but he was also the city manager of departments on a day-to-day basis and maintained strong contact with political leadership in the city. He worked a full 10- to 16-hour day, day after day, seven days a week. Into this incredible schedule, how were we to cram 30 monthly, 90-minute management reviews? In addition, since Zuccotti hated to approach situations without having the facts, we had to find time to brief him, as well as find the time for the reviews themselves.

Somehow the schedule adjusted. We did not have a management review every month. Smaller departments were scheduled for every three months. The schedule also had a tremendous amount of slippage in it so that if we met six times over a nine-month period with a major department, we were pleased. We tried every kind of device to circumvent or deal with the reality of not enough time and unpredictable demands. In the middle of a briefing, the phone would ring or the mayor would appear at the door (the first deputy mayor's office was next door to Mayor Beame's) and Zuccotti would disappear. He might reappear in a minute or he might not reappear at all.

Under the tremendous stress with which we were all operating, it took many weeks to evolve a workable format for the briefings and the material. We learned to tie each item on the agenda to a specific page in the monthly report. We began some effort to reduce the volume of paper, moving toward more summary formats. As the system matured, the interplay among performance measures, improvement projects, and critical issues became clearer. We could look at a performance problem in a particular mission in relation to an improvement project to change the way service was delivered in relation to a critical issue involving permission to fill vacant positions.

Gradually the agendas moved more and more toward current critical issues, and very often an attempt was made to solve the problem on the spot. As the system began to work, the emphasis shifted from premanagement review preparation to postmeeting follow-up. Whereas at the beginning we spent weeks putting together an agenda and only five minutes working on follow-up, as the system matured, putting together the agendas became more straightforward (many of the issues did carry forward from one meeting to the next) and we began to develop more systematic procedures for identifying and tracking follow-up responsibility.

The review meetings varied in tone. Sometimes, a department

head would bring only senior staff and no line managers. Other department heads would bring only senior line managers. At the beginning, we encouraged department heads to bring more staff because that was a way to get the message out to the middle managers of the city: the first deputy mayor really cares about performance and the system was really being used to make decisions. Having real numbers on the table and real issues on the agenda prevented most of the meetings from deteriorating into show and tell ceremonial waltzes. Very often, for the most sensitive questions the department head would request a few minutes alone with the first deputy mayor. We never really quantified it, but I believe that because meetings were held, department heads did save up their pet peeves and concerns, and there was much less day-to-day erratic pressure on the first deputy mayor.

When the city's first director of operations, Lee Oberst, was appointed, he took over the direction of the system. Because he was an unusually talented operations manager, and the operations of city departments were his primary obligation, some things improved. The meetings began to run on schedule, and many of the discussions became more sharply focused on operational improvement. But the cost was substantial. As the management plan and report system moved away from the power center which was city hall, the director of operations did not have authority to make many of the important policy judgments and high-level decisions that had to be made in city hall. The first deputy mayor was in a unique position to evaluate the tradeoffs between what seemed to make sense from a management or operational point of view and what made sense from a political policy point of view. The feedback that he got from political leadership and from the mayor meant that he could bring a broader perspective to the table than the operations group could. So if he pressed hard on catch basin cleaning as a priority it was probably because the mayor was picking up complaints in important areas of outer Queens about flooding problems. None of the rest of us were positioned to make that connection. So the system gained stability but lost clout and subtlety.

As we went into the second and third years of the system there were many changes and enhancements. First, there was an effort to get departments to develop plans of their own for internal management purposes, and the citywide executive level was trimmed down somewhat. Second, substantial effort was invested in the development of citywide indicators to lay the groundwork for inter-departmental comparisons: standards were established for the support functions of the city so that we knew we were measuring the same thing in different departments. The efforts of the office of operations to work with departments generated newer and more ambitious improvement projects.

The system was far from perfect. A key weakness was the partial separation of planning and review of the *finances* of the city from the planning and review of the *operations* of city departments. The former was staffed by the Budget Bureau and related through the budget director and also involved overhead agencies such as the Financial Control Board. The latter of course worked through the management plan and report unit and later through the office of operations. Even though budget and personnel staff participated in management review meetings, and each meeting began with a review of the department status vis-à-vis its financial plan, the basic split made it difficult to do more than cursory analysis of that crucial relationship between what the city was spending on a program and what it was getting.

The second key problem was that there was no systematic capacity to deal with interdepartmental or citywide issues. Many of the important citywide issues were constantly on the agendas of many of the individual departments. This was cumbersome and repetitive. Vehicle maintenance, for example, was a problem in several different departments. Interdepartmental issues needed a larger arena for resolution. For example, problems with the IV-D program—the city was required to try to locate absent fathers of children on welfare—were due at least in part to interdepartmental conflict between the probation department and the Human Resources Administration as to how the program was to be operated.

Both of these weaknesses were substantially modified by the development of one other institution which turned out to be tremendously important in improving the performance management effort.

The Operations Committee—February 1977

Along with the appointment of the director of operations in the spring of 1977, it was decided to organize an operations committee composed of the first deputy mayor, the director of operations, the director of budget, the director of personnel, and the director of labor relations to meet on a regular basis to review important concerns. While set up as an intelligent way for the director of operations and the first deputy mayor to communicate, it rapidly turned into more than that.

The operations committee met weekly. On the agenda were the highlights of all the management review meetings held the previous week and a prospective on all the meetings coming up. Then there was a discussion of the important citywide management improvement issues, including relationships between budget and operations planning. The third part of the agenda was devoted to review and discussion of the high-priority improvement projects, including citywide projects such as the installation of the new integrated financial management system (IFMS) as well as special improvement efforts sponsored by city hall in key troubled departments. The meetings worked. Each of the participants was a seasoned veteran of city government battles (with the exception of Oberst, who brought enough to the table to hold his own). Zuccotti and later Donald Kummerfeld were strong leaders and, clearly, it was their team. There was very little bickering over turf, and there were few attempts to pass the buck or to subvert each other's activity.

In order to support the operations committee, a monthly list of all the important citywide management improvement efforts was put together and kept up to date. When I think of this list now, which covered about 35 separate operations, I am struck anew by how widespread and deep the effort was to reshape the city's management and how poorly it was understood by the citizenry at large or the media. It was the rare reporter who had the patience and intelligence to try to penetrate our often heavy jargon to get to the root of what was being accomplished. Steve Weisman from *The New York Times* and Ken Auletta were such reporters, who worked hard at making the important management issues understandable.[2] For the first time, one saw serious articles about the state of the city's management on the front page of *The New York Times*.

We struggled throughout this two-year period with the effort to

[2] See Ken Auletta, "A Reporter at Large: More for Less," *The New Yorker*, August 1977, pp. 28–48; Steven R. Weisman, "New Management System Tightens Beame's Control," *The New York Times*, Sept. 27, 1976, p. 1.

relate the installation of a performance management system to tangible, visible results. Was it making any difference? The good reporters were always pressing us for examples or proofs that all this effort to change the way government worked really mattered, or that in fact we were making any headway. We ourselves often wondered, but we were usually too busy to talk about it.

I remember one morning when John Zuccotti's car wouldn't start over in Brooklyn and those of us waiting in city hall for a 7:30 A.M. meeting drove across the Brooklyn Bridge to pick him up. As we headed back toward the city, the early morning sunshine illuminated the various citizens going about their business as they started their day. Zuccotti began musing out loud about the connection between what we were doing and what was going on out there in the world. Suddenly the unspoken had become the spoken: what difference did the management program make in the quality of life in the city? When would results be visible in the world of the indivudal citizens seen from our car as we headed toward a management review prebriefing? No one had any answers beyond agreeing that there was probably a long time lag. An improvement in a management procedure this year probably would not impact the cost or quality of service until next year or the year after. Of course, the question came up at other times as well; but this scene is etched in my memory because the sharp contrast between the outer world of people, streets, sights, and smells and the inner world of meetings, reviews, data, and procedures made the size of our challenge suddenly come into focus.

Conclusions

By the end of 1977, we had an *impression* that while the city reduced its workforce by 60,000 the available measures of service seemed to indicate that things had improved slightly or stayed the same in most service areas. It is likely (but not certain) that so radical a reduction in the size of the available workforce would have had a paralyzing effect on city services without the systematic management improvement efforts which were under way. Don't get me wrong. The fiscal crisis did hurt, primarily in the area of infrastructure as the city lost the capacity to invest either in the rebuilding or heavy maintenance of its bridges and streets and mass transit system. As we went from a street replacement cycle of once every 30 years to once every 200 years, there were visible costs to the city's welfare, but in the area of ongoing services more things improved than got worse. The fire department, the income maintenance program, and the highways program seemed to be successful at doing more with less.

Part V

Implementing
Public Management Improvement:
Making It Happen

A special effort is required to make management improvement a way of life in state and local government. There are very few automatic self-correcting devices in the usual government operation. With all its imperfections, the competitive marketplace in the private sector does offer some stimulus to individual companies and firms to keep improving their own operations. The electoral process is too infrequent and the public is too poorly informed to perform the same function for government. We vote every two or four years; we buy groceries every week. The grocery store whose service declines and whose prices creep up is going to be reminded of its sloppy operation by a loss of customers. Since the stimulus for management improvement in government is not automatic, it needs to be explicitly designed and built in. Management improvement needs to be kept on the public agenda where it competes with crises, political pressures, and the inertia of business-as-usual—"this is how it has always been done."

Speeches about management improvement are a dime a dozen. And war stories about foul-ups that occur in state and local government make good cocktail party talk—and are almost as numerous as are exhortations from civic leaders, often linked to public scorn of the quality and intelligence of public servants. None of this will change government one iota. Someone, somewhere, and it almost doesn't matter who, needs to surface an intelligent and coherent agenda for management improvement that people inside and outside of government can rally around. The agenda needs to be specific enough so that it can be followed, stated clearly enough so that it can be understood, and well founded so that it cannot be easily dismissed.

The first ingredient for achieving management improvement—developing a specific improvement agenda—is discussed in Chapter 14. Change in government is made in response to pressure from constituencies, those who demand and who are vocal. The principle in government often is "he who yells the loudest gets." This ancient maxim of practical politics is as real today as ever. Unless there are folks out there yelling for better government, it can't happen. A constituency for effective public management is a corollary to a specific improvement agenda.

In the final analysis, it is the government itself that must be able to change the way it operates if improvement is to take place. But a government, like any other institution, is notoriously difficult to change. One way to move an institution forward is through a network of change agents all committed to roughly the same objective. Such a network of determined and effective managers is key to implementing management improvement. Building management improvement capacity into the government is discussed in Chapter 15.

14

Creating an Agenda and a Constituency for Effective Public Management

Most American cities and states experiencing fiscal pressure back into management improvement. Whether the fiscal stress is a result of growth, inflation, and tax revolt (the western model) or whether it is the result of inflation, declining revenues, and increasing pressure for expenditures (the eastern model), there is rarely a considered approach to the problem of reducing costs. Someone, usually a budget director, makes up a hit list of relatively quick available savings.

A more reasoned response to fiscal pressure is to systematically derive a management improvement agenda. In this chapter a two-step approach is suggested: (1) a process of diagnostic analysis to identify improvement opportunities, and (2) a process of operations analysis to translate opportunities into solutions.

Diagnostic Analysis: Identifying Management Improvement Opportunities

The management improvement specialist, like many another hot shot, may come riding into town with guns blazing, and there are likely to be a lot of misses and a lot of wrong hits. As in many other endeavors it probably makes sense to slow down and take aim. It's hard to improve what you can't see and don't understand.

The best approach to identifying management improvement opportunities is a comprehensive performance measurement system of the type discussed in Part IV. With such a system in place and with a regular flow of information, problems will begin to be defined. A monthly management report may show that the welfare error rate might be above national standards; street cleanliness might be seen to be lower than the goal established by the commissioner together with the mayor. Or the cost per square foot of asphalt placed by city crews might be rising without any simple or obvious explanation.

In most jurisdictions such a performance management system does not exist, exists on paper, or operates at so low a level of usefulness as to provide very few clues to where significant management problems exist. Without a useful system in place the sources of information about management problems are more diverse. A newspaper series comparing the cost of service in city A to those costs in two comparable cities in the same region might focus attention on that issue. A barrage of complaints about the slow response of police to citizens' calls would focus attention on that problem. Or a new federal initiative to fund energy conservation programs in schools and hospitals might focus attention on energy conservation. Any one of a number of different sources can trigger the perception of a management improvement opportunity.

An improvement opportunity exists wherever there is a reasonable probability that something can be made to work better. It may be caused by dissatisfaction with an existing service level or cost level, or it may be a new source of funding. The focus on the concept of improvement opportunity rather than on the concept of "problem" is more than a semantic difference. It reflects a mind set or attitude that is crucial if services are in fact to be improved. One can spend endless amounts of time trying to understand a problem without arriving at a solution. For example, the causes of absenteeism are complex and involve social, psychological, managerial, and workplace issues, but one does not need a total understanding of the interplay of these forces in order to conclude that a reasonable program of management controls is likely to reduce the absence rate. In time of great fiscal constraint the largest expenditure categories themselves are almost by definition targets of opportunity.

Once an improvement opportunity is identified, whether via a comprehensive reconnaissance or a newspaper article, a second phase of analysis is called for. This involves in-depth study of each area of opportunity and the development of alternative approaches to capitalize on management improvement potential.

Operations Analysis: From Opportunities to Solutions

Thousands of management project studies or operation reviews have been carried out in public and private organizations. In fact, every management consultant called in to help solve a management problem uses a variation of the same basic approach: Facts are gathered, people are interviewed, sometimes mathematical models are used or built, options are tested with regard to probable consequences. The costs and benefits of alternative solutions are quantified, and proposals are developed. The experience with this kind of analysis in the public sector suggests that there are some do's and don'ts that seem to have some bearing on the quality of the results.

The process seems to work better with a team or task force rather than an individual. A three- or four-person team virtually guarantees multiple perspectives on what are basically fairly complicated problems with significant controversy about both fact and value judgments. Such a team probably works best if it has both vertical and horizontal diversity. Thus a task force analyzing police department organization is probably going to be more effective if it includes a patrolman as well as a sergeant or lieutenant and captain or inspector, and is far superior to one composed exclusively of captains. A good task force includes both staff and line personnel. Staff people are likely to be more sophisticated about data analysis; line people are likely to have a much better understanding of what makes things really work. The best teams include people from both inside and outside the organization. The insiders bring understanding of the subtleties of the environment and the process, the outsiders bring a fresh perspective. An operations review is a great way for top management to evaluate the capacity of younger managers for growth and development. People who can handle both the human relations and technical aspects of coming into another person's shop and suggesting improvements probably have pretty good potential for managerial growth inside their own operation. A strong team captain is essential.

A good alternative to the mixed team is a group of people trained in operations improvement who have worked together before or have had similar training. A team drawn from a trained operations improvement group is likely to bring considerable analytic skill as well as considerable ability to relate to "client" managers without making the latter feel that they are on the carpet. Its members are trained to be project-oriented and change-oriented; the typical line manager will require substantial reorientation to be either. The experience with such teams, drawn from private industry, in the Hartford Management Study was outstanding. In most cases a team was drawn from a single company. This meant that the company's flag was on the effort and increased the probability of getting good people. The project also tried individual experts working alone: they got lonesome and confused in the forests of government. Part-time people don't have their heart in it; their rewards depend on the other half of their work.

The essential quality of a good operations review or management improvement study is that it is a bottom-up effort. The team that spends substantial time interviewing the workers themselves and asking them about their problems and suggestions for how to do the job better is going to be immeasurably more effective than the team that spends all its time in the executive suite interviewing the director, in the library, or on the telephone consulting with colleagues in other cities. This appears to be a perfectly obvious common-sense dictum. The team that spends a significant portion of its time in direct field observation of the work process is likely to draw a substantially better flow chart of the work being analyzed than the team that relies on the secondhand evidence of senior managers or the study that was published five years before—again, common sense but often ignored.

In the best projects, the client of the analysis is a decision maker who has at least some control over the implementation of explicit management improvement recommendations. Good management improvement projects involve substantial ongoing interaction at every stage between the task force and the client. The classic mistake of all management consultation is a situation where the client and the analyst reach what appears to be initial agreement on the mandate at the beginning of the process and the consultant delivers a finished plan at the end. In the complex environment of public management analysis, subtle changes in the needs of the client accumulate over time so that at the end of three or six months the client's expectations bear almost no resemblance to the work product of the analysts. Close consultation on an ongoing basis does not mean flying in the face of available evidence to give the decision maker the answer that he or she prefers. If the recommendations are distorted this way then the work is essentially useless as the analysis brings nothing new to the decision-making process. In an effective process of management study and review, very often different participants will attempt to reach agreement on facts and will agree to disagree about recommendations.

A management improvement agenda can be developed inside a government or outside; it could be incremental or comprehensive with some mix. The New York City management improvement agenda was all of these. It started out as an incremental agenda partly developed inside the city and partly developed by outside forces; gradually as the ship of state began to come under control and as management improvement efforts multiplied, an attempt was made to fit the whole into the comprehensive framework described in the previous chapter.

A largely implicit management improvement agenda, based on hunch rather than on systematic analysis, can still be an effective guide to action if the key public and private decision makers agree on what is to be done. But such implicit agendas are likely to be overturned or undone, either by political constituencies competing for scarce public resources or by the thousands of decisions and actions of the individual workers and managers in government.

Far better is an agenda that is explicit rather than implicit and which is pragmatic, analytic, and strategic. The approach needs to be pragmatic in the selection of management improvement tools, analytic in the definitions of the questions to be asked, and strategic in its focus on those areas where management improvement efforts are most likely to yield significant dollar savings and/or substantial improvements in service. Such a program was developed for the city of Hartford between 1978 and 1980.

Case Study: Hartford's Management Improvement Agenda

In the summer of 1978, a number of forces in the city of Hartford coalesced to focus attention on the general question of how well the city government was being managed and how it could be improved.

On one side, there was the business community paying a substantial portion of the property tax bill for the city (the 20 largest taxpayers pay 40 percent of the local bill). On another side was a city administration facing the scorn of a state legislature which apparently believed that no matter how much money it gave Hartford it would be wasted. On the third front, a series of newspaper articles had indicated that in a number of areas Hartford seemed to substantially outspend its neighboring cities of Bridgeport and New Haven.

Out of these forces came an agreement for a comprehensive management study of the city government. Political leaders hoped that the city would get a clean bill of health but recognized that in order for the results to be useful the study had to be objective and they had to subject themselves to searching scrutiny. The business community felt that this would give them an opportunity to make sure that their money was being spent well. A nonprofit corporation called the Citizens' Committee for Effective Government (CCEG) was formed to undertake the Hartford Management Study.

The environment was not one of overt crisis. Thus the CCEG had the luxury of a comprehensive approach from the beginning. In a 13-week reconnaissance, all city operations were reviewed. Previous studies and reports on the management of the city and its departments were collected and analyzed. Key city officials were interviewed at length. Basic information on the city's population, economy, and public services was collected.

Priorities for study were defined by reviewing potential studies from the point of view of probable benefit (in terms of reduced costs, increased revenue, or improved service) and the relative level of constraint (policy sensitivity and the relevance of private sector experience). No single management area clearly dominates; significant tradeoffs exist. For example, potential management improvement studies in the service delivery area appeared likely to have the most significant potential benefits. At the same time such areas are by their very nature highly policy sensitive. Further, private sector expertise is not as obviously relevant.

This analysis was helpful in deciding not only what to study, but when: less sensitive areas (such as support functions) earlier in the study, and the most sensitive studies—police and fire—saved for last. As a result of this reconnaissance, 16 targets for study were identified as appearing to present the greatest opportunity to im-

Figure 12. Procedure used by each task force in the Hartford Management Study.

Initiation	Analysis and Recommendations	Transition	Implementation and Report
• Company Commitment	• Bi-weekly Progress Meetings	• Preliminary Implementation Issues	• Detailed City Implementation Plan
• Task Force Leader Identified	• Preliminary Findings	• Implementation Agenda	• Implementation Plan Summary
• Task Force Selected	• Study Director Review	• Implementation Strategy Meeting	• Technical Assistance Program
• Preparation of Fact Sheet	• Findings and Preliminary Recommendations	• Identification of Technical Assistance Needs	• Public and Press Conference Report
• Press Conference	• Review to Chairman of Citizens' Committee	• Briefings with Municipal Department Heads and Others	• City Manager's Response
• Start Date			
• Contact with City Liaison	• Review with City Officials		• Legislative Recommendations
• Orientation Meetings	• Revised Recommendations to Citizens' Committee		
• Development of Briefing Book	• Preparation of First Draft Technical Report		
• Scope/Objectives Statement	• Task Force Documentation		

Source: *Hartford Management Report, Working Draft* (Hartford: Citizen's Committee for Effective Government, Hartford Management Study, 1980), p. 3.

prove service and/or reduce costs through improved management. In the second phase of the program, lasting 12 months, task forces were formed to analyze each high-priority area in depth. A typical task force was made up of three or four loaned executives from one of 14 major Hartford area employers working full-time for three to four months. Wherever possible, a company's own in-house management improvement experts were used. Over 300 recommendations were forwarded to the city manager in 16 reports and memoranda. The Hartford Management Study evolved a detailed procedure for use by each task force, which is outlined in Figure 12.

The three-year management improvement program published in the *Hartford Management Report,* abstracted in Figure 13, is a good example of a comprehensive management improvement agenda. It outlines 38 major recommended improvement areas; key actions that need to be undertaken; and a three-year projection of anticipated results in dollar savings, expenditures needed to implement the program, and anticipated qualitative benefits.

Figure 13. Portion of a recommended three-year management improvement program, Hartford (1980–81 through 1982–83).

Improvement Programs	Key Actions		Probable Impact		
	1979–80	1980–81 through 1982–83	1980–81	1981–82	1982–83
	SOCIAL SERVICES		SOCIAL SERVICES		
1. Quality Control	Photo I.D. Quality control unit.	Pilot program. Full-scale program.	$58,000 / 85,000 / 5% reduction in caseload cost savings to State.	$53,000 / 170,000 / 10% reduction in caseload cost savings to State.	$53,000 / 255,000 / 15% reduction in caseload cost savings to State.
2. Case Management	Develop plan.	Training and demonstration. Upgrade referral system. Case specialization.	$35,000 / 35,000 / Improve staff morale, reduce turnover.	$20,000 / 85,000 / 5% reduction in caseload, improve client access to jobs/services.	$20,000 / 170,000 / 10% reduction in caseload, improve client access to jobs/services.
3. Automate Paper Flow	Caseload report.	Master file. Automate State billing. Integrated system.	$40,000 / 70,000 / More staff time for clients.	$40,000 / 130,000 / More staff time for clients.	$40,000 / 170,000 / More staff time for clients.
4. Service Areas	Develop plan.	Restructure service areas. Decentralize intake.	— Better supervision and service, reduce travel and waiting time for clients.	— Better supervision and service, reduce travel and waiting time for clients.	— Better supervision and service, reduce travel and waiting time for clients.
5. Customer Service	Complaint record system.	Complaint response system.	— Better staff morale and client service.	— Better staff morale and client service.	— Better staff morale and client service.

REVENUE MANAGEMENT

		1980–81	1981–82	1982–83
34. Cash Management	√ Reduce demand accounts. Negotiate banking services. Lock-box for tax payments. Formal cash forecasting.	Develop and implement more formal cash management system. Negotiate banking services on continuing basis	**$10,000** / *245,000* — Timelier deposits of taxes. Improved cash forecasting	**$10,000** / *245,000* — Timelier deposits of taxes. Improved cash forecasting	**$10,000** / *245,000* — Timelier deposits of taxes. Improved cash forecasting
35. Tax Collections		Implement accelerated tax collection schedule. Collect motor vehicle taxes in single payment, or raise minimum to $100	— / *$600,000* — Administrative efficiency. Increased revenues from short-term investments.	— / *$600,000* — Administrative efficiency. Increased revenues from short-term investments.	— / *$600,000* — Administrative efficiency. Increased revenues from short-term investments
36. Grants Financial Management		Formalized grants financial management program. Speed up submissions for indirect costs.	**$25,000** / *145,000* — Administrative efficiency. Timelier reimbursements.	**$25,000** / *145,000* — Realize full revenue potential from grants.	**$25,000** / *145,000* — Realize full revenue potential from grants.
37. Parking Revenues	√ Review fine levels.	Review of fine and fee levels. Increased enforcement.	— / *$350,000*	— / *$350,000*	— / *$350,000*
38. Non-tax Revenues		Periodic reviews of non-tax revenue in budget process. Ensure that fees cover administrative costs.	— / *$60,000* — Assurance that fees cover costs. Increased revenues	— / *$60,000* — Assurance that fees cover costs. Increased revenues	— / *$60,000* — Assurance that fees cover costs. Increased revenues.

Summary

	1980–81	1981–82	1982–83
Estimated Annual Costs	**$2,849,000**	**$2,263,000**	**$2,388,000**
Estimated Annual Savings	*3,337,000*	*4,764,000*	*6,032,000*
Net Annual Savings	488,000	2,501,000	3,644,000

Key:

√ = City has completed this action
Boldface = Estimated annual costs
Italic = Estimated annual savings

Source: *Hartford Management Report, Working Draft* (Hartford: Citizens' Committee for Effective Government, Hartford Management Study, 1980), pp. 14–15.

In a third phase of analysis, a similar study was undertaken of Hartford's school system management.

Other Examples

In Allegheny County, a similar effort under the sponsorship of Com-PAC resulted in nine reports to the county commissioners of Allegheny County, the result of the work of 12 area corporations. ComPAC studies covered purchasing, cash management, personnel, computer services, management information/program budgeting, construction management, records management, business/industrial development services, and financial management.

Other examples of management improvement agendas for cities and states abound, although few involve as large-scale and painstaking an effort as a Hartford Management Study or a ComPAC. In Cleveland, an actual default was the trigger for setting up an operations improvement task force in the spring of 1980. Ninety loaned executives participated in a three-month comprehensive review of the city government's operations. Sometimes management improvement agendas are national, such as the publications of the Committee on Economic Development.[1] Public expenditure councils all over the country have published at least partial agendas for management improvement.[2] Warren King Associates has carried out dozens of studies of state government management.[3]

Having a thoughtfully prepared, clearly articulated management improvement agenda by itself hardly ensures results. For every improvement agenda which sees the light of day, there are two that remain in the drawer. Of those that do see the light of day, for every item implemented there are probably ten which are not. There are two other crucial ingredients: a public constituency for better management and in-house management improvement capacity in government.

---

[1] For example, *Improving Productivity in State and Local Government* (New York: Committee for Economic Development [CED], 1976).

[2] For specific examples, see the annual *Bibliography of Governmental Research* (Ocean Gate, N.J.: Governmental Research Association, 1979).

[3] Warren King Associates is a Chicago-based consulting firm specializing in management studies of state governments using local business task forces. Since 1963, it has studied such governments as Indiana (1969), Tennessee (1971), and Florida (1974).

A Public Management Constituency

Cities and states do not appear to have an informed, vocal public constituency for improved public management. Without the support of large numbers of citizens, no elected official, no matter how well intentioned, can carry out the program of management improvement that is needed. Things will not improve simply because some people believe that they should. The management of state and local government will change *if* large numbers of people perceive that it is in their interest to have such a change. But without specific effort to heighten public consciousness, perceptions will not change. The average citizen does not now perceive that a process of appointment which takes many months to fill a needed position, a vehicle maintenance system which tolerates 35 percent downtime, or a crucial shortage of personnel for data-processing positions all adversely affect the quality of the services they receive and are taxed for.

We seem to be blessed (or cursed) with many groups interested and willing to battle for *more* government spending—each group in society legitimately wants to see more done to meet its own real needs, so there is much support for more spending. Conversely, there are groups clearly pressuring for less spending. There seems to be a great gap between these extremes. Where are the groups arguing forcefully for the middle ground—for more careful spending and greater accountability for results—in short, for more effective government? This constituency seems to be absent.

A constituency is a group of people who care enough to be *for* something (it is easy to find folks against things, which is why progress, however measured, is slow). It is constituencies that make things happen. The blueberry growers in New Jersey, the chamber of commerce in Iowa, and the Gray Panthers all operate out of specific self-interests. But doesn't better state and local management respond to large numbers of people's self-interest? If better management does mean better services at lower costs, then shouldn't taxpayers and the users of local services be out there fighting for better management? While many people might agree that it is broadly in their interest to have more effective government, almost any public management improvement is likely to hurt some group and to step on somebody's toes. The very same people who are broadly in favor of more effective government are likely to be strenuously against specific improvements on the basis of their specific interests. Unless there is a vocal and strong constituency for better services at lower cost, almost any management improvement issue will tend to get resolved on the basis of a struggle between the specific interests of competing groups.

A typical issue illustrating this dilemma is the question of contracting out a public service or activity. Highway resurfacing, for example, is sometimes done by outside contractors, sometimes by city or county crews, and sometimes a mix. If one introduces cost-effectiveness analysis into this environment, one may conclude that it is cheaper and better to contract out; one may conclude that it is better to do the resurfacing work with city or county employees; and one may even conclude that a system of bidding in which outside and inside crews compete on a project basis is the most cost-effective option. If the analysis shows that it is better to contract out, then the municipal union will be angered; if the analysis indicates that it is better to do the work with the city workforces, then the outside contractors get angry. Typically, the decision will depend on who has the best access to the decision makers and the most influence on the media. The third option, contracting-in—bidding public against private and picking whoever is best for each job—is likely to have little or no public support. Rather than wringing our hands and saying isn't it too bad that no one is representing the public interest in this decision, it is more useful to ask how we can stimulate a constituency that will join the issue and speak for the third position.

Good government constituencies are not unknown. There are many historical examples: the political reform movement in Philadelphia developed a new charter and revolutionized the way the city was run in the late forties and early fifties. The city manager form of government itself was a good government reform, and even in 1980, with the movement somewhat embattled, there were over 2,000 local jurisdictions with a city manager in place. The City Beautiful movement and the City Efficient movement of the turn of the twentieth century were not always successful, but were active on the scene. Citywide reform groups like the Citizens Union in New York, which used to elect mayors, now have virtually no power. The growth of neighborhood groups exacerbates the difficulty of creating statewide or citywide constituencies.

Can such a constituency for better public management be created? If there weren't a groundswell of concern for the quality and cost of public services, even if crudely expressed through the tax revolt, the answer would probably be no. But with the backdrop of the tax revolt, and the survey findings discussed in Chapter 1 indicating that the root of the issue is people's perception that government is inefficient, there is some hope, although the challenge is substantial and the probability of success not necessarily high. There are two possible strategies which could begin to open the door: building constituency through involvement, and building constituency through greater accountability for results.

Building Constituency Through Involvement

The more citizens who are involved in government, the better the understanding of the problems and the potential for doing better. The sources for such involvement are now possible. The business and financial community has substantial stakes in the financial viability of America's great urban centers and is becoming increasingly concerned with the need to improve government operations. Enlightened labor leaders recognize that management improvement is virtually the only way that government can find the resources to pay reasonable salaries to their members. There are good government groups and public economy groups which have rallied behind legislation limiting government expenditure out of a frustration in not having any better flag to rally around.

A critical side benefit of the efforts described above to build a public agenda is the involvement of those who work on the agenda in the actual workings of government. Groups such as the MMAB in New York, ComPAC in Allegheny County, and CCEG in Hartford indirectly or directly involved hundreds of people in a firsthand experience with and exposure to government. Not all members of every task force come away with greater empathy for those in government trying to solve public problems or with a clearer image of how government can be improved; but most do.

In a few instances, citizens have organized to better inform themselves about particular public services and have had some impact on management issues. Transportation and environmental protection are two functional areas that have seen a significant rise in informed public action or public interest groups. Part of any effort to improve government needs to be an explicit strategy for involving as many citizens in as many walks of life as possible. One of the limitations of business-dominated groups is the lack of experience of private industry leaders with operating in public view. Involvement strategies are time-consuming and subject to risk; there is always the possibility that personal political ambition in a highly participatory environment will take over and subvert any management improvement agenda.

One important way for an involved constituency to make an impact is simply through demonstrations of support by groups and individuals, particularly in the legislative arena. The number of letters, phone calls, and visits that reach a state assemblyman or senator on legislation for civil service reform, countering the perfectly appropriate lobby that will typically be organized to defeat such legislation, is a crucial element in the ability of a city or state to move forward.

There are increasing numbers of other arenas for citizen participation. New local advisory boards (from health through education) open opportunities for citizen involvement. Who serves on these boards, who volunteers for committees, and who speaks before them will have a dramatic impact on the future government of the city. If significant numbers of people committed to public management improvement involve themselves in these arenas, then the overall quality of public governance is bound to improve.

Building Constituency Through Accountability

In theory in a democracy, elected officials are accountable to the citizens who express their views via the polls, just as, in a roughly analogous way, corporate management is responsible to its stockholders. But even in private business, where there is a relatively clear performance bottom line, the relationship is largely mythic. In the political process, without a clear performance measure, and in an adversary environment where politicians are prized for their ability to create impressions (which may or may not be contrary to the evidence), citizens lack the information with which to hold elected officials accountable for results. One way to promote management improvement in state and local government is to improve the quality of information available to citizens on how good a job is being done. Hopefully, this will arm people with the ammunition to punish those who perform poorly and reward those who perform well, using the ballot box as the instrument of reward and sanction.

There has been some movement in this direction in the area of financial information on cities and states, fueled in part by the impact that New York City's near collapse had on the bond market and the sudden realization that in fact investors knew very little about the cities and counties they were investing in. The concern for greater financial accountability is reflected in national legislation requiring that cities and counties have an outside audit and that their financial statements meet generally accepted accounting principles (GAAP). Beyond the area of financial accountability, the waters grow murky. Although accounting theoreticians still have many issues to work out in the application of GAAP to the public sector, their task is relatively straightforward compared with the more difficult problems of measuring results.

Some cities have public reports on their performance. New York City's *Mayor's Management Report* as mandated by the charter was an attempt to get city leaders to publish their anticipated and actual performance achievements. Despite valiant attempts to produce a meaningful document, even in the midst of political campaigns, the effort was not particularly successful. It was extremely difficult to prepare a document that would be comprehensible yet comprehensive, that would provide enough information so that the intelligent reader could make some judgments but not so much that the reader would be deluged with pages and pages of statistics. In commenting on the first report, the League of Women Voters, which maintained an active interest in the new charter and its implementation, commented that the *Mayor's Management Report* seemed more useful for internal management purposes than as a public document. They were wrong about the former—it was not detailed enough for internal management—but they were right about the latter.

A more sophisticated approach to presenting the public with information necessary to make judgments about the quality of their city administration was presented in the *Hartford Management Report.* Substantial effort and expense were put into a document which would be attractive and understandable to large numbers of people. Over 50,000 copies of the report were distributed—about half as a

Sunday supplement to the major newspaper, the Hartford *Courant*, and the remainder in a variety of other ways. An attempt was made to elicit public interest by labeling the report a working draft and by explicitly seeking comments.

The response was underwhelming. Even with all the effort to make the format attractive and to reduce many hundred of pages of separate reports and memorandums into a simple 16-page format, most people were unmoved. Only a handful of written responses were received. The notion of a comprehensive program of management improvement seemed to be understood by some individual managers within the government but received little public support and attention. Obviously, much more work needs to be done to crack the problem of getting the management message to the citizenry.

15

Building the Capacity for Management Improvement into the Government

In the best of all possible worlds, all managers in an organization are trying to do more with less and working at it creatively all the time. In the real world, even the best-managed organization, with the highest-caliber people, needs structure, stimulus, and support to make improvement happen. In government, with intense political pressure and antimanagerial traditions, a specific capacity-building effort is crucial.

The strategy of a capacity-building effort is threefold: (1) to develop managers committed to managerial self-improvement; (2) to educate and train managers in the concepts, methods, and techniques of better management; and (3) to establish and staff an organization with a mandate for, and expertise in, operational improvement.

Management Development

Most managers in government, no matter how competent or intelligent, are not systematically prepared for their job. Most of them have come up through the ranks, and there is little recognition that the shift from worker to manager represents an important change in role and identity. Moving up the hierarchy, they gradually pick up new tasks and responsibility, but it is rare for someone to clearly define for them what is involved in becoming a manager. "Political" managers come and go with each administration. Unless they have held the managerial role somewhere else, it is likely that they will be even more poorly prepared than their counterparts in the civil service. They have the added disadvantage of being flushed with victory in the political arena, which obscures their judgment and willingness to learn.

The task of managing government is increasingly complex, and the pressure to cut costs and improve service and productivity leaves the manager frustrated and demoralized. A public official commented to me recently on the mismatch between managerial capacity and his expectations in relation to his managers: "I guess I've been a little bit like my son's football coach. I have been growing increasingly angry at the coach because he keeps telling him to block more without teaching him how to block." The official realized that he, too, had been telling his subordinates to manage without a systematic development effort to help them become managers.

In any organization, the most able people are attracted and retained if they feel there are opportunities for individual growth. Such people are also motivated to perform if they are being challenged and their horizons expanded. The trick is to tap this motivation for the good of the organization, building the reputation of the organization as a place where good people want to come and stay because they believe they will be challenged and helped to grow: in short, where they are developed.

In an ideal world, development is not a program at all. It is just something that happens as part of the ongoing business of government. A manager is evaluated periodically; in consultation with his or her superior, methods are worked out to enhance and build on strengths and reduce or eliminate weaknesses in a way that makes sense to that individual. Promotion is awarded to high-performance individuals in a very visible process so that all are motivated to work harder and to grow. In the current world of government, however, declining resources reduce the real opportunities for promotion and other forms of growth, and, hence, motivation. In this environment, specific attention to management development is even more important than in a growth environment where opportunities are plentiful.

The objectives of a development program are threefold: to develop new managers; to watch, support, and move the best managers along on some sort of fast track so as not to lose them; and to make sure that most of the managers who have reached their level and/or are gradually moving ahead don't run out of gas and run down instead of up.

Developing New Managers

In the well-managed private company, development of managers is a high-priority activity. While each company has its own strategy for management development, most work on the premise that the vast majority of actual development occurs on the job, and substantial importance is given to the role of coaching on the job by an employee's immediate superior. In some companies, a new manager may spend as much as 18 months in carefully designed on-the-job training and rotational assignment before assuming a regular managerial position.

Cities and states, which have management problems at least as complex and challenging as private industry, should provide the same level of rigorous preparation for new managers as industry does. Initial management development should consist of a mixture of training courses and rotational assignments. Those with little or no previous work experience might spend several months each in a central budget office, another overhead department (such as personnel), a line agency field operation, and a centralized line department, in order to get exposure to different types of perspectives within a government.

A step in the direction of a full-fledged management development effort for new managers is a management intern program. Typically for one year, these programs are rarely explicitly integrated into the regular job-promotion system; at the end of the year, often the intern seeks employment elsewhere. The absence of a specific postinternship job reduces the commitment on both sides. Yet there are examples of notably effective programs. Kansas City, Missouri, had one of the earliest programs, which operated between 1950 and 1959 and was reinstituted in the early 1970s. Of the initial group of 42 interns, 35 became city managers at some time during their careers.

Fast-Tracking the Best

In an effort to find and keep the best young managers, New York City's Urban Academy has, since 1977, operated the Top 40 Program.[1] Yearly, 40 individuals who display outstanding leadership potential are selected from the city's management ranks. Over a three-year period, they are exposed to a blend of job-related educational and professional experiences. The goal is to give the city, over time, a group of managers with training comparable in sophistication to that provided to topflight corporate and federal government executives. People chosen must be young enough to assure they will continue to pursue long careers of distinguished service to the city. At the same time, they must have been in the city organization long enough to gain recognition from their superiors as the "movers and shakers" of the future.

The Top 40 selection process works in four steps: (1) Approximately 200 names are elicited from city leaders including all commissioners whose departments participate. (2) Personal data are cross-checked with the department of personnel, prior superiors, and peers. (3) An interview team consisting of Urban Academy faculty members and city practitioners review qualifications and pose questions in a structured interview. (4) In a final screening, candidates recommended for acceptance are subject to final review by the Urban Academy policy committee. In the first year, participants take part in performance assessment exercises followed by introductory policy analysis workshops. Case studies are based on actual New York City practice. Additional monthly seminar luncheons bring participants together with distinguished practitioners. In the second year, participants receive varied internship experience in responsible positions in staff departments. In the third year, students take weekly problem-solving workshops on major policy issues.

Steady-State Management Development

Beyond the objectives of initial management development to get managers off to a fast start and the ongoing efforts to identify and move along the best of the middle-management people, there is the third objective of management development which consists in stopping them from losing ground. Sunnyvale, California, has developed

---

[1]Launched in 1974 and originally established as a joint venture of New York City and the City University, the Urban Academy is the most ambitious city-sponsored training program in the United States. Currently organized as an independent nonprofit institute, the academy has trained tens of thousands of city personnel, has prepared hundreds of training documents, and has been a full participant in the city's management improvement programs.

a management rotation plan, probably the most ambitious program of any in the United States to keep public managers on their toes. Between 1971 and 1973, the groundwork was prepared: information was exchanged between departments, and interdepartmental task forces were used extensively. In 1973, the city manager asked each of the eight department directors to make a first and second choice of other departments for a 60-day job rotation. Three weeks before the actual rotation, department directors notified all management personnel, who in turn announced the rotation plan to all other employees. One year after the first rotation, 15 additional managers, primarily at the division head level, were rotated for 60 days. Seven supervisors and administrative assistants were rotated to new assignments in May 1975 for six weeks.

The management rotation program cut across all functional and operational areas of city government. It encouraged a total city approach rather than simply a departmental approach to problem solving. Managers consistently reported renewed interest, professional development, and better understanding of the relationships of specific programs. Management rotation also facilitated structural change. Department directors analyzed the structure of the city and recommended consolidation of several programs. The program is claimed to have improved communication, city services, and individual job performance.

Management Education and Training

Even in the private sector, there are skeptics on the question of the effectiveness of training, but most well-managed companies view training and education of managers as an integral part of their operation. A recent study by The Conference Board estimates that during 1974 the nation's largest companies (those with over 500 employees) spent over $2 billion on employee education and training. Almost one out of eight of the 32 million employees in these companies participated in some formal off-the-job program sponsored by the company.[2]

Fire and police departments traditionally do quite a bit of technical training but very little managerial training. In New York City before the fiscal crisis, 14 city agencies carried out some kind of

[2]Seymour Lusterman, *Education in Industry* (New York: The Conference Board, 1977).

ongoing training to address job-specific skills, The sanitation department, transit authority, department of corrections, finance administration, and housing department all carried out substantial job-specific programs around technical skills, but only the fire department had a considerable training effort in the supervisory and managerial area.

There is no widespread tradition of systematic management training or education in government. Such programs are the exception rather than the rule. Thousands of government employees are enrolled in various courses aimed at self-improvement, but there is a crucial distinction between training and development in the private sector and in government. Whereas training of a manager in business is an element of the corporate program, training in government is viewed as an element in the individual's program. Whether a manager gets training or not is seen as his or her business rather than as a key element in the business of the government.

Education and training in government should be seen as a key instrument for implementing management improvement. This orientation needs to pervade the content of the program itself. The purpose is not to teach management but to teach management improvement. The difference is a subtle but important one. For a well-managed company, training the individual manager is a matter of helping that manager to learn, first, how to function effectively within an established management system, and second, how to improve it—that is, to change methods, procedures, or concepts. In large measure what is being taught is an established body of knowledge and skills that correspond to models in the real world. The public sector manager needs to be helped to learn how to improve existing public management practices. Because they must always work within an existing system, public sector managers—to a far greater extent than their private sector counterparts—are change agents.

There are many different ways to think about training and education for better public management. In one model, articulated by James Hayes, the president of the American Management Associations, public management training and education should be divided into two components, each with a different emphasis: Part 1 is an immediate, fast indoctrination of people so that they have a common language and an exposure to basic management principles. This would involve massive short-course activity involving everyone in government under the same umbrella of concepts and approaches. In Hayes's view this is best done in a cascade. First the mayor and/or governor and his or her top staff are "brought on board," then department heads, then the senior managers, and so on down through the first-level supervisor.

Part 2 is a longer-term intensive program involving training and skills as well as deeper management concepts. This second, long-range program would focus on key needs and might proceed very rapidly and intensively in some departments or levels of management and rather slowly in others.

Another approach to training is to try to use the process of governmental transition itself, that is, to try to build training and education heavily into the early months of a new administration. In principle, the time between election and inauguration is ideal for preparing the administration for a fast start. The governmental transition offers a unique opportunity for systematic rigorous training and orientation for high-level city or state managers, who, once in office, are typically too burdened with ongoing responsibilities and crises to spend much time in training courses no matter how valuable. Such training courses could present the philosophy and goals of a new administration; teach fundamental management principles; explain how government works—that is, how to make things happen in a bureaucratic environment; and provide an analysis of the current policy environment and key operational and fiscal issues (such as budget and labor relations).

This concept has several problems which are probably generic to the transition process. It usually takes much longer to get key appointments made than anyone anticipates; preinaugural jockeying may knock some of the early participants out of the box. Elected officials flushed with victory do not understand, psychologically, that they need to be taught. Similarly, department heads, believing that they were recruited because they knew their job, are not likely to take kindly to the notion that they need to go to school. Oddly enough, new judges don't seem to have any difficulty in going off to judicial college in order to learn how to be a judge. I guess the executive branch has not learned that lesson yet. Lower-level people are busy trying to get and hold on to their jobs and adjust to the new team. Altogether, people in the early weeks of an administration are more likely to want to see themselves as teachers than learners. It's too bad. Conceptually, it's the ideal time. In practice, it requires an extremely secure leader to be willing to try to make it happen.

Another way to think about management training and education is to think in terms of kinds of learning or curriculum. Education and training for public managers falls into three basic categories: general management, functional management, and service delivery management.

General management includes basic skills, concepts, methods, and attitudes that go along with the development of managerial identity. General management could be subdivided by the level of management: executive management, senior/middle management, and entry-level management.

Functional management is subdivided into four major groups: personnel, financial management, management systems, and support (such as data processing, purchasing, vehicles). Within this area, the stress is on the specific managerial skills and concepts identified with each of these generic management functions.

Service delivery management covers two groups of courses in managing service delivery: courses in the generic art of how to make public services work better (work process improvement, technology, and customer service), and courses in specific industries or types of service.

These are broad strategies for using management training and education as an instrument for improving a government. Yet the comprehensive organization for training is still a rarity in American government. The private sector has been struggling to define useful models: to find an intelligent middle ground between those who view training as a luxury on the periphery of corporate organization and those who see it as a central function.

Among the bewildering variety of ways to approach this issue, four principles can be identified in the best private sector practice: (1) Responsibility for administration and monitoring of the activity is usually clearly fixed. (2) Support for the entire process comes from the very top; the CEO either participates in the process at appropriate points or monitors it closely and makes the interest visible. (3) Funds for the purpose are built into the budget and protected in times of downturn; it is recognized that when the activity is cut off or curtailed, it may cost at least three times as much to reinstitute. (4) Although some very large firms build a capability for providing all needed resources, increasing numbers count on building a small group of highly skilled professionals who function as project managers; they write specifications and monitor performance of outside training professionals.

To bring management training to bear in government, four key elements must be in place: (1) a specific process to identify training needs; (2) a method for planning and controlling training and development, including an accountable organization and a training budget; (3) a way to identify and evaluate training and development resources (expertise and funds); and (4) an organizational entity to help match training needs and resources and to monitor results. It is the rare government that has all of these elements in place.

Organizing and Staffing Operations Improvement

The well-managed private company is likely to have available substantial resources for improving operations. First, there are one or more managers on the executive level whose sole responsibility is operations; second, senior executives have access to analytic staff to diagnose, analyze, and solve operational problems; and third, there are technical experts to implement planned solutions.

In the crisis atmosphere of state and local government, on the other hand, these resources are often unavailable. Implementing management improvement requires a network of change agents who have an understanding of and commitment to a common management improvement agenda, as well as intellectual capacity and technical expertise. They should also have time in the form of relative freedom from line duties and/or crisis fire fighting, should be in a strategic position to influence decision making, and should be sufficiently numerous for their presence to be felt.

There are three approaches (not mutually exclusive) that may be needed to build improvement into government management. One is to set up executive management for operations; the second is to add analytic operations improvement staff; and the third is to develop an ongoing technical assistance program from industry.

In most large governments, there is no one at the executive management level who cares about nuts and bolts operations. Such a person is a professional manager whose explicit mandate is improving quality of service and reducing costs. The city manager form of government was meant to remedy this deficiency, but even the city manager is often too busy with policy-relevant issues to pay much attention to day-to-day operations, and few large governments have a manager.

High-level coordination is especially important on interdepartmental issues. It is a mistake to equate high-level with policy-level. Simple-sounding operational issues, if they cross the boundaries of turf-conscious departments, require the same level of power and authority to resolve as matters of constitutional significance. For example, effective street cleaning requires close coordination between parking enforcement, traffic control, street repair, garbage collection, and street cleaning crews. Unless there is someone who can *direct* the interaction of police, traffic, and sanitation, coordination is likely to be episodic and the results mediocre.

The managing director's office, established in Philadelphia's reform charter of the late 1940s, seems to have worked fairly well. Even through highly politicized administrations, the office maintained basic operating responsibility over the city's departments in Philadelphia, keeping the city positioned for managing operational improvement. Of course, only genuine political leadership can make operational improvements happen; but an appropriate structure can help implement political will and a poor structure can frustrate it.

A second approach to building operations improvement into government is to establish a staff dedicated to this mission. Government headquarters staff is traditionally relatively weak, particularly at the local level. Analytic staff in general is woefully thin in both line departments and city halls of most cities and counties. Central staffs tend to be more on the model of the political "assistant to," and a genuine professional staff available to help top management operate is rare. Even at the state level, where combined management and budget staffs seem to work fairly well, there is usually no one specifically assigned to identify management improvement opportunities and implement solutions.

In-house management consulting, which private industry has been using successfully in the last ten years, may be a useful resource for government. Whether called a management staff group or an operations improvement group, the concept is the same: These are the management generalists whose specific assignment is to define improvement opportunities and to work with individual department or division heads in seeing them implemented. Such an operations improvement unit was organized in Hartford to implement the recommendations of the Hartford Management Study.

If the thesis of this book is even partly right, state and local government in 1980s can save a good deal of time and energy by building on what service industries were learning in the 1960s and 1970s about better management of soft products. One way to bring this expertise to bear is via ongoing technical assistance, perhaps through a broker who maintains a list of technical assistance requirements and matches it with a list of people prepared to provide assistance. In New York City during the fiscal crisis, technical assistance from industry ranged from the loan of individual executives to fill key spots for six months to a year to an after-hours consultative (free) service organized by the Harvard Business Club in New York.

In Hartford, where major management improvement studies were carried out by a company and relationships developed between the relevant department and that company, the basis for an ongoing informal relationship was set. For the first time, there was direct communication between city departments faced with particular problems and giant companies only blocks away. To be able to call up someone with whom one has a relationship of trust to kick around a complex management problem can be tremendously reassuring to a harrassed line manager who rarely has the time to think management problems through clearly.

Technical assistance can take a variety of forms. A city may decide to try to do something about the increasing number of incidents against individuals and property and may appoint a security coordinator. Security coordinators from a number of companies make time available to meet with that person and guide him toward available materials. Six months later, the city's security coordinator plans an all-day seminar with key city officials, and the security coordinator from company X helps plan the conference and actually participates.

The city may decide to install a system for custodial performance rating. The inspector is sent to a local company for training. At a later stage, the company provides a monitor or evaluator to find out how well the program is going.

A city official may decide to change the way the city deals with its banks. He invites a variety of representatives of local companies to orient him and his staff on how they negotiate for banking services.

The city may be given a computer package which it needs to convert to a programming language compatible with its own equipment. The city has critical vacant programmer positions. Company Y lends the city a programmer for three weeks to make the necessary modifications.

These adjustments to staffing and organization—adding an executive manager for operations and/or adding operations improvement staff and using technical operations assistance from industry—will not make or break an operations improvement program. But along with and in support of the other capacity-building efforts discussed earlier, such investments are likely to be quite beneficial.

Conclusions

In this chapter and the previous one, an approach has been presented for implementing public management improvement. Implementation is not automatic: Each city, county, or state needs its own specific improvement agenda that makes sense in the context of its own management history and style and that fits its traditions of governance and decision making.

To carry out the agenda, an outside-inside coalition is needed. Outside of government there needs to be an active and vocal good government constituency willing and able to make more effective management one of its key concerns. Inside the government, through management development, training, and education, and supported by necessary organizational and staffing adjustments, the managers themselves need to become the advocates and creators of better management.

A constituency for more effective public management must be made; it is not born. In the largest sense, this book is aimed at helping to inform those interested in better public management and to stimulate them to create such a constituency.

This, then, is the challenge—to develop an approach to public management that blends the historic imperatives of a democratic society to respond to the electorate through the political process together with the new imperatives to reduce costs and improve public services. The difficulties are real, but so are the opportunities.

Index